Contemporary World Cinema

Contemporary World Cinema

Europe, The Middle East, East Asia and South Asia

Shohini Chaudhuri

Edinburgh University Press

© Shohini Chaudhuri, 2005

Edinburgh University Press Ltd
22 George Square, Edinburgh

Typeset in Monotype Ehrhardt by
Servis Filmsetting Ltd, Manchester and
printed and bound in Great Britain by
Antony Rowe Ltd, Chippenham, Wilts

A CIP record for this book is available from the British Library

ISBN 0 7486 1798 1 (hardback)
ISBN 0 7486 1799 X (paperback)

The right of Shohini Chaudhuri to be identified as author of this work has been asserted
in accordance with the Copyright, Designs and Patents Act 1988.

Contents

Acknowledgements

I am enormously grateful to those who read chapter drafts: Margherita Sprio, Julian Stringer, Asuman Suner, John Haynes, Erna von der Walde, I-Fen Wu, Takaharu Saito, Howard Finn, Joseph Allard, Oradol Panbhat, Eunju Hwang, Rita Lampen, Frida Wigström, Sam Hellberg, Matt Prodger and Amal Chaudhuri. Many others offered help, support or advice at other stages – in particular, Tony Mitchell, Lance Rickman, Jon Cheetham, Christelle Bossard and Hamish Ford. I owe special thanks to John Cant, who stepped in to teach at a difficult time, and to my students. I would also like to thank the British Film Institute library staff, who were always very helpful.

The University of Essex enabled my research by granting me two terms of study leave, one of which was supported by the University Research Promotion Fund. The University of Technology, Sydney, offered me a Visiting Fellowship during the other study leave.

Oliver Craske read all my drafts and was incredibly supportive, even while writing his own book. He knows how challenging it has been for me to complete this work – and I don't think I would have been able to do it without him.

Introduction

At the 1998 Academy Awards ceremony, James Cameron declared that he was 'king of the world'. His film *Titanic*, at $200 million the most expensive of its time, not only surpassed US box-office records but more than doubled its receipts abroad, becoming a mammoth hit even in post-socialist territories such as China.[1] Superlative (like the ship itself) in size, expense and impact, the movie quickly became a symbol for Hollywood's ascendancy as global entertainment. Yet, in Japan, the animation film *Spirited Away* (2001) snatched *Titanic*'s record for highest-grossing film. In Sweden, Norway and Finland, the Swedish film *Show Me Love* (1998) outdid *Titanic*, as did *Shiri* (1999) in South Korea. Meanwhile in India, the world's most prolific feature-film-producing nation, *Titanic* made only a 'disappointing splash . . . before sinking without a trace'.[2]

One major motivation for writing this book is to convey that Hollywood is not the only form of global entertainment. 'World cinema' is a term which has gained currency in recent years although its usage and meaning is far from settled. It is sometimes deployed as a catch-all term, designating all cinemas around the world, including Hollywood. This book, however, adopts it in a more specific sense, not only to refer to national cinemas outside Hollywood – another common use of the name – but also to assert the importance of placing the national within regional and global perspectives. In an age where film practices and film audiences are increasingly globalised, 'world cinema' raises a distinct set of problems and issues and invites a different critical approach from national cinema studies – although there are many overlaps between the two. This often produces tensions between cinemas, as some are more internationally formed than others.

This book focuses on feature-filmmaking in Europe, the Middle East, East Asia and South Asia since the start of the 1990s. Its aim is not to represent *all* cinemas in these regions, but to make the field more approachable to students through (1) overviews of regional aesthetic styles and modes of production and (2) case studies of particular nations, showing how they inflect regional patterns, with close analysis of films chosen either for their high local impact or for their international resonance. This will, it is hoped, provide an introduction to the variety of world cinema and inspire readers to consider further works by specialists who cover these areas in more detail. The chapters can be read separately by readers interested in a particular national or regional cinema, but they have also been written to offer comparisons between regions and to enable readers to transfer ideas developed in one region to the themes and practices of another.

In order to look at cinema in a regional context, chapters outline shared features (socio-historic, geographic, religious, linguistic) in their territories' backgrounds, enabling insights into a given region's shared cultural sphere. However, the book also recognises that geographical location does not necessarily confer affinity, and emphasises diversity as well as unity. Each chapter traces major industrial and aesthetic trends, focusing on significant genres or leading figures and filmmaking movements. Due to its economic and culturally dominant position, Hollywood has defined the choices available to other cinemas, which have frequently reshaped or countered its models. Aesthetic and industrial comparisons with Hollywood form one linking thread between the chapters, yet these cinemas have also developed in relation to each other, making Hollywood only one node (albeit a formidable one) in a global network of cross-cultural influences.

The rest of this introduction looks at some of the broader frameworks of world cinema, making a case for the usefulness of this term for Film Studies. Film now belongs to an enormous multinational system consisting of TV networks, new technologies of production and distribution, and international co-productions. It is no longer a separate art but part of the digital convergence with other media. Through these transnational processes of film production, financing and distribution, it increasingly makes sense to think in terms of 'world cinema'.

Film Production and Distribution

According to Benedict Anderson, a nation is an *imagined* community: although members of a nation do not know most of their fellow members, they carry an 'image of their communion' in their minds.[3] Other writers have since emphasised that a nation is a created artefact, an imaginary ideal, underneath which there are disparate, conflicting interests and groups, and that this is becoming more obvious in the era of globalisation and the transnational.[4] Most of today's national populations are more heterogeneous than previously – although not all, as the age of globalisation has also witnessed the rise of sub-nationalisms and the break-up of multi-ethnic states (as in Yugoslavia; see Chapter 1).

Recent national cinema studies emphasise that national identity is not a fixed and unchanging 'essence' but is actively constructed in films, which project national imaginaries, creating imaginary bonds holding the nation together.[5] Films are frequently produced in national languages, drawing on national situations, literatures and folklores.[6] In all these respects, films are undoubtedly often 'national'.

Nation-state policy (or lack thereof) is often pivotal in setting the climate and conditions that enable films to get made.[7] A nation-state's involvement in cinema can take the form of state investment (film subsidies, film foundations), state protection (for example, through quotas stipulating a required number of national productions, or through taxes on foreign imports), industrial assistance (training institutes), intervention (censorship boards), national festivals with prizes and inducements conferring prestige to filmmakers, or co-operation with another state.

However, as film financing and production becomes increasingly transnational, what defines a film's 'nationality'? Film Acts often stipulate nationality in terms of who makes the film or where the film is made, yet film personnel frequently migrate from one industry to another, and filmmaking by exiles can blur or disturb these categories (see Indian Expatriate Filmmakers in Chapter 8). International co-productions further challenge notions of national cinema. Historically, they have been used to combat Hollywood dominance, enabling partners to pool financial and other resources to produce works with greater international appeal. Co-productions fall into different categories including 'full co-productions', when more than one participating country is involved creatively, and 'co-financing', where the various foreign partners' role is limited to investment.[8] Within Europe, the main co-producers are France, Spain and Germany (the UK co-produces more with the USA and Canada than with the rest of Europe).[9] In Asia, Hong Kong and Japan are among the leading co-producers.[10] Middle Eastern filmmakers often participate in co-productions with European (especially French) partners.

Globalising processes have increased social exchange between different parts of the world, with new technologies such as VCRs, satellite and fibre-optic cable networks, digital signal compression, the Internet, VCDs (video CDs) and DVDs accelerating the flow of films to diverse audiences internationally. Under these conditions, it becomes even more problematic to think of cinema solely in national terms. However, global screen traffic is full of inequalities. Although the majority of the world's films are made outside Hollywood, US films flood the world's screens, while hardly any 'world cinema' reaches US screens. International co-productions also contribute to uneven power relations; for example, Middle Eastern films co-produced with European partners often obtain international video or repertory distribution, while mainstream local production often remains unseen by foreign audiences.[11] Film Studies has yet to address properly the extent to which current critical coverage manifests the inequities of global film distribution.

At the 1993 Uruguay Round of the General Agreement on Tariffs and Trade (GATT), non-US delegates under a coalition led by the French campaigned against US demands for unlimited access to the world's screens and succeeded in exempting audio-visual products from trading terms imposed on other goods.[12] They argued that films and other audio-visual products are works of 'culture' and therefore 'non-commodifiable'.[13] This battle for the world's screens is often presented as a case of Hollywood versus 'the world', as in the cultural imperialism thesis, which claims that the USA is using culture to extend its influence and to project American goods, values and way of life globally. The actual situation is more complex, as the globalisation of Hollywood's film industry is tied to the growth of media giants in Germany, Italy, France, the Netherlands, Japan, Australia and the UK, which share similar competitive interests to US companies. For example, Rupert Murdoch's News Corporation owns Twentieth Century Fox – together with the pan-Asian satellite broadcast service Star TV – and is a major shareholder in British Sky Broadcasting (BSkyB). Columbia Pictures belongs to the Japanese conglomerate Sony, and Universal Studios to the European giant Vivendi Universal (which also owns France's pay-TV network Canal Plus). These giant transnational entertainment and leisure conglomerates dominate the world's cultural flows.

Since 1986, the US majors have been fostering the growth of multiplexes internationally as part of their blockbuster release strategy.[14] Apart from Western Europe (which has the largest number of multiplexes outside the USA), multiplexes have gradually been built in Eastern Europe, and there has been an 'explosion' of multiplex construction in parts of Asia – including Japan, Thailand and India, while China has been relatively untouched, as indeed has the Middle East.[15] Multiplexes are mainly owned by US studios or have close ties to US studios' distributors, but in Asia other exhibitors from Australia, Hong Kong and Malaysia are expanding their global presence.

Through their control of distribution networks around the world, the US majors can make sure that their films reach exhibitors and audiences everywhere. However, the same distribution technologies that enable Hollywood films to be screened in different parts of the world also have the potential to circulate films from elsewhere. Multiplex development lured audiences back to the cinemas, creating record-breaking box-office revenues and opportunities for seeing non-Hollywood product. Multiplexes tend to exhibit films that are most profitable for their locality. In Britain, the multiplex chain Cineworld, launched in 1995 by the American Steve Wiener, has made an extremely lucrative business screening Bollywood films in locations with high densities of South Asian populations. Similarly, in Bangkok, shopping-mall cinema complexes screen Thai and Korean as well as Hollywood blockbusters.

The dynamics of global cultural flows can make a 'core' of popular works widely available, but force the rest to eke out a parallel existence in alternative theatrical venues.[16] In Britain and the USA, theatre releases of world cinema have traditionally received a limited art-house distribution. Due to the US majors' powerful position in the global markets, many small independent distributors have either folded or forged alliances with the majors or with each other to survive. Such alliances give independents access to large-scale distribution facilitated by integrated corporate structure, but this can limit the range of films chosen for distribution.[17]

Although US films dominate video and broadcasting markets as well as the domestic box office in many parts of the world, VCRs and satellite TV allow viewers to opt out of the limited choices offered by regulated broadcast TV and theatrical releases.[18] Video and satellite TV are hugely popular among immigrants and other groups who have traditionally been badly served by public sectors. Indians, Chinese and Turks are all great video-users; as Ien Ang writes, 'the circulation and consumption of ethnically specific information and entertainment on video serves to construct and maintain cross-national "electronic communities" of geographically dispersed peoples who would otherwise lose their ties with tradition and its active perpetuation'.[19] Within India, since skies were opened up in the early 1990s, satellite networks have penetrated fast among urban middle classes, but video and DVD are less common. In Asia, generally, VCDs are more common – and cheaper – than DVDs and are bought legitimately in record shops (like HMV in Hong Kong and Music World in India) or illegally on the black market. Like other examples in this section, piracy testifies to the numerous ways in which films cross national borders and reach audiences around the world – with or without the media conglomerates, and often in defiance of national censors.

Film Festivals and Prizes

Film festivals are important to considerations of 'world cinema', as they facilitate cultural exchange between different 'national' cinemas and provide an alternative global distribution network. As the vagaries of international distribution get more fraught and regular theatrical markets become more impenetrable, festivals perform an indispensable role in enabling a diverse range of films to be seen by audiences around the world. For filmmakers and national film establishments, festivals are a means of gaining international visibility and kudos; filmmakers often take their films to festivals in the hope of attracting distributors, although 85 per cent of films shown at festivals never reach commercial screens beyond the festival circuit.[20]

Nonetheless, films distributed in festivals may not be representative of the situation of filmmaking in their originating country, nor of the kinds of films that are popular with that country's audiences. Certain film industries and filmmakers, mainly in non-Western countries, have been accused of targeting their films specifically for festivals. Some critics think that the choices of subject matter, style and visual imagery in these films cater to Western/international film-festival tastes, packaging Third World cultures in Orientalist or 'tourist-friendly ways'.[21] Positive response at festivals then stimulates further production of the same kinds of films. Others view the targeting of the festival circuit as a strategic necessity for surviving in the global marketplace and for raising production funds difficult to obtain at home.

The 'Big Three' competitive festivals are Cannes, Venice and Berlin, which offer as their top prizes the Palme d'Or, Golden Lion and Golden Bear respectively. Other prizes at Cannes include the Caméra d'Or, awarded to debut features. Such prizes are valuable for catching the attention of international audiences and distributors, although judging decisions can be arbitrary and lack transparency.[22]

Unlike film festivals, the Academy Awards ceremony does not specialise in world cinema – indeed, it is mainly a Hollywood industry event. As Ella Shohat and Robert Stam scathingly note, it corrals all the world's non-English-language film production into the restrictive category of 'Best Foreign Film', for which each competing country enters one film.[23] Yet it provides another realm in which works of world cinema can break through internationally. As a global spectacle, attracting billions of television viewers, the Oscars ceremony has come to be valuable for the profile of world cinema, offering crucial publicity for any film or filmmaker lucky enough to win or be nominated.

Art and Aesthetics

All films, regardless of whether they are classified as 'art' or 'popular entertainment', follow established aesthetic and discursive practices. One of the insights to be gained by the concept of 'world cinema' is that such practices, which are so often naturalised as conventions, are variable and contingent. The study of world cinema therefore enables us to re-perceive our own cultural positioning, as well as discovering 'alternatives'.

Entertainment cinema is characterised by the forms of textual continuity upon which it relies. For example, the key characteristics of Hollywood film are fast-paced linear narratives, goal-motivated protagonists, stars, narrative closure and, increasingly in the present age, big budgets, special effects and spectacular action. This is the broad narrative genre that Hollywood industry insiders believe has 'universal' appeal across the world.[24]

Far from being 'universal', genres are unstable, a litmus of their historical and geographical situation, and they have never been the sole property of Hollywood. In the age of globalisation, they 'mutate and cross-fertilise as a result of their worldwide circulation', creating 'international variants of recognised or designated film styles'.[25] The action film is a recurrent example, as is the blockbuster, a 'genre' which is being reconstructed in other parts of the world, for example in the three-hour omnibuses of Indian popular cinema.[26]

Certain genres, such as melodramas, have long pre-cinematic traditions – Hollywood melodrama is only one of the many sources of melodramatic inspiration in the cinemas covered in this book. Melodrama is associated with polarised representations of heroism and villainy, song and dance, stylised acting and emotional excess, and is popular in Asian cinemas.

Hollywood films deploy an 'invisible' style (such as continuity editing) and psychologically credible narratives in order to promote an illusion of realism and to facilitate audience identification. There are, however, competing conceptions of realism – most influentially, Italian neorealism, a 1940s film movement which used location shooting, naturalistic performance styles (with unknown or non-professional actors) and low-budget visual styles to emphasise authenticity. Similar kinds of 'realism' can be found in New Iranian Cinema and India's 'Parallel Cinema'. Yet realism is just one convention in cinema, and Western realism 'only one band on a wider esthetic spectrum'.[27] In Asia and the Middle East, the most popular forms of indigenous cinema have strongly anti-realist tendencies, thriving on entertaining fantasy and spectacle – for example, India's popular cinemas, Chinese and Hong Kong swordplay films, Japanese *anime*. Common trends in Asian arts involve a rejection of realistic imitation; they evoke through means of abstraction and manifest the belief that time is cyclical instead of linear.

David Bordwell and Steve Neale have provided two influential accounts of art cinema, defining it as (1) a genre with a body of textual characteristics and (2) an institution with its particular sources of finance, modes and circuits of production, distribution and exhibition, forms of publicity and promotion, relationship to the state and the international film industry.[28] Bordwell defines the textual characteristics of art cinema by measuring them against classic Hollywood 'norms', from which art cinema purposefully deviates.[29] For example, narratives do not follow a linear causal chain – events are more haphazard, more like 'real life' than Hollywood's rationally ordered narratives – and there is no firm closure. Narratives promote uncertainty, often in the form of an open-ended quest.

Art cinema is '*auteur*' cinema – that is, the director is identified as the main artistic creator of the film. Its aesthetic influences derive from the early twentieth-century Euro-American movement, modernism, which fully impacted on cinema from the 1960s onwards. European modernist directors include Michelangelo Antonioni (Italy), Ingmar Bergman (Sweden), Rainer Werner Fassbinder (Germany) and Jean-Luc Godard (France). Non-European directors who have been added to this 'canon' include Satyajit Ray (India), Youssef Chahine (Egypt), Akira Kurosawa (Japan), Yilmaz Güney (Turkey) and Lester James Peries (Sri Lanka).

Originating from theology, the word 'canon' refers to the list of 'great works', 'classic authors' and privileged 'moments' that form a national or cultural tradition. Film Studies textbooks, film courses and art-cinema retrospectives are all informed by notions of the film 'canon', which is composed of 'great' movements such as Italian neorealism, French New Wave and New German Cinema, as well as 'great' directors. Canonformations result from decisions taken at particular times by scholars, critics and teachers. They are never immutable and always subject to revisions. The process of canonisation also creates gaps in film history: the bias is nearly always towards white male directors, and a lot of 'mainstream' world cinema gets excluded.

This is one reason to view art cinema as an institution with its own set of institutional discourses promoting and supporting it, as Neale proposes. This approach understands the concept of the *auteur* not in the 'genius' or 'masterpiece' tradition but in an industrial context: for instance, the director as originator of the film, screenwriter and financier rolled into one. Art cinema is usually dependent on patronage from state institutions and is bound up with value judgements produced by such institutions (hence the term 'quality films' frequently used in state legislation). The tension between art cinema's 'international' and 'national' aspects is felt at many levels, including the market, film-critical discourses, policy legislation, and in the films themselves.[30] Neale points out that art cinema is a mode of production as well as a mode of consumption, an international market niche, where the director becomes a brand name that sells the film. Art cinema can be seen as a form of product differentiation, a useful marketing device targeting audiences seeking something different from the Hollywood 'norm'. Films that are sold as 'popular' in their home territories are often rebranded as 'art' when exported abroad.[31]

Art cinema has mutated considerably since its 1960s heyday – and so has Hollywood. During the 1960s, the borrowing of art-cinema models was part of Hollywood's reorganisation after the collapse of the studio system. Art cinema was a big influence on New Hollywood directors such as Francis Ford Coppola and Martin Scorsese, who adapted its narrative and stylistic forms into their films. This symbiosis between Hollywood and art cinema contributed to the development of post-classical Hollywood film language. These developments have affected the textual features of art cinema which, according to Neale, primarily have a product-differentiating function and therefore 'change in accordance with which features of Hollywood films are perceived or conceived as dominant or basically characteristic at any one point in time'.[32] The institutional relationship between mainstream and art cinema has changed too as cultural hierarchies of taste become less fixed.

Postmodernism and Post-colonialism

Postmodernism and post-colonialism are two critical discourses through which world cinema is repeatedly discussed. Postmodernism is the cultural manifestation of the period known as postmodernity, which is defined by the shift from an industrial economy based on manual labour to an information and service economy based on computerisation and electronics (and of which globalisation is an integral feature). Postmodernism emphasises the plural, the partial and the provisional, the relativity of all 'truths', thereby challenging orthodox historiography. Postmodern works react to perceptions that modernist works are 'difficult' by playfully mixing high and low culture, thereby addressing a broad audience. Postmodernism thrives on simulation (using parody or pastiche to imitate former genres or styles), prefabrication (reworking what is already there rather than inventing materials), intertextuality (texts exist in relationship to other texts and are tissues of quotations from other texts) and bricolage (assemblage of works from eclectic sources).[33] Distinction is often made between 'popular' postmodernism and 'resistance' postmodernism; the latter uses these techniques 'to 'deconstruct' and subvert old meanings as well as to 'construct' new meanings through the repositioning of artistic and cultural discourses.[34]

Although films portray images of postmodern society, adopt postmodern techniques and are increasingly reliant on postmodern technologies, it is television which is seen as the primary medium of postmodern culture.

The music video has been called 'the postmodern turn' in television, and the twenty-four-hour all-music cable channel MTV is a prime example of postmodern TV.[35] Now in common usage, the term 'MTV aesthetic' refers to the stylistic conventions of music video, where editing follows the tempo of popular music. 'Synaesthesia' or 'cross-sensual communication' is its perceptual basis: MTV presents 'the look of sound'.[36] In a music video, segments of visuals from other contexts are rearticulated and recombined, condensed in the video in the form of pastiche and palimpsest – part of what makes it postmodern. Disruption and speed are basic to MTV's sensual impact; its quick-cut style broke with the norms of classical Hollywood narrative and television realism, but is now integral to post-classical Hollywood, TV and advertising. Targeted at the youth market, MTV is all about embodying attitude, tying an appeal to young people's identification with rock musicians and subcultures with the capitalist ideology of conspicuous consumption.[37] The MTV aesthetic is an influential postmodern aesthetic for many cinemas considered in this book.

Post-colonial theory helps to locate these issues in a global perspective which is not confined to Western perspectives, as discourses of postmodernism so often are. In parts of the world where societal modernisation has been late and ultra-rapid, modernity and postmodernity have unfolded more or less simultaneously. Modernity, broadly speaking, implies a break with tradition (namely feudalism). In Europe, the epoch of modernity stretches from the advent of capitalism in the sixteenth century to the nineteenth and twentieth centuries when modernising trends were intensified by industrialisation, urbanisation, mass communications, political mass movements and the rise of nation-states. Arising in the West under specific socio-historical circumstances, modernity has spread slowly to different parts of the world, 'awakened by contact; transported through commerce; administered by empires, bearing colonial inscriptions; propelled by nationalism; and now increasingly steered by global media, migration, and capital'.[38] Now modernity no longer solely emanates from the West, but it does not unfurl in the same way in all places, producing multiple, hybrid, alternative modernities.[39]

Post-colonial theory looks at the after-effects of the age of empires as well as the ways in which those power relations have not been fully transcended. Its inaugural text is Edward Said's *Orientalism*, which analyses colonial discourse, revealing how the West projects its own fantasies onto the Orient, construing it as a dangerous, backward place, full of unbridled sensuality, exoticism and inscrutable mystery.[40] By 'othering' colonial subjects as ignorant, sinister or savage, the West legitimates its own claim to superiority. Colonialism defamed indigenous culture and exalted

European culture. Eurocentrism – the belief that Europe is the centre of the world and that European culture is superior to other cultures – is therefore a key element of Orientalism. Language can betray Eurocentric positioning – for example, in terms such as the 'Middle East', which is only 'east' in relation to Europe. In India, the government and media refer to this region as 'West Asia', and geographers elsewhere have tried to introduce the term 'South-West Asia' (both of these, however, exclude North Africa). 'World cinema' looks at cinema from a non-Eurocentric perspective, although the term 'Middle East' has been retained in this book in the absence of satisfactory alternatives (this issue is discussed further in Chapter 3).

Some post-colonial critics have questioned the validity of applying Western discourses such as Marxism, psychoanalysis and feminism to non-Western contexts, stating that these discourses are Eurocentric. However, the influence of these discourses extends beyond the West, so there are good reasons for adapting them to transcultural perspectives. They have been contrasted with Third Cinema theory, 'the only major branch of film theory that did not originate within a specifically Euro-American context'.[41] The concept of Third Cinema arose amid a revolutionary call to arms against social inequalities and neocolonial exploitation in Latin America, North Africa and South Asia. In their manifesto 'Towards a Third Cinema', Argentinian film directors Fernando Solanas and Octavio Getino differentiate between First Cinema (commercial, studio-based cinema on the Hollywood model), Second Cinema (European art cinema and the cinema of *auteurs*) and Third Cinema (cinema of militant collectives).[42] Here, Third Cinema refers to Third World film production, but not *all* Third World films; for example, Bollywood and India's other popular cinemas fall into the category of First Cinema. Third Cinema is ideologically opposed to the filmmaking practices of both First and Second Cinema. Political issues as well as issues relating to the cinematic medium itself are paramount. Films about revolutionary anti-colonial struggle such as *The Battle of Algiers* (1965) exemplify the early definition of Third Cinema.

Recent Third Cinema theorists have grappled with the problematic distinctions of the original three-cinema model.[43] The concept of Third Cinema now generally includes non-Third World films and today's diasporic cinemas such as Black British Cinema (see Chapter 1). Despite the demise of the politicised cinemas of the 1960s and 1970s, the concept of Third Cinema remains valid as an inspiration for contemporary filmmaking. As a transnational film practice, it undoubtedly lays the critical framework for 'world cinema'. In the contemporary era, however, the concept of 'world cinema' better encapsulates the dispersed and decentred model of film production and distribution that increasingly prevails, especially if it is used to emphasise the interplays between national, regional and global levels of cinema.

Notes

1. By October 1998, *Titanic*'s non-US sales had reached $1,214 million, about twice as much as it had earned in the USA at that time. When adjustments are made for inflation, however, the all-time US box-office record would go to *Gone with the Wind* (1939).
2. Guneratne, 'Introduction', p. 24.
3. Anderson, *Imagined Communities*, p. 6.
4. Rosen, 'Nation and Anti-Nation', p. 399.
5. Higson, 'Idea of National Cinema', p. 7.
6. Shohat and Stam, *Unthinking Eurocentrism*, p. 285.
7. Crofts, 'Concepts of National Cinema', p. 5.
8. Hoskins et al., *Global Television and Film*, p. 23.
9. Miller et al., *Global Hollywood*, p. 84.
10. Anon., 'Global Film Production and Distribution', p. 203.
11. Shafik, *Arab Cinema*, p. 42.
12. GATT was a global trade organisation which aimed to implement multilateral trade agreements. The World Trade Organisation replaced it in 1995.
13. Miller et al., *Global Hollywood*, p. 36.
14. Acland, *Screen Traffic*, pp. 18, 162.
15. Ibid., p. 138.
16. Ibid., p. 244.
17. Jäckel, *European Film Industries*, p. 142.
18. Hoskins et al., *Global Television and Film*, p. 29.
19. Ang, *Living Room Wars*, p. 147.
20. Stringer, 'Regarding Film Festivals', p. 141.
21. Ibid., p. 134.
22. Ibid., p. 174.
23. Shohat and Stam, 'Media Spectatorship', p. 148.
24. Miller et al., *Global Hollywood*, p. 95.
25. Stringer, 'Regarding Film Festivals', p. 125.
26. Stringer, *Movie Blockbusters*, p. 10.
27. Shohat and Stam, *Unthinking Eurocentrism*, p. 295.
28. Neale, 'Art Cinema as Institution', p. 13.
29. Bordwell, 'Art-Cinema Narration', p. 213.
30. Neale, 'Art Cinema as Institution', p. 34.
31. Forbes and Street, *European Cinema*, p. 40.
32. Neale, 'Art Cinema as Institution', p. 14.
33. Hayward, *Cinema Studies*, pp. 277–8, 283.

34. Hill, 'Film and Postmodernism', p. 100.
35. Williams, *Why I [Still] Want My MTV*, p. 3.
36. Ibid., pp. 11, 19.
37. Ibid., p. 23.
38. Gaonkar, *Alternative Modernities*, p. 1.
39. Ibid., p. 17.
40. Said, *Orientalism*, pp. 206–7.
41. Guneratne, 'Introduction', p. 7.
42. Solanas and Getino, 'Towards a Third Cinema', pp. 51–2.
43. See Guneratne, 'Introduction', pp. 12–18.

CHAPTER 1

European Cinema

For most of its history, European cinema has evolved in 'fraught' but creative tension with its main rival, Hollywood.[1] During the globalisation of the 1990s, Hollywood held Europe – its most valuable export market – in its grip and expanded its influence into former communist territories in Eastern Europe, where the lifting of trade restrictions created unprecedented levels of competition from US films. France, Britain, Germany, Spain and Italy are Europe's biggest film-producers, yet even their domestic markets are largely captive to Hollywood. Despite that, increasing competition from Hollywood has acted as a powerful catalyst for innovative strategies in some of the region's cinemas. An outstanding example is the Danish film movement Dogme 95, explored separately in Chapter 2, alongside other Scandinavian trends. This chapter also looks at developments elsewhere in Europe, firstly in Britain, France, Germany and Spain, then in the ex-communist territories of Poland, the Czech Republic and former Yugoslavia.

These territories' recent histories are linked by the rise of nationalism in the nineteenth century, the decline of empires (including the Austro-Hungarian, Ottoman, French and British empires) in the twentieth century, the experience of two World Wars, the Cold War and the formation of the 'new' Europe. During the Cold War, East Germany, Czechoslovakia, Poland and (briefly) Yugoslavia were members of the Soviet Bloc – satellites of the Soviet Union inhabiting a separate cultural sphere largely isolated from the West but not without cultural exchange with each other. However, since the momentous events resulting from the policies of *glasnost* (openness) and *perestroika* (restructuring) launched by Soviet leader Mikhail Gorbachev in the mid-1980s – namely, the fall of the Berlin Wall in 1989 and the collapse of the Soviet Union in 1991 – the 'iron curtain' which divided Europe has gone. As a result of this shared post-Cold War and post-colonial background, there are a number of similar themes across the region's cinemas. These include nationalism and national identity, borders and frontiers, migration, issues of history, politics and morality.

European cinema's defining aesthetic is realism. It is possible to trace this tendency to the British documentary movement or to French poetic realism (both from the 1930s) or even further back to some of the earliest moving pictures shown by the Lumière Brothers. European realism also has pre-cinematic origins in the nineteenth-century European realist novel and in pre-twentieth-century Western visual arts which can be seen – at least since the Renaissance – as progressive attempts to represent a concrete 'reality'. The ideology of 'realism' is one of the means by which European cinema has traditionally sought to differentiate itself from Hollywood. Hollywood realism is guided by character motivation and causal relationships ('realism' seen in terms of 'plausibility'). In European cinema, realism is often conceived as an appeal to national or cultural 'authenticity', offering an alternative to Hollywood by addressing cultural specificities unavailable in Hollywood.

The Italian neorealist movement of the 1940s had an enormous impact on the French and British New Waves of the 1950s and 1960s and has a continuing influence on conceptions of realism today. So too has the 1960s French documentary movement *cinéma-vérité*, which has come to epitomise cinematic attempts to capture reality. *Cinéma-vérité* techniques were incorporated into the French New Wave's narrative cinema. While heavily stylised, French New Wave films cultivated a 'slice of life' approach to filmmaking and became a determining influence on 1960s New Wave cinemas throughout Europe. In contemporary European cinema, realism has reformed into further varieties; as John Orr notes, one type strives to get under 'the skin of the real' through techniques like hyperactive camerawork and decentred close-ups that disrupt normal perception – *Blue* (1993), *Morvern Callar* (2002), *The Last Resort* (2000) – while another, 'hyperrealism', absorbs the real into the spectacular, transforming normality into a stylised surface, for example *Trainspotting* (1996) and the French *cinéma du look*.[2] However, as we shall see, realism is not always the favoured vehicle for the expression of European national or cultural identities. The cinemas of former Soviet-bloc countries often disregard realism, partly as a reaction to the communist doctrine of Socialist Realism, which prescribed clear-cut, idealised depictions – life as it 'should be' according to Party ideology. Surrealism, which emerged as a 1920s avant-garde movement in France, is still a defining force in many parts of Europe, especially Spain and the Czech Republic. Surrealism aims to represent the forces of the unconscious, including dreams. The fantastical countertendency in European cinema further emerges through magic realism, which has Latin American novelistic roots and combines historical realism with myth and fantasy.

Although the heritage film, Second World War film and comedy may be considered pan-European genres, contemporary European films borrow extensively from international neo-noir, Hollywood thrillers and Vietnam war films. These, together with stylistic influences like MTV, modify the realist impulse. Many of the examples discussed in this chapter attest to the emergence of a hybrid aesthetic in the European cinema of the 1990s which is, to varying degrees, *anti*-realistic.

The major current funding sources for European cinema are: private and state-run TV channels, state subsidies (including lottery funding and earnings from taxes on box-office receipts) and intra-European funding bodies.[3] Most European countries offer some form of state protection for their cinemas, showing that even in today's capitalist heyday they deem cinema to be too culturally important to be left entirely to the mercy of market forces.[4] However, it was the communist governments which best understood the importance of film because of its usefulness for propaganda, and were most dedicated to developing an infrastructure for film production, exhibition and distribution. The issue of state censorship looms large in discussions of communist film industries – periods of relative freedom alternated with periods of extreme repression and state intervention – yet full state control also had advantages, including high production levels and less reliance on commercialism.[5] Now these film industries are grappling with the new problems of market economics. There is no longer any state interference; the state-controlled studio system has been replaced by producer-led enterprises. The decrease in state subsidies means that film producers often have to compete for these funds or raise money from national TV networks or international co-producers, as in other European countries. The constraints of working under state censorship have given way to comparably tough commercial constraints.

Pan-European co-productions and the exchange of film personnel between various European film industries have origins in the 1920s, their aims being to counter Hollywood, promote good relations between European countries, share the burden of costs and resources for film production, and guarantee international distribution and box-office success. In 1989, the Council of Europe, a pan-European body spanning West and East Europe, created the Eurimages fund for co-productions between its members. Eurimages also aids exhibition and marketing. In the 1990s, the European Union launched further initiatives, including MEDIA programmes to tackle film production and distribution. The EU has evolved into an economically powerful supranational bloc with a single market and common currency, and by 2004 it had grown to twenty-five states. Its most recent new members include former Eastern-bloc countries, which have made reorientation to the West their top priority. Thus, we find filmmakers from these countries increasingly seeking alliances with the West rather than, as was previously the case, with each other.[6]

British Cinema on the Margins

Through its 1960s New Wave, British cinema became known for its 'kitchen-sink' realism, which typically focused on the working class and England's industrial North. This legacy can be seen in popular hits like *The Full Monty* (1997) as well as in the work of Ken Loach and Mike Leigh, who use location shooting and often improvise with their ensemble casts (rather than using stars). Alongside 'gritty' realism, the other dominant strands in contemporary British film are heritage pictures (exemplified by Merchant Ivory films) and comedies like *Four Weddings and a Funeral* (1994) and *Notting Hill* (1999). There is also, however, a partly submerged fabulist or visionary tradition in British cinema, harking back to the elaborate sets representing utopian or fantasy surroundings constructed in British studios in the 1940s and 1950s – as in *A Matter of Life and Death* (1946) and *Black Narcissus* (1947) directed by Michael Powell and Emeric Pressburger, or Hammer horror productions – and continued in the 1970s and 1980s in the films of Nic Roeg and Ken Russell. The sumptuous use of colour in Peter Greenaway's *The Cook, the Thief, His Wife and Her Lover* (1989) is one outcome of this tradition; so too are reinventions of the heritage genre: *Orlando* (1992), *Wings of the Dove* (1997), *Elizabeth* (1998) and *Shakespeare in Love* (1998). Recent British gangster films, including *Lock, Stock and Two Smoking Barrels* (1998) and *Sexy Beast* (2000), also lean towards fabulist traditions.

Important contributions have come from Black British cinema – films dealing with the experiences of, and mainly made by, South Asian and Afro-Caribbean diasporas. Black Britons (the term 'Blackness' being adopted to articulate a political and 'de-biologised' identity) created common bonds as a result of the shared history of colonialism and contemporary experiences of British racism.[7] Black British filmmakers emerged through workshops, such as Retake and Sankofa, supported by the British Film Institute and by Channel 4, which was launched in 1982 with a remit to address Britain's cultural diversity. They made low-budget films, often described as countering Hollywood models; but, according to Sarita Malik, 'this often had as much to do with the funders' cultural expectations than with any conscious decision by the film-makers themselves to refuse commercial fictional treatments'.[8] Channel 4 commissioned the feature film *My Beautiful Laundrette* (1985), which explored facets of British cultural identity that at the time were perceived to be transgressive – it depicts gay love between a Pakistani and a white ex-National Front member. It became a mainstream success and a landmark for gay and lesbian cinema. The writer, Hanif Kureishi, has since been involved in making other films based on his books, including *My Son the Fanatic* (1997) and the TV series *The Buddha of Suburbia* (1993).

The Conservative government led by Margaret Thatcher (1979–90) favoured deregulated market-led enterprise, ultimately driving Channel 4, the BFI and other public institutions to abandon their commitments to independent filmmaking. With the arrival of Channel 5 and multi-channel TV in the 1990s, Channel 4's commissioning and programming became less ambitious due to its attempt to win larger audiences and higher adver-tising revenues. Meanwhile, Black British cinema itself began to go main-stream, with films such as *Young Soul Rebels* (1991) and *Bhaji on the Beach* (1993) carrying a populist appeal and – like *My Beautiful Laundrette* – crossing over from minority and art-house crowds into larger commercial audiences.[9] Despite their success, Black British cinema was still thought to be a minority cinema, and throughout the 1990s financiers were unwilling to back Black British films. The phenomenal popularity of *East Is East* (1999) – its initial marketing divested of references to Asian themes – and *Bend It Like Beckham* (2002) has again proved them wrong.

These recent mainstream successes are hybrid films. Apart from *Young Soul Rebels*, they are all British Asian films that draw on influences from British cinema – the social realism of the New Wave and Ealing Studio comedies of the 1940s and 1950s – and the emphatically non-realist colour, spectacle and narrative conventions of Indian popular cinema (see Chapters 7 and 8). For example, *East Is East* uses a working-class Northern English setting and contains a homage to the Bollywood film *Pakeezah* (1971), while *Bhaji on the Beach* follows a diverse group of Asian women to Blackpool, a typically 'English' seaside resort. A rich vein running through these films, including *Young Soul Rebels*, is their enlarged defini-tions of Britishness. They reinscribe the distinctive experiences of Black Britons into the discourse of British cultural identity, where they are so often absent. In this sense, they are 'de-defining' Britain, or redefining British cultural identity.

With Jess, a West London Indian girl who wants to play football and who worships David Beckham, the English football star famous for curving his free kicks, *Bend It Like Beckham* exemplifies this trend. It is also a riposte to British realist traditions – director Gurinder Chadha stated that she did not want to make a 'grey British movie', so *Bend It Like Beckham* adopts a bright look and tone.[10] Moreover, its colourful Punjabi wedding and love-triangle plot – Jess and her friend Jules vie with each other for the affec-tions of football coach Joe – establishes generic continuity with contemporary Bollywood (see Chapter 8). When the film cross-cuts between Jess's big match and her sister Pinky's wedding, both scenes are joyful, despite the graphic contrast; the film eschews stereotypical choices between 'Indian' traditions and 'Western' modernity. The film makes subtle reformulations of national identity – without being nationalistic. The term 'English' is used among Punjabis as a marker of difference; for example, Pinky refers to Joe as being English. Yet, ironically, Joe is actually Irish and calls *Jess* English – losing to the Germans on penalties in the team's Hamburg match makes her part of English footballing tradition! *Bend It Like Beckham* topped the UK box office, proving even more popular than *East Is East*. A good example of a film with 'legs' (appropriately, given its subject), it also had a long and profitable overseas run, particularly in Australia, South-East Asia and India. Funded by British Screen Finance, the satellite TV channel BSkyB, Germany's Road Movies and Helkon SK, it was aided by a vigorous marketing strategy, opening on 460 UK screens – the cost of this distribution was three times the production cost – while punning headlines in press coverage of Beckham's metatarsal injury before the 2002 World Cup boosted its publicity.

While *Bend It Like Beckham* counters the bigoted extremes of English nationalism by mobilising the multicultural potential implied in football as a 'national' sport, *The Last Resort*, a BBC TV production directed by Polish-born Pawel Pawlikowski, probes issues of British national identity through the treatment of asylum-seekers. When her fiancé fails to turn up on her arrival at Stansted airport, a Russian woman, Tanya, pleads political asylum to avoid deportation and is sent, with her son Artiom, to a detention centre surrounded by barbed wire, police patrols and surveillance cameras in a dismal seaside town called Stonehaven – actually Margate. Tanya is imprisoned in a nightmarishly bureaucratic system which takes 'twelve to sixteen months' to process applications, makes her wait 'three to six months' for clearance when she decides she wants to return to Russia, and does not permit her to work, thereby making her prey to an Internet pornographer who lurks around offering quick cash. The film uses documentary realist techniques such as handheld camera and some non-actors, including 'real' asylum-claimants, yet the Margate that we see is abstract and stylised – emptied of traffic and people, filmed in desaturated colours to enhance its visual bleakness. This abstraction makes some sequences dreamlike, as when Alfie, an arcade manager who befriends Artiom and Tanya, helps them escape on a yacht, and in the final bleached-out shot through the airport tunnel. As Les Roberts states in a reading of the film, 'overwhelmingly white, Conservative and mono-cultural' British towns and seaside resorts like Margate are the 'temporary home and "last resort" of asylum claimants' – a situation which provokes hysterical, xenophobic rhetoric from local and national British newspapers, right-wing politicians and neo-Nazi groups.[11] Their imagery revolves around notions of overflowing – typically 'floods' of 'bogus' asylum-seekers, often from Eastern Europe – and aims at flushing out 'impure' excess. *Last Resort* avoids explicitly delving into this, yet shows the effects of xenophobia and politicians' 'resort' to nationalism on issues of asylum and immigration.

A similar process of 'de-defining' is at work in the cinemas of Britain's Celtic fringes, which are likewise concerned to assert the particularities of their cultural identity and their difference from British cinema 'norms'. These issues came to a head during the 1980s, when Thatcher's policies were perceived as favouring southern and English interests. When the Labour Party took power in 1997, it held referendums leading to devolution in 1999, giving Scotland and Wales some self-determination. Administered by the Arts Councils of England, Scotland, Wales and Northern Ireland, lottery funding (introduced in the mid-1990s) helped the resurgence of these newly devolved film industries. Scottish cinematic revival, moreover, was propelled by the success of *Shallow Grave* (1994) and *Trainspotting*, both made by the same creative trio: director Danny Boyle, producer Andrew MacDonald (grandson of Emeric Pressburger) and scriptwriter John Hodge. *Trainspotting* follows heroin-users in Edinburgh and London during the 1980s. It was funded by Channel 4 and targeted at youth audiences – its innovative poster campaign downplayed the heroin story and gave British cinema an energetic, hip, confrontational image. Visually flamboyant, with hallucinogenic images and a pulsating techno, Britpop, retro-punk and ambient soundtrack, *Trainspotting* launched new stylistic, cultural and industrial trends as well as leading a wave of films about club and drug culture, including *Human Traffic* (1999), *24 Hour Party People* (2002) and *Morvern Callar*. Rejecting stereotypes of British realism, *Trainspotting* produces the marvellous and fantastic from the mundane, as when the protagonist Renton dives into 'the Worst Toilet in Scotland' to retrieve his opium suppositories and finds himself in an underwater paradise, with Brian Eno's 'Deep Blue Day' playing on the soundtrack.

This fantastic element can be related to Celtic myths and legends, the Gothic and the supernatural.[12] There is a visionary twist in Scottish cinematic realism, best exemplified in the work of Lynne Ramsey, who came to prominence on the strength of the films she directed for Tartan Shorts, including *The Gasman* (1997). Contemplative, aesthetically subdued and emotionally intense, her films subtly defamiliarise everyday reality through unexpected angles and decentred framings. *Ratcatcher* (1999), her first feature, is set during the 1973 Glasgow dustmen's strike, and follows a boy who watches his friend drown. In *Morvern Callar*, the eponymous heroine finds her boyfriend dead, with a suicide note asking her to publish his novel. Pretending the novel is hers and disposing of the body in a shallow grave (a Scottish cinema in-joke), Morvern keeps his death a secret, not even telling her best friend Lana. The film evokes the cynical, wasted mood of fin-de-siècle rave culture when Morvern and Lana go on holiday to Spain with proceeds from the dead boyfriend's bank account. Morvern drifts through the resort's nightclubs much as she did in the supermarket in her Highland fishing-port home, the strobed lighting reminding us of the flashing Christmas-tree lights on her boyfriend's corpse and highlighting Morvern's liminal, disenchanted state. The film can be read in terms of Julia Kristeva's theory of abjection, which describes a state suspended between objecthood and subjecthood – the abject is the 'in-between, the ambiguous and the composite'.[13] A corpse is the 'ultimate of abjection'. The narrative of *Morvern Callar* emanates from this perspective; Morvern adopts the abject as a 'safeguard' in a world otherwise emptied of meaning.[14]

French *Cinéma du look*

France has the biggest film industry in Europe and extensive state protection measures, including a film quota system which restricts US imports, and a levy on box-office receipts which funds local films. Like Britain, France has strong realist traditions. Although the naturalistic legacy of the French New Wave and *cinéma-vérité* has recently been reasserted through films such as *The Dream Life of Angels* (1998) and *Être et Avoir* (2002), this was swept aside in the 1980s by a trend favouring elaborate, sensuous spectacle filled with pastiches of American film genres and influences from music video, advertising and French comic strips (*bandes dessinées*) that was far more popular among youth audiences. Critics call it the '*cinéma du look*', usually in pejorative reference to its emphasis on style over (political) substance. Its primary exponents are Jean-Jacques Beineix (whose *Diva* [1981] launched the style), Luc Besson and Léos Carax. Their films are populated with characters who are 'a curious mixture of the chic and down-at-heel, the attractive and the grotesque, the intellectual and the brutish' – types drawn intertextually from fairy tales, cartoons and generic conventions rather than from 'life'.[15] This is a cinema that foregrounds light, colour, sound and space in ways that divert sharply from naturalistic practices, as can be seen in Luc Besson's use of anamorphic widescreen to show his protagonists in alienating urban surroundings in *Léon* (1994); this format uses a wide-angle lens that greatly accentuates the horizontal axis at the expense of the vertical, resulting in a distortion of the *mise en scène*. With its stylish violence, *Léon* also intersects with international neo-noir genres and marks the evolution of *cinéma du look* internationally – and Besson has taken it further in his science-fiction blockbuster *The Fifth Element* (1997).

The fantasy film branch of *cinéma du look* is exemplified by the work of Jean-Pierre Jeunet and Marc Caro, who collaborated on *Delicatessen* (1991) and *City of Lost Children* (1995); Jeunet also directed the Hollywood film *Alien: Resurrection* (1997) and the Oscar-nominated *Amélie* (2001). These films utilise bizarre camera angles, distorting anamorphic lenses and elaborate set design to present defamiliarised worlds. They are full of virtuoso choreographed set pieces, such as sex scenes synchronised with other rhythmic actions and sounds in *Delicatessan* and *Amélie*, and lyrical surrealist moments, as when characters play a duet with a saw and cello in *Delicatessan*'s final rooftop scene. Jeunet's favourite actor, Dominique Pinon, stars in each film. While *Delicatessan*, *City of Lost Children* and *Alien: Resurrection* can all be seen as variations on the theme of dystopia, *Amélie* represents a utopia no less artificial in its style and setting than the other films. Created with extensive computer graphics and interiors shot on stages in Germany, it depicts an unreal Paris, evoking the 1950s, with all the 'bad' bits (such as racism) gradually filtered out.

Another important film relating to *cinéma du look* is *La Haine* (1995), which won Matthieu Kassovitz the Best Director's Award at Cannes in 1995 and became a massive hit internationally. Kassovitz is an actor; he appears in *Amélie*, *A Self-Made Hero* (1996) (a film satirising the myth of French wartime resistance heroes), and in a minor role as a skinhead in *La Haine*, his directorial debut. *La Haine* is set in the Parisian *banlieue* (suburbs) populated by working-class and immigrant families, and explores race, class and gender relations in a society where both government and police face pressures from France's popular National Front Party. Thematically, *La Haine* connects with a tendency called *cinéma beur* – films directed by, or dealing with the experiences of, second-generation immigrants from France's former North African Arab colonies; *beur* is French backslang for *Arabe*. However, in contrast to *beur* films' understated social realism, *La Haine* is stylistically hyperbolic. Despite the *cinéma-vérité* connotations of its 'gritty' black-and-white street-riot footage, it uses wide-angle lenses to foreshorten perspective (making characters look 'larger than life'), fluid tracking, and image sequences edited to music (as when DJ Cut Killer plays Extreme-NTM's song 'Fuck the police'). These MTV influences give the film its sensory appeal. *La Haine* also fills the screen with homages to Martin Scorsese and Spike Lee. Ginette Vincendeau has argued that this combination of locally specific concerns with the iconography of spectacular male violence – familiar to audiences from the neo-noir territory of Scorsese, John Woo and Quentin Tarantino – was what propelled its global success.[16]

Post-Wall German Cinema

Any account of contemporary German cinema has to refer to the New German Cinema movement, which started in the Federal Republic in the 1960s. Its directors included Rainer Werner Fassbinder, Werner Herzog and Wim Wenders, whose films showed empathy with society's outsiders and an ambivalent relationship with America and Hollywood genres. They were not generally liked by domestic audiences but were highly esteemed abroad, especially for interrogating the country's Nazi past. The movement began to decline after Fassbinder's death in 1982, partly because the new Helmut Kohl-led Christian Democrat government withdrew subsidies. Some New German cinema directors have gone to work abroad – including Wenders, who made films in Germany (*Wings of Desire* [1987]), Hollywood (*Paris, Texas* [1984] and *End of Violence* [1997]) and Australia (*Until the End of the World* [1991]).

A year after the fall of the Berlin Wall, East Germany reunified with the West. Around the same time, a new generation of filmmakers emerged, who distance themselves from New German Cinema's overt socio-political critique. They aim to make films that are liked by, and accessible to, the German public. These films are generally unconcerned with Germany's Nazi past and reflect the 'normalisation' and Americanisation of Germany since reunification.[17] Although popular at home, they do not travel well, being perceived as too parochial; a notable exception is the Oscar-nominated *Nasty Girl* (1990), which dramatises the true story of a schoolgirl who was ostracised for uncovering her town's Nazi secrets. However, two directors who have departed from 'parochial' concerns differently, achieving popular success at home and abroad, are Tom Tykwer and Wolfgang Becker.

Produced by Tykwer's company X Filme, together with West German Radio, ARTE, various German regional funds and Germany's Ministry of the Interior, on a small budget of $1.8 million, *Run Lola Run* (1998) – Tykwer's third film – was Germany's most successful 1990s movie. With a fast-paced, techno soundtrack-driven thriller narrative and a goal-directed flame-haired heroine, *Run Lola Run* combines Hollywood-like entertainment values with European art house, referencing an eclectic range of films from *Blind Chance* (1981) to *Pulp Fiction*. Lola has only twenty minutes to find DM100,000 to save her boyfriend Manni from his drug-dealer boss. The film gives her three chances to complete her quest, with characters and events configured slightly differently on each round.

It renders the multiple outcomes through influences from computer games, hypertext, animation, MTV and chaos theory. Lola has the power to change her fate, yet her actions spring partly from contingency. This stresses the unpredictability of cause and effect, especially in snapshot flash-forwards of passers-by whose brief contact with Lola generates random repercussions.

For German audiences, *Run Lola Run* is distinctively a Berlin film. It opens with a prologue showing Berlin's East and West halves being soldered together. The reason why Lola must run, rather than take a taxi, is offered in the first few minutes: a previous taxi journey took her to the wrong destination, a street in the East with the same name. When Lola runs, she passes well-known Berlin locations, but not Nazi landmarks. The film plays with space in these sequences, juxtaposing parts of Berlin which are geographically disparate in order to show a city in the process of being remade and reconstructed: a new Berlin unfettered by the past in which Lola is a dynamic agent of change, sprinting into the future despite the odds stacked against her and despite her initial failures. Released in the same year as the elections that ended Kohl's sixteen years as Chancellor, the film was interpreted as a call for political rejuvenation.[18]

Becker's *Goodbye, Lenin!* (2003), also produced by X Filme, starts in the German Democratic Republic (East Germany) before the fall of the Berlin Wall. It is narrated from the perspective of Alex Kern, whose mother – a Communist Party faithful – has a heart-attack when she sees him in an anti-government demonstration. She falls into an eight-month coma, waking up after the Wall has fallen and the GDR no longer exists. Alex protects her from shock by pretending that these events have not occurred. He and his friend Denis record fake TV reports to explain the chinks appearing in the illusion, as when his mother witnesses Lenin's statue being freighted away and an enormous Coca-Cola advert unfurling next door; Alex has East German astronaut Sigmund Jähn pose as the new GDR president, declaring that the Wall has been pulled down to welcome Western refugees disillusioned by capitalism – a hilarious inversion of actual events. Signs of globalisation and multinational capital flood the landscape everywhere except in his mother's flat; Alex himself becomes a satellite-dish salesman, and his sister works at Burger King. The supermarkets stock foreign produce, so Alex rummages in bins for old GDR jars in which to repackage his mother's food, including the 'Spreewald gherkins' she craves.

In earlier films, including *Wings of Desire*, the Wall created complications, whereas here its non-existence does.[19] *Goodbye, Lenin!* comes in the wake of films such as *Sun Alley*, the best-selling German film of 1999, feeding a growing nostalgia for the GDR – a fad known as '*Ostalgie*', which includes the reissue of GDR brands, GDR theme parks, and the wearing of communist-style uniforms as fashion statements. There is a similar romanticisation of the communist era in cinemas of other former communist territories, as we will see. The keenness of former GDR citizens to assert a distinct 'East German' identity is often attributed to the hardships of adapting to Western market economies. *Goodbye, Lenin!* makes it clear that the GDR lost out economically. Alex finds his mother's hidden savings when it is too late to convert them into West German marks. The football scores tell it all: 'the exchange rate was two to one, and Germany won one-nil'. However, *Goodbye, Lenin!* maintains a critical edge on the *Ostalgie* phenomenon by having Alex realise that the fake picture of the GDR that he paints for his mother is the GDR he dreamed of – a country that acknowledges its faults and welcomes outsiders.

Post-Franco Spanish Cinema

Spanish cinema hosts a wide range of traditions from the surrealists Luis Buñuel and Salvador Dalí (*Un Chien Andalou* [1929]) to the contemplative visionary Victor Erice whose *Spirit of the Beehive* (1973) uses the image of Frankenstein's monster to refract the horrors of life under General Franco's dictatorship. Franco died in 1975 after ruling for forty years. Censorship was lifted in 1977, ushering in an era of liberalism, consumerism and democratic transition, resulting in an explosion of explicitness and experimentation in the nation's cinema. Rob Stone writes: 'Filmmakers found themselves in an unsupervised candy store of previously forbidden treats, and either stood there gawping at all the bare flesh and blasphemy or gorged themselves sick on the new permissiveness'.[20] The legacy of Franco's patriarchal, Catholic autocracy did not disappear overnight; the new consumer society was still male-dominated, although movements favouring women's rights, feminism, divorce, homosexuality, abortion and contraception emerged.[21] Some filmmakers tried to retrieve cultural histories and identities buried or distorted under Franco's censorship; this increasingly took the form of sexual identity politics. Masculinity is one such contested area; under Franco, popular genres glorified Spanish masculinity, hence some contemporary films pit the 'New Spanish Man' against the 'Iberian macho'. However, in a similar way to former communist countries, commercial demands proved more constricting than censorship for some directors like Erice, who has made few films over the last thirty years; the post-Franco era favours entertainment cinema capable of competing with Hollywood.[22] Film policies increasingly aimed to make film-producers independent of the state. During the rule of the right-of-centre People's Party (1996–2004), state subsidies ended.

The People's Party were elected because of growing disillusionment with the governing Socialist Workers Party, amid a climate of general strikes, rising abortion rates and escalating violence from the Basque separatist group ETA. Many Spaniards became doubtful whether their economic marginalisation under capitalism was any better than living under Franco.[23] This disillusionment manifests in 1990s Spanish films reflecting themes of nostalgia, abstinence and family values; or, in the work of internationally celebrated *auteurs* like Julio Medem and Alejandro Amenábar, a general apathy towards socio-political concerns, driving an attention to 'personal issues' or playfulness with cinematic genres.[24]

The work of Pedro Almodóvar encapsulates the dominant trends – a steady turnover of commercial hits paving the way for his Oscar triumph with *All About My Mother* (1999). Almodóvar draws on Hollywood influences and Spain's theatrical and literary traditions, as well as the *movida*, an underground cultural movement known for its drug-use and sexual liberalism, to create genre pastiches which portray gender and sexuality as stylised performances.[25] His films affirm post-Franco liberties with only a cursory backward glance at the past, as seen in *Live Flesh* (1997). They are playful and camp, with a bright, glossy look appealing to 'how post-Franco Spain liked to see itself and how it liked to be seen'.[26] While the homoerotic thriller *Bad Education* (2004) explores male relationships, most of Almodóvar's other films since the 1990s have focused on heterosexual couples, although films like *Tie Me Up! Tie Me Down!* (1990) and *Talk to Her* (2002) emphasise sexual deviance within heterosexuality, showing that all gendered positions are complex, fluid and playful, not just those of homosexuals, drag queens and transsexuals.

Beyond the Polish Cinema of Moral Concern

Polish cinema held a strong international presence from the 1950s to the early 1980s through figures such as Andrzej Wajda, Krzysztof Zanussi, Agnieszka Holland and Krzysztof Kieślowski. In 1980, Solidarity – the first free trade union to exist in the communist bloc – shook the foundations of state socialism, leading to the imposition of martial law from 1981 to 1985. In this period, these Polish directors made films dealing with the conflicts of personal interest and socio-political demands which highlighted the cracks in the state socialist system.[27] Avoiding direct political critique, they expressed dissent through images of stagnation and dull routines. None has been more influential than Kieślowski, who died in 1996.

Often hailed as the most important contemporary European director, his career set the precedent for an emerging breed of transnational European *auteurs* including Tom Tykwer, who filmed Kieślowski's script *Heaven* (2002), and Austria's Michael Haneke.

Kieślowski began as a documentarist during the 1970s. His early fiction films *Camera Buff* (1979) and *Blind Chance* satirise the way in which life under state socialism determines or limits their protagonists' life options. *Blind Chance* depicts three possible outcomes when a medical student runs to board a train. With its musings on fate, chance and ethical choice, it became a big influence on Tykwer's *Run Lola Run* and the British film *Sliding Doors* (1998). In the ten films belonging to *Decalogue* (1988–9), Kieślowski explores the Ten Commandments through characters on a Warsaw housing estate. He gradually moved from exploring moral concerns in determinate socio-political contexts (namely, Polish state socialism) to 'universal' existential themes, including coincidence and parallel destinies, enabling him to reach a larger audience.[28] The style of his films also changed, giving more emphasis to colour, lighting, unusual camera angles and music (he began collaborating with composer Zbigniew Preisner on *No End* [1985]). The realist depictions of 'grey' Poland in his early works gave way to tendencies towards stylisation.

Kieślowski's 1990s films, *The Double Life of Véronique* (1991) and the *Three Colours – Blue*, *White* and *Red* (1994) – were internationally financed and backed by Marin Karmitz of MK2 Productions, France's most powerful independent producer. They feature major European stars: Juliet Binoche, Julie Delpy, Jean-Louis Trintignant and Irène Jacob. The *Three Colours* trilogy meditates on the broad social theme of European unification: *Blue*, *White* and *Red* take place in France, Poland and Switzerland respectively; these are the countries of the films' financiers. Yet they remain focused on the personal level, interweaving the main characters' destinies so that they all turn up as ferry-disaster survivors in *Red*, the final film. They are also loosely based on French Revolution ideals – Liberty, Equality, Fraternity. For example, *White* deals with equality, transposing a skit on communism – nobody wants to be equal, they want to be more than equal – into a Polish man's vendetta against his French ex-wife.

Czech Surrealism and Historical Films

Czech culture is known for its black humour, pessimism and cynicism as well as its interest in fantasy, magic and surrealism. The propensity for pessimism was intensified by the political traumas of Stalinism and the 'thwarted hopes' of the popular movement called the Prague Spring which rose up in response to Soviet leader Nikita Khrushchev's 'thaw', a gradual process of post-Stalinist liberalisation.[29] The Prague Spring was crushed in 1968 by invading Soviet-led forces, and was followed by a period of extreme repression throughout the Soviet Bloc, ironically called 'normalisation' in Czechoslovakia. Communism finally collapsed peacefully in the 1989 'Velvet Revolution', leading to liberal democracy and then the country's partition into the Czech and Slovak Republics in 1993.

During 'normalisation', many films were banned, including those of surrealist animator Jan Svankmajer, who started making films in 1964 but only became internationally known after *Dimensions of Dialogue* (1982). Czech surrealism started in the 1920s and was made illegal after the Second World War. The same events made Czech surrealists more sober in their attitude to the fantastic than their French and Spanish counterparts. Svankmajer explains: Czech surrealism 'could not react to this absurd reality and therefore all creation during this period was evidently less "poetic" and "lyrical" and was more "sarcastic", full of black and objective humour'.[30]

Svankmajer uses both clay and puppet animation. His films are greatly influenced by local folk puppetry, a stylised puppet art form comparable to Japanese Kabuki and Chinese opera. Although his films are now shown on Czech television, Britain – not the Czech Republic – is the keenest promoter of his work. Channel 4 helped to fund his first full-length feature film *Alice* (1988), while the BBC participated in financing his second feature, *Faust* (1994). These, together with his more recent films *Conspirators of Pleasure* (1996) and *Little Otik* (2000), combine animation with live action. They are filmed using the same method as Svankmajer's animated short films – editing together short and single-frame shots. These films mine the underside of horror, dream and infantilism in myths, fairy tales and children's stories. Eating and dismemberment are recurring motifs. In *Little Otik*, for instance, mouths – whether speaking or eating – are filmed in tight close-ups. The live action, like the animation, makes viewers react to tactile images on screen with their imaginations and evokes perverse, even libidinous, attitudes towards seemingly innocuous activities.

Historical films are a major trend in Czech and Polish cinemas. These generally focus on the two World Wars, the Holocaust and the Stalinist era.[31] Within this trend, there is a new leaning towards revisionist films that either express nostalgia for communism or unearth stories suppressed during the Stalinist era – *glasnost* emboldened filmmakers to investigate this previously restricted area. In the nostalgia category, there is a tendency to humanise the former colonisers, the Russians, turning them into vulnerable beings, like the little boy in the Oscar-winning *Kolya* (1996), or showing them trapped into prostitution. This trend even applies to films made outside the former Soviet Bloc, including Pawlikowski's films and Lukas Moodysson's *Lilya 4-ever* (2002) (discussed in Chapter 2). With the collapse of the Soviet Union, Dina Iordanova remarks, 'the tyrant has disappeared', leaving its former occupied territories in a competitive capitalist world where they find themselves being the losers.[32] The sentiment of forgiveness rather than resentment permeates *Kolya*, where a Prague bachelor who hates everything Russian finds his attitudes softening after he is forced to look after the boy. The director, Jan Svěrák, is the Czech Republic's most commercially successful filmmaker. Few films from the former Soviet Bloc reach global audiences, but Svěrák established his own production company, Biograf Jan Svěrák, to make sure that *Kolya* did.[33] Funded by Biograf with the Czech TV network CZTV, Czech Republic state funds and other sources including Eurimages, it was acquired by seventeen international distributors, including Miramax, and successfully released in forty countries. It also became the most popular film of the year in the Czech Republic.

Svěrák's *Dark Blue World* (2001), reportedly the most ambitious movie in Czech film history, belongs to the other revisionist category. Narrated in flashback from the 1950s Stalinist terrors, it follows two Czech pilots, Franta and Karel, who arrive in England in 1939 from Nazi-occupied Czechoslovakia. They join the Royal Air Force in the Battle of Britain, and fall in love with the same English woman. With amazing aerial dogfights, filmed using special effects with live-action aerial photography and outtakes from *The Battle of Britain* (1969), the film celebrates the Czechoslovak servicemen who fought with the Western Allies – a glorious moment which was buried when the communists took control of Czechoslovakia in 1948 and made the West a capitalist enemy. Czech airmen, no longer considered patriots, were arrested as traitors, like Franta in the film, who is condemned to a labour camp. In its funding and international cast, as in its revisionist history, *Dark Blue World* is symptomatic of the former Soviet Bloc's westward turn.

Yugoslav War Films

Yugoslavia's Communist Party leader Tito broke with Stalin in 1948 and opened up channels with the West, thus the history of Yugoslav filmmaking followed a different course from other former communist territories. Filmmakers succeeded in decentralising film production into smaller units, which gave them greater control. But, as in some other former communist countries, the collapse of communism gave way to ethnic rivalries and nationalist obsessions. In Czechoslovakia, partition along ethnic lines was peaceful; in Yugoslavia, it was catastrophic. Tito was widely credited with holding together the Yugoslav federation like a glue; his dogma of 'Brotherhood and Unity' outlawed nationalist movements. The Communist Party of Yugoslavia disintegrated a decade after his death, when Slobodan Milošević came to power supporting the cause of Serbian nationalism. This led in 1991–2 to the break-up of Yugoslavia into the independent nations Croatia, Slovenia, Bosnia and Macedonia – leaving only a rump Yugoslavia consisting of Serbia and Montenegro – and to the ethnic slaughter of Serbs, Croats and Muslims. International opinion perceives Milošević's Serb government to be the primary aggressor; Milošević and other leaders such as Bosnian Serb Radovan Karadžic have been indicted for war crimes involving 'ethnic cleansing' in Croatia (1991–5), Bosnia (1992–5) and Kosovo (1999).

This bloody conflict put the international spotlight on the territory's cinemas as well as evoking responses from outsiders, including the UK/US co-production *Welcome to Sarajevo* (1997). The most controversial film from the territory is *Underground* (1995), which won Emir Kusturica, a Bosnian Muslim, his second Cannes Palme d'Or. During the war, Milošović's regime prioritised film funding, aware of cinema's importance as a weapon for rewriting history and disseminating it around the world. It is likely that it endorsed *Underground*, a French, German and Hungarian co-production made in Belgrade with an undisclosed investment by regime-controlled Radio-TV Serbia.[34] An internationally acclaimed filmmaker like Kusturica does not need to seek state aid from Belgrade, yet he chose to. Yugoslav commentators accused him of betraying his native Bosnia and spreading Serbian nationalist propaganda with portrayals of Croats as pro-Nazi (these nationalist clichés are reflected in regional slang, where Croats are called 'Ustaše' after Nazi-affiliated Croatian nationalists who slaughtered Serbs during the Second World War, while Serbs are called 'Četniks' and Muslims 'Turks'). Exhausted by controversy, for his next film *Black Cat, White Cat* (1998) Kusturica returned to the apolitical topic of the Roma lifestyle which he had earlier covered in *Time of the Gypsies* (1988), for which he earned his first Palme d'Or.

Kusturica's films characteristically revel in absurdity and use magic realism to highlight the limits of naturalism for capturing the chaotic events in the Balkans. In *Underground*, he relates the escapades of Marko, Blacky and Natalia; Marko and Natalia trick Blacky into hiding underground during the communist era under the pretext that the Second World War is still going on, while the two of them become international arms-dealers. After an apocalyptic finale, the characters reassemble for the epilogue, a wedding in which they continue celebrating even when the section of land on which they stand breaks and drifts away from the mainland. The film traces contemporary problems to Tito's communist era, which kept people in a 'metaphorical cellar'.[35] However, as well as blaming the communists, it suggests that the troubles result from ancient quarrels. Kusturica articulates this in interview, describing war in the Balkans as 'a natural phenomenon . . . an earthquake which explodes from time to time . . . [N]obody is able to locate the roots of this terrible conflict.'[36]

These metaphors obfuscate the deliberate military and propagandistic planning behind the war – for example Milošević's incendiary rhetoric, spreading rumours about attacks on Serbs. They also repeat certain Western myths about the Balkans, which were used to justify nonintervention in the recent crisis: 'let them resolve their own quarrels'. Slavoj Žižek argues that the same myths are used in Serb propaganda to prevent analysis of 'the *political* calculuses and strategic decisions which led to the war', making the conflict's origins seem mysterious and unknowable.[37] For him, Kusturica's statements are 'an exemplary case of "Balkanism", functioning in a similar way to Edward Said's "Orientalism": the Balkans as a timeless space onto which the West projects its phantasmatic content'.

During the war, Tito's 'Brotherhood and Unity' dissolved into bloody fraternal rivalry, as former neighbours and 'brothers' turned on each other, determined to differentiate themselves in narrowly conceived, ethnic terms.[38] The theme of Self versus Br(Other) is treated in a number of films, including Srdjan Dragojević's *Pretty Village, Pretty Flame* (1996). Subsidised by Radio-TV Serbia and the Serbian Ministry of Culture – and also accused of being Serbian propaganda, yet thought by some to 'slander' the Serbs – this film follows two boyhood friends, Milan (a Serb) and Halil (a Bosnian Muslim), who play outside a disused Brotherhood and Unity tunnel. Neither dares enter the tunnel, imagining that an ogre inhabits it. During the Bosnian War, however, Milan and other Serb soldiers shelter in it and find themselves besieged by Muslim soldiers; among them is Halil, who Milan now believes killed his mother: their friendship, so solid during peacetime, is renounced in the expedient of war. Told in flashback from Milan's perspective, as he lies injured in a Belgrade military hospital in 1994, the film represents Serbs as more than just murderers, yet it gives them a share of the blame along with others. This moral complexity aided its international success, as did its deployment of Vietnam War movie motifs.[39] It delights in the pyrotechnics of destruction; hence the title, which translates more literally as *Pretty Villages Burn Nicely* – an ambivalent statement, as 'ethnic cleansing' takes place through the burning of villages.

International accolade also went to *No Man's Land* (2001), the debut feature by Bosnian Muslim Danis Tanovic, praised for its clear and thought-provoking treatment of the conflict. It won the 2002 Best Foreign Film Oscar, beating *Amélie* and the Bollywood film *Lagaan* (2001) (see Chapter 8). It is set in the Bosnian War, when UN peacekeepers were sent in but ordered not to intervene, and centres on two soldiers – a Bosnian Muslim, Ciki, and a Serb, Nino – trapped together in a disused trench between enemy lines, with a third soldier, Ciki's friend Cera, lying on the trench floor booby-trapped to a mine that will explode if he moves. A French UN sergeant tries to help the soldiers, but is initially stopped by UN Headquarters. The UN was much criticised for its policy of non-intervention during the Bosnian War, especially when the 1995 Srebrenica massacre occurred after French UN commander General Morillon had declared the town a 'safe haven' – like Sergeant Marchand in the film, Morillon wanted to help but was badly compromised.[40] In the film, British journalist Jane Livingstone (played by Mike Leigh actress Katrin Cartlidge) rushes to the trench along with other reporters, baying for a hot story. Tanovic ambivalently portrays the combative power of the global media training their lenses on the conflict; they pressure the UN to take action, yet their presence has a distorting effect. When Cera's mine proves impossible to defuse, the UN pretend they have rescued him for the media's benefit. The film ends with the camera floating over the trench where Cera still lies, fading into darkness as night descends, his plight of no more concern now that the media circus has departed – without verifying their reports.

The film crystallises wider issues relevant to other contemporary conflicts through its tight focus on the trench – a 'microcosm' of the Bosnian War. Its dark humour expresses the war's tragic and painful absurdity. Ciki and Nino are like 'brothers' or neighbours who now mistrust each other, quarrelling over who started the war and shooting each other as soon as they are evacuated. Yet ironically they have more in common than any of the other characters – they once dated the same girl in the same town, and they understand each other without translators.

Notes

1. Forbes and Street, *European Cinema*, p. xiv.
2. Orr, 'New Directions in European Cinema', p. 301.
3. Ezra, *European Cinema*, p. 15.
4. Jäckel, *European Film Industries*, p. 1.
5. Iordanova, *Other Europe*, p. 22.

 6. Ibid., p. 145.
 7. Malik, 'Beyond "The Cinema of Duty"?', p. 204.
 8. Ibid., p. 205.
 9. Ibid., p. 210.
10. Forde, 'Winning Team', p. 9.
11. Roberts, '"Welcome to Dreamland"', p. 87.
12. Petrie, *Screening Scotland*, p. 8.
13. Kristeva, *Powers of Horror*, p. 4.
14. Orr, 'New Directions in European Cinema', p. 306.
15. Harris, 'The *Cinéma du Look*', p. 222.
16. Vincendeau, 'Designs on the *banlieue*', p. 323.
17. See Rentschler, 'The Post-Wall Cinema', pp. 260–77.
18. Sinka, 'Tom Tykwer's *Lola Rennt*'.
19. Iordanova, 'East of Eden', p. 27.
20. Stone, *Spanish Cinema*, p. 110.
21. Ibid., p. 120.
22. Ibid., p. 10.
23. Ibid., p. 129.
24. Ibid., p. 130.
25. Ibid., pp. 125–6.
26. Arroyo, 'Pedro Almodóvar', p. 108.
27. Iordanova, *Other Europe*, p. 109.
28. Ibid., pp. 111–12.
29. Hames, *Dark Alchemy*, p. 2.
30. Ibid., p. 102.
31. Iordanova, *Other Europe*, p. 150.
32. Ibid., p. 160.
33. Jäckel, *European Film Industries*, p. 82.
34. Iordanova, *Cinema of Flames*, p. 123.
35. Ibid., p. 118.
36. Cited in Žižek, *Plague of Phantasies*, p. 62.
37. Ibid., p. 62.
38. Krstić, '"Showtime Brothers!"' p. 58.
39. Iordanova, *Cinema of Flames*, p. 147.
40. Horton, 'No Man's Land', p. 39.

CHAPTER 2

Scandinavian Cinema

During the silent era, Sweden and Denmark were among the world's leading film-producers. Scandinavian directors such as Victor Sjöström and Mauritz Stiller and stars like Greta Garbo and Asta Nielson became internationally famous. With the advent of sound, Scandinavian cinema's international prominence declined, although it continued to boom domestically throughout the studio era (1930s–1950s). Abroad, it became known mostly for its art cinema, especially Carl Dreyer's and Ingmar Bergman's dark films about religion, faith and doubt. In the 1990s, Scandinavian cinema leapt back into the international limelight with Dogme 95, the Danish film collective launched by Lars von Trier and Thomas Vinterberg. At the start of the twenty-first century, Scandinavian films prospered again at home and abroad. This chapter will look at factors underpinning this revival and will focus on representative figures, including the Danish provocateur von Trier, Sweden's popular *auteur* Lukas Moodysson and cult Finnish director Aki Kaurismäki. It will argue that these small film-producing nations acutely exemplify the struggles of European cinema against Hollywood domination.

Situated in Europe's far north, the Scandinavian nations – also known as Nordic nations – are Denmark, Sweden, Norway, Finland and Iceland. The sparsely populated northernmost parts of Sweden, Norway and Finland are inside the Arctic Circle, where winters are long, dark and extremely cold while in high summer the sun never sets. Apart from geographic and climatic features – integral to many Scandinavian films – the countries have commonalities based on shared histories of occupations and empires. Sweden ruled over Finland from 1155 to 1809; Norway was owned by Denmark, then governed by Sweden in the nineteenth century, and became independent again in 1905; Iceland was a Danish colony from the late thirteenth century until its independence in 1944.[1] Finland, annexed by Russia after being ruled by Sweden, became independent in 1917 and has cultural affinities with Eastern Europe as well as with the rest of Scandinavia. There are differences alongside the similarities; in film contexts, this is evidenced by differing receptions of the same films in different countries. Moreover, all Scandinavian languages share Germanic roots except Finnish, which belongs to a rare language group known as Finno–Ugric. These linguistic and historic factors affect the export of films within countries – for example, many Swedish movies are exported to Finland, where Swedish is a common second language, while Finnish films are rarely exported to Sweden.

The roots of many films discussed in this chapter lie in the region's theatre traditions – particularly the *Kammerspiel* (German for 'chamber drama'), a naturalistic Northern European theatrical tradition originating in the late nineteenth century and associated with playwrights August Strindberg and Henrik Ibsen. *Kammerspiele* are family dramas which use a small number of characters and sparse sets, working by means of realism and understatement to emphasise 'revelatory nuances of gesture and expression'.[2] Dreyer was one of the *Kammerspielfilm*'s early practitioners. His *Passion of Joan of Arc* (1928) is famous for its many close-ups intimately scrutinising faces for unspoken intensities. Bergman revived this expressive use of the close-up in his own chamber dramas of the 1960s and early 1970s, especially in *Persona* (1966). The *Kammerspiel*'s legacy especially impacts on Danish Dogme films about families or tight-knit groups.

In *Nordic National Cinemas*, Tytti Soila, Astrid Söderbergh Widding and Gunnar Iversen hold that 'typical' cinematic themes are complicit with outsiders' stereotypical images of Scandinavia – filmmakers often draw on these to market their work abroad.[3] This Scandinavian 'imaginary' includes: nature and its mythical or exotic meanings, landscape and changing seasons shaping characters' affairs; Scandinavian depression; Lutheran austerity and self-denial, together with the release of buttoned-up emotions, including the breaking of sexual taboos. Such themes are represented differently, and in varying degrees, in each national cinema. Films of rapidly urbanised nations like Finland, Norway and Iceland often contrast 'an unspoilt wilderness environment' with 'the ugly, inhuman face of the city', while in Danish films the country offers less respite from urban corruption and decadence.[4] Themes of social conformity and group mentality, the flipsides of the social conscience and egalitarianism of Scandinavia's welfare-state societies, are most emphasised in Danish cinema.

As in the rest of Europe, comedy is Scandinavia's most popular locally produced genre, particularly light comedies. Contemporary filmmakers have enlivened the genre of romantic comedy in films such as *Mifune* (1999), *Italian for Beginners* (2000) and *Jalla! Jalla!* (2000). Darkly humorous movies, blending depression with farce, are often more popular abroad. These include *Songs from the Second Floor* (2000), *Nói Albínói* (2003) and Aki Kaurismäki's works. Scandinavian cinema frequently adapts established Hollywood genres to its own landscapes. For example, the dazzling snow-capped Midnight Sun landscape and inescapable light form the perfect backdrop for the detective's paranoia in the Norwegian film *Insomnia* (1997), transforming the American film *noir* genre into a film *blanc*. In terms of ideology and narrative style, however, Scandinavian films differ vastly from their Hollywood counterparts, as many of them (but not *Insomnia*) focus on collective action rather than on the individual.

Scandinavia's film industries operate on capitalistic models but also benefit from generous state subsidies similar to those of former Eastern European states; this combination of capitalism and socialism reflects the region's Social Democratic governments. State influence includes censorship, varying in nature across the region; for example, in Finland, due to its Cold War relationship with Russia, there was political censorship prohibiting criticism of Russia as well as censorship concerning sex, alcohol and violence, while in Sweden – renowned, like Denmark, for sexual liberalism – violence is censored more than sex.[5]

Without state support, today's Scandinavian film industries would not survive Hollywood domination. Low population densities mean that films rarely recover their costs at home, while linguistic factors limit their reach abroad. Official state support began in 1963 with the establishment of the Swedish Film Institute, which allocates grants for the production, distribution and exhibition of Swedish films in Sweden, and promotes Swedish cinema abroad. Other countries followed Sweden's model: the Finnish Film Foundation was founded in 1969, and the Danish Film Institute and Icelandic Film Fund (now the Icelandic Film Centre) in 1972.

There is a 'high degree of integration and exchange' between Scandinavian film industries.[6] Long before the EU implemented its vision of a borderless Europe, the Nordic Council (established in 1952) initiated various pan-Nordic ventures enabling Scandinavian citizens to move freely around the region without passports and to work in other Scandinavian countries. Scandinavian nations have successfully undertaken co-productions for decades, and Scandinavian film personnel regularly lend their talents to neighbouring industries. In 1990, the Nordic Council created the Film and Television Fund, which receives money from Scandinavian governments, national TV stations and film institutes.[7] Initially intended to back Nordic co-productions, the fund now invests in any project likely to be distributed in at least two Nordic countries. In order to recover its loans, the Nordic Fund (like MEDIA and Eurimages) increasingly finances projects that demonstrate commercial potential. Some films discussed in this chapter have received money from this fund and from national film institutions. They have drawn on other sources, too, as will be detailed below.

Lars von Trier and Dogme 95

Dogme 95 started out as a collective involving four Danish directors: Lars von Trier, Thomas Vinterberg, Søren Kragh-Jacobsen and Kristian Levring. It was launched with a manifesto in 1995, although the films – financed by Danish TV station Danmarks Radio in return for broadcasting rights after von Trier's arrangement with the Danish Film Institute fell through – did not appear until a few years later. The manifesto sets out ten filmmaking rules, known as the 'Vow of Chastity', which stipulate: location shooting using only props and sets found on site; diegetic sound; handheld cameras, with the camera following the actors rather than actors moving to where the camera is; colour film stock and natural lighting; Academy 35mm format; and contemporary stories set in the 'here and now'.[8] They prohibit optical work and filters, 'superficial' action involving guns and murders, and genre movies. Most provocatively, they insist that 'the director must not be credited'; according to von Trier, this is 'a punch in the face of all directors'.[9]

So far, there have been two waves of Danish Dogme films. The first consisted of films made by the founding directors: Vinterberg's *Festen* (1998), von Trier's *The Idiots* (1998), Kragh-Jacobsen's *Mifune* and Levring's *The King Is Alive* (2000). The second wave, currently ongoing, includes Lone Scherfig's *Italian for Beginners*, Susanne Bier's *Open Hearts* (2002), Ole Christian Madsen's *Kira's Reason* (2001) and Åke Sandgren's *Truly Human* (2001). The Dogme concept has, moreover, spilled across national borders and inspired filmmaking outside Denmark. Non-Danish Dogme films include *Julien Donkey-Boy* (USA, 1999), *Lovers* (France, 1999) and *Fuckland* (Argentina, 2000). However, with the exception of *Julien Donkey-Boy*, these have not equalled the Danish films' success, either critically or commercially. This inevitably leads to speculation that Danish Dogme films are 'grounded in a specific location and sensibility' which the foreign films lack.[10] John Orr, for example, sees Dogme's emphasis on restrictions as recalling Lutheran denial and suffering.[11]

Dogme 95 claims to be a 'rescue action' designed to counteract 'certain tendencies' in cinema today.[12] According to some reports, von Trier and Vinterberg drew up the manifesto in 'a mere twenty-five minutes, amid gales of laughter'.[13] Both solemn and playful, the rules are designed to provoke the film establishment and to give filmmakers fresh inspiration through the creative use of limitations. The idea that creativity can flourish when one has constraints rather than complete freedom has a long history and is shared by other filmmakers working under completely different circumstances, including Abbas Kiarostami, whose films must comply with strict Iranian state censorship (see Chapter 4). Removing the director's credit, however, has done little to shake the *auteur* concept, which remains attached to all Dogme films.

Dogme has become known for its 'back-to-basics' realism. The Dogme filmmakers desire to force 'the truth' out of their characters and settings, swearing to do so 'at the cost of good taste and any aesthetic considerations'.[14] Dogme's emphasis on contemporary stories, location shooting and handheld cameras recalls Italian neorealism, while the idea of the camera following the actors, and not vice versa, evokes American independent filmmaker John Cassavetes, whose 16mm Arriflex cameras achieved an intense intimacy with actors in films like *Faces* (1968). With even more flexible camera technology, Dogme takes emotional closeness with actors yet further. Dogme also subverts 'fly-on-the-wall' documentary film conventions, where the cameraman is a passive observer, and makes the cameraman a participant in the action. Shaky, hyperactive camerawork and abrupt jump-cuts abound in the early films, conveying 'raw, truth-telling qualities' but also emphasising confusion and highlighting the limits of their 'truth'-capturing potential.[15]

Filmmakers in small nations like Denmark can never compete with Hollywood. However, Dogme 95, with its ten filmmaking rules that oppose Hollywood rules, has effectively changed the 'rules of the game', as Mette Hjort has argued.[16] In the age of Hollywood mega-blockbusters, most people's idea of a legitimate film is defined by high production values, expensive special effects, established genres like science fiction, disaster movies, or thrillers involving violent, 'superficial action'. Dogme 95 offers an alternative, freeing filmmakers from the costly technical apparatus of mainstream filmmaking and making low-tech productions more acceptable to wider audiences. It therefore levels the playing field on which world cinemas compete with Hollywood. As von Trier himself asserts, films like *Festen* lend incentives to filmmakers in other small nations, who can see that 'if *that's* a film, then we can make films too'.[17]

Dogme 95 has revitalised the entire Danish film industry, even outside the production of Dogme films. *Italian for Beginners* broke Danish box-office records and helped to raise the market share for domestic films in Denmark to 30 per cent in 2001. Over the next three years, Danish films retained these market-share levels – a considerable achievement compared with other European cinemas. In 2002, Denmark was second only to France; but, while France's national market share of 33 per cent was achieved on the basis of 200 features, Denmark's was based on nineteen.[18] High admissions for Danish films can be further attributed to the appeal of a younger generation of stars, including Paprika Steen, Thomas Bo Larsen and Mads Mikkelsen, who have all appeared in Dogme films.

Dogme 95 has also helped make cinema Denmark's most visible export. Although *Italian for Beginners* was extremely successful abroad – including in America – *Festen*, a box-office hit in Denmark, did even better in its foreign sales, which accounted for 99 per cent of the film's overall admissions![19] Dogme 95 has undoubtedly blazed a trail for European cinema in the age of globalisation and increasing competition from Hollywood.

Unquestionably, the main impetus behind Dogme is Lars von Trier. Widely recognised as Denmark's most notable director since Dreyer and as Europe's most important living director after Kieślowski's death, von Trier has played an invaluable role in raising Danish cinema's profile. Provocation is central to his methods, earning him the reputation of being a fraudster and a cynical manipulator. He is also renowned for his fraught relationships with actors – most famously for the dispute with Icelandic singer Björk, whom he cast as the lead in *Dancer in the Dark* (2000), a musical which won the Palme d'Or and Best Actress Award at Cannes 2000.

Von Trier shot to international cult fame with his early films *Element of Crime* (1984), *Epidemic* (1988) and *Europa* (1991). Meticulously realised, these films are very different from his Dogme works but are formative for Dogme in crucial respects. They also brought about a sea-change in official definitions of what counts as a Danish film. The 1972 Danish Film Act stipulated that a film had to be shot in Danish, using mainly Danish actors and technical crew, in order to qualify for state funding. In 1989, largely because of von Trier, who shot his films in English, the law was changed so that a film can be Danish if it is shot in Danish *or* if it has 'a particular artistic or technical quality which contributes to the advancement of film art and film culture in Denmark'.[20] Other Danish filmmakers have since adopted English-language filmmaking as a globalising strategy, including Scherfig for her post-Dogme film *Wilbur Wants to Kill Himself* (2002).

In 1992, von Trier and producer Peter Aalbaek Jensen formed their own film company, Zentropa, which gave von Trier full artistic control over his films and enabled their partnership to instigate other film and TV projects. Zentropa's first project was the *Twin Peaks*-inspired Danish-language TV series *The Kingdom* (1994) (later followed by *Kingdom 2* [1997]). Set in Copenhagen's biggest hospital, the Rigshospitalet ('hospital of the Danish Kingdom'), *The Kingdom* blends the supernatural with black comedy and was massively popular with Danish and Swedish audiences, as well as internationally.[21] A major source of humour is the cantankerous Swedish head doctor Stig Helmer, who affirms his national identity by extolling Swedish icons and brand names – Tetra-Pak, Volvo and Björn Borg! – and ranting against Danes.[22]

For *Kingdom*, Von Trier adopted what he calls a 'left-handed' approach. Gone was the meticulous storyboarding and technical perfection of his early films; in their stead appeared a handheld pseudo-documentary camera style influenced by US TV shows *NYPD Blue* and *Homicide*, a fast shooting schedule (necessitated by on-location shooting at the hospital), use of available light and a new emphasis on characters with some improvised performances. Von Trier's new method of working – to be fully articulated in the Dogme 95 manifesto – was taking shape; like his next project, *Breaking the Waves* (1996) (analysed below), *The Kingdom* is a proto-Dogme work.

With *The Idiots*, von Trier takes 'left-handed' filmmaking even further. The story is about a collective of young people who pretend to have learning disabilities and who challenge each other to 'spazz' in public. *The Idiots* is also about 'spazzing' at the level of film technique – von Trier shot most of the film himself, and purposefully sloppy framing abounds, as it does in von Trier's next film *Dancer in the Dark*, in which he also operates the camera.

Von Trier claims never to have travelled outside Europe, due to his phobia of flying. *Dancer* and *Dogville* (2003), the first in an anticipated USA trilogy, are both shot in Trollhätten, Sweden, despite their American settings. Both *Dancer* and *Dogville* provocatively break with Dogme rules while continuing to be informed by them. For example, *Dogville* – starring Hollywood actress Nicole Kidman – is filmed on a sound stage with minimal props and locations chalk-marked on the floor. *Dogville* evokes Scandinavia's minimalist theatre traditions but in a different way from Dogme 95: while stripping down the *mise en scène*, it makes extensive use of lighting and sound effects. With laconically edifying voiceover narration and 'chapter headings', *Dogville* implies a Brechtian reworking of *Breaking the Waves*, more technically controlled (with von Trier operating the camera again) but equally powerful.

Swedish Cinema after Bergman

Bergman's towering presence as the figurehead of Swedish cinema is long thought to have hampered the creativity of younger Swedish filmmakers. But, since the turn of the millennium, Swedish cinema has been flourishing, and the director most credited with removing it from Bergman's shadow is Lukas Moodysson, whose films *Show Me Love* (1998) and *Together* (2000) (analysed below) were conspicuously more popular with Swedish audiences than *Titanic*. Starting out as a poet, Moodysson began making films after joining the Swedish film school Dramatiska Institutet in Stockholm. *Show Me Love*, his debut feature, was the first film released by

Film i Väst, an organisation which runs the Swedish film industry based in Trollhätten, south-west Sweden – the hub of Swedish cinema's current revival. Moodysson's subsequent movies *Together* and *Lilya 4-ever* (2002) were also made there. Film i Väst gets half its income from the government, a quarter from Europe, local councils and the SFI, and another quarter from self-generated income. It has cultivated successful relationships with the Swedish company Memfis (which produces Moodysson's films), Zentropa and Illusion Films by awarding them greater investment with each successive feature, and it has played an important role in Sweden's cinematic revival by backing fresh projects like *Show Me Love*, which the SFI was initially hesitant to support.[23]

Moodysson shares affinities with British filmmakers Mike Leigh and Ken Loach insofar as he works with ensemble casts and sometimes improvises scenes (although he always starts with a complete script). His raw pseudo-documentary shooting style with available lighting and wobbly camera is not dissimilar to Dogme 95. Yet his films also contain expressive soundtracks and a Hollywood-like appeal to a broad audience. Moodysson is known for his skill with child performances; this aligns his work with Sweden's strong tradition in children's films, many of them based on books by Astrid Lindgren, creator of Pippi Longstocking. Tytti Soila notes that Swedish children's films of the 1970s to the 1990s, including Lindgren adaptations, all look back to a utopian past, taking place in peaceful middle-class provincial communities, and mainly focus on boys; for example, Lasse Hallström's *My Life as a Dog* (1985), which is about a 1950s boyhood.[24] Moodysson's *Show Me Love*, however, focuses on teenage girls in small-town Åmål in contemporary Sweden. It romanticises neither the place – its Swedish title is *Fucking Åmål* – nor teenage years, which are seen as an ordeal that teenagers would rather put behind them. Elin, an aspiring Miss Sweden, despairs when she reads in a magazine that raves are unfashionable: 'when something's in, it takes so long to get here it's out already!' With school outcast Agnes, who loves Elin, the film questions traditional gender and sexual identity formations. The girls share a brief epiphany, kissing in the back seat of a car with Foreigner's *I Wanna Know What Love Is* blaring on the radio. Elin subsequently succumbs to peer pressure and begins to ignore Agnes, losing her virginity to a boy called Johan; but the girls finally reunite, making their relationship public by literally coming out of the closet. *Show Me Love* met with unprecedented critical and commercial success. One-tenth of Sweden's population went to see it, and it became a sensation in Norway, Finland, the Netherlands, Russia and Switzerland.[25] Bergman called it 'a young master's first masterpiece'.[26]

Moodysson's recent film *Lilya 4-ever*, a story about sex-trafficking, received ecstatic reviews in the UK press and marks Moodysson's shift to overtly political filmmaking. It follows Russian teenager Lilya, who is abandoned by her mother then promised a new life in Sweden by a boyfriend who is actually a pimp. Imprisoned in a Swedish apartment block, Lilya is hired out as a prostitute, then escapes, apparently jumping off a bridge to her death. Moodysson wrote the script after hearing about a girl in Malmö, Sweden, who committed suicide under similar circumstances. In one affecting scene, Lilya's pimp shepherds her through a shopping mall which, with its glittering consumer goods, epitomises the promise of the West; the ordinary Westerners with whom she brushes shoulders there have no idea that she is being sold in a darker corner of the same market. *Lilya 4-ever* shows that the growing phenomenon of sex-trafficking from East to West is the product of economic gaps created by neoliberal capitalism.

In 2000, the market share for Swedish films peaked at 25 per cent. One of the major hits that year was *Jalla! Jalla!* Directed by Lebanese-born Josef Fares and produced by Moodysson, the film treats its theme of arranged marriages with an explosive energy – *Jalla! Jalla!* means 'hurry, hurry' in Arabic. Sweden opened its borders to immigrants in the 1950s.[27] Many economic and political refugees from Turkey, Iran and Arab countries have settled there, making Sweden an ethnically mixed nation, although it is still in the process of formulating its multicultural identity. There have been films portraying immigrants in Sweden since the 1970s.[28] However, *Jalla! Jalla!* belongs to a significant new trend of successful features made by first- or second-generation immigrants. Other examples include Reza Parsa's *Before the Storm* (2000) and Reza Bagher's *Wings of Glass* (2000). *The New Country* (2000), originally a TV series co-scripted by Moodysson and Peter Birro, also treats the lives of immigrants in Sweden and concerns two asylum-seekers, one Iranian and one Somali.

Although *Dancer in the Dark* won the Cannes Palme d'Or, there were two other Scandinavian contenders for the award in 2000: Liv Ullman's *Faithless* (2000) and Roy Andersson's *Songs from the Second Floor*. Both these films could be considered stylistic antitheses to Dogme 95, favouring stillness and long takes. Ullman, a Norwegian, built her reputation as an actress in Bergman's films. A story revolving around an adulterer's confession, *Faithless* is based on Bergman's script and contains many Bergmanesque motifs. Erland Josephson, who frequently played the director's alter ego, appears as 'Bergman', an old recluse living on the island of Fårö. *Songs from the Second Floor*, by contrast, is a blackly humorous surrealistic satire of corporate conformity. Its characters are buttoned-up middle-aged Swedish bureaucrats who let go of their eccentricities. Each scene is filmed in single, deep-focus static takes, boxing in the set, while open doors leading into other rooms give the impression of a many-layered hallucinatory reality behind routine façades.

Kaurismäki and his Fellow Travellers

Aki Kaurismäki is the best-known of Scandinavia's dark humorists. Aside from his work, Finnish cinema is scarcely known outside Finland. For this reason, Kaurismäki actively promotes Finnish films abroad. He organises the Midnight Sun Film Festival with his brother Mika, also a filmmaker, and they produce other Finnish films through their company, Villealfa. The opening of multiplex cinemas has given Finnish cinema a further boost. In 1999, Finnish films took 25 per cent of the national market share, figures based on twelve domestic releases out of a total of 431 films in distribution.[29] The biggest Finnish hit that year was Olli Saarela's *Ambush* (1999), which deals with Finland's Continuation War (1941–4) with Russia, a traumatic topic rarely treated before in Finnish cinema; Finland allied with Nazi Germany to fight the Russians and lost, thereafter having to appease Russia through its Cold War foreign policy – hence the term 'Finlandisation', which describes 'situations in which a small state appeases its more powerful neighbour'.[30] Joshua Siegel writes: 'The indignities of this label did much damage to Finland's national pride'.[31] In many respects, *Ambush* is an anti-war film – yet, coming after the full extent of Stalin's plans for annexing Finland were revealed under *glasnost*, it allows Finnish resistance and sacrifices to be re-evaluated, therefore restoring national pride.

Kaurismäki's films are totally different from period films with glamorous actors like *Ambush*. They probe beneath the surface illusion of Finland's affluent society, exploring the lives of those disadvantaged by Finland's transition from traditional heavy industry to a high-tech consumer and information economy. Kaurismäki's protagonists are drifters, alcoholics, deadbeats and blue-collar workers. Endearingly glum, reticent and awkward, they draw on and parody Finnish stereotypes – shyness, reclusiveness, uncommunicativeness, quirkiness – characteristics thought to be bred by Finns' seclusion on Europe's Arctic outreaches!

Scandinavian cinema is generally orientated towards naturalism. By contrast, Kaurismäki's films give priority to external realism through ascetic settings, but indulge in fanciful turns, especially through music. Finnish tango, a crucial element of Finnish popular culture, often plays diegetically on jukeboxes, on radios or with a live band – expressing characters' melancholia and utopian dreams in a deliberately kitsch fashion. Finnish rock and roll is another influence – including the Leningrad

Cowboys, who appear in *Leningrad Cowboys Go America* (1989) flaunting elongated quiffs and winkle-picker shoes. Kaurismäki combines social realism with stylised comedy filled with pastiches of popular genres: road movie, gangster film and film noir. Understatement is his key technique, supporting minimal dialogue and deadpan acting. With a face that Kaurismäki affectionately compared to 'a sad rat', Matti Pellonpää (1951–95) is the actor who best personifies Kaurismäkian gloom, especially in *Ariel* (1988) and *Take Care of Your Scarf, Tatjana* (1994).[32] Pellonpää won the European Felix prize for Best European Actor in 1991. Kati Outinen, another Kaurismäki favourite, specialises in the female version of Kaurismäkian despondency. She won the Best Actress Award at Cannes for her role in *Man Without a Past* (2002).

Kaurismäki's recent films belong to his new 'Finland trilogy'. The first instalment, *Drifting Clouds* (1996), shows ordinary Helsinki workers persisting with quiet determination while their routine lives are shattered by wider economic trends – high unemployment and multinational takeovers of local businesses. *Man Without a Past*, the second instalment, articulates the social problem of homelessness – another overlooked aspect of contemporary Finland. Here, a nameless protagonist travels to Helsinki in search of work, is robbed and beaten up, loses his memory and begins a new life among the city's homeless who live in Helsinki dock containers – a virtual compendium of Kaurismäki's earlier films, where the city is invariably a hostile place, full of hoodlums and crooks.

Extensively used as a film location throughout the twentieth century, Iceland only began to produce its own films in 1979 and has a large film industry given the country's small population size – about 280,000.[33] Iceland also boasts one of the world's highest per-capita rates of cinemagoing. Its films have a distinctive look and tone – especially with their bleak but stunningly photographed landscapes. The sagas from Iceland's ancient literary heritage are a key influence, imparting otherworldly, dreamlike, mystical qualities to the landscape; so too are contemporary novels. Iceland's best-known director is Fridrik Thór Fridriksson, whose *Children of Nature* (1991) was Oscar-nominated. His films use deadpan black comedy, doleful characters and pastiches of American genres (film noir and the road movie). In *Cold Fever* (1995), a Japanese man, Hirata (Masatoshi Nagase), travels to Iceland to perform rites for his parents. A horizontal enlargement of the film frame marks his arrival, spectacularly displaying the Icelandic landscape. The film was popular in the USA and also in Japan, where Masatoshi Nagase is a big star.

Iceland is even more secluded than Finland, the rare winter daylight hours apparently offering little recreation except – as portrayed in

Fridriksson actor Baltasar Kormákur's *101 Reykjavik* (2000) – drinking and sex. Its protagonist Hylnur lives at home with his mother, doing nothing except surfing internet porn, sleeping and getting drunk, until his mother's flamenco teacher and lesbian lover Lola (played by Almodóvar star and sex icon Victoria Abril) arrives. In Dagur Kári's *Nói Albínói*, teenager Nói longs to escape his small town in Iceland's West Fjords, far removed from the capital in the south. Shots of a snowy mountain, which looms over the town and isolates its inhabitants from the rest of the world, reinforce Nói's sense of incarceration. Nói is younger than Kaurismäki's protagonists; but, with his albino bald-headed looks and a question mark over whether he is the school dunce or genius, he is an oddity and a match for any Kaurismäki hero. The deserted provincial café where Nói meets city girl Iris is a Kaurismäkian topos, and their romance gets under way with humorously clipped dialogue. On a 'date', they break into a museum to find an interactive world map with buttons lighting up different countries; there is no button for Iceland, they dryly observe.

Close Analysis

Breaking the Waves (Lars von Trier, 1996)

Set in a strict Presbyterian community in the isolated, windswept Scottish Western Isles during the 1970s, *Breaking the Waves* is the first part of von Trier's *Golden Hearted* trilogy, inspired by a children's story where a girl gives away all her possessions to needy passers-by, declaring she will be all right even when she has nothing left. The second and third parts of the trilogy are *The Idiots* and *Dancer in the Dark*. *Breaking the Waves'* golden-hearted heroine is Bess (Emily Watson), who believes she has a personal 'hotline' to God in a church where women are formally forbidden to speak. Bess marries Jan, an 'outsider' to the community; when Jan is paralysed in an accident at work on a North Sea oil-rig, she feels guilty, as she requested God to send Jan home. Jan persuades Bess to have sex with other men and report to him; initially reluctant, Bess sees her actions as a sacrifice to aid his recovery. Her community ostracises her as a fallen woman. She dies, tortured by a sadistic sailor; and Jan does indeed recover, witnessing giant bells pealing in heaven (while on earth the Presbyterian church has no bells). A critical and commercial success, the film won the Grand Jury Prize at Cannes 1996, but its sexual politics disturbed feminist critics.

Von Trier's funding sources for this English-language production include the Danish and Swedish Film Institutes, Canal Plus, Eurimages and the European Script Fund. Von Trier asked Watson to study Marie Falconetti's performance in Dreyer's *Passion of Joan of Arc* – a major inspiration, as it, too, depicts a young woman accused by religious, patriarchal authority. In *Breaking the Waves*, we see church elders oppressively hunched over Bess, and extreme close-ups of her looking up to heaven when she talks to God, adopting low, forbidding tones when 'he' replies. The film realises its narrative and style with a Dreyer-like asceticism. The community's puritanical austerity is symbolised in the church tower without bells and reflected in the harsh and unforgiving environment, the echoes of typical Scandinavian themes enabled by the fact that Scotland is a Northern European territory 'similarly shaped by extreme Protestantism'.[34] Jan's miraculous recovery, rising from his bed and walking again, moreover recalls *Ordet* (1955), another Dreyer film, where a dead woman is resurrected.

Slavoj Žižek has argued that 'the key' to *Breaking the Waves* lies in 'the tension between the narrative and the way it is shot'.[35] On the one hand, we have a melodramatic story about miracles; on the other, a style that follows naturalistic conventions, that is, conventions we have learned to associate with 'truth'-telling: gritty images, restless, handheld camera, swish pans instead of shot/reverse-shots, and overlaps in continuity presenting the same event from slightly different angles. All this gives an impression of raw immediacy, as if we were 'eavesdropping on the characters before the camera person has had a chance to edit the film'.[36] Von Trier himself states that if he had shot *Breaking the Waves* in a 'direct' melodramatic fashion, audiences would have found the film 'too suffocating': 'What we've done is to take a style and put it over the story like a filter . . . The raw, documentary style which I've laid over the film, and which actually annuls and contests it, means that we accept the story as it is.'[37] Naturalism is not readily identified with the supernatural or miracles, yet the film's style urges the viewer towards a naturalistic interpretation of events. Some viewers may be led to suspend their disbelief willingly throughout, while others may feel cheated when the naturalistic illusion decisively gives way to the supernatural in the final shots.

Watson's performance as the hysterical child-woman Bess is pivotal. The handheld camera scrutinises her facial expressions, testifying to her joy and pleasure during her sexual awakening with Jan and her anguish when she 'sacrifices' herself to brutalities of other men.[38] Her occasional glances into the camera, rather than breaking the cinematic artifice, give further credence to our belief in her as a 'real' character, whom we know intimately. However, in the film's extreme widescreen Cinemascope format, faces – even in close up – never fill the screen. No matter how close the camera gets, the image breaks up. This is enhanced by the grainy images resulting from shooting interiors in available light. The film was made consistently grainy in post-production by transferring the film to video, electronically draining it of colour, and accentuating the grain in correctly exposed exterior shots before outputting it back to film. As well as implying pseudo-documentary rawness, the grains visible on screen accentuate the limits of documenting 'reality'. The film's frenzied hand-held style constantly encircles this abyss, implying a loss of meaning and creating an unbalancing effect overall.

The film strives to recover stability in the final heavenly shot and in the digitally created romantic landscape panoramas illustrating its chapter titles: (1) Bess Gets Married, (2) Life with Jan, (3) Life Alone, (4) Jan's Illness, (5) Doubt, (6) Faith, (7) Bess's Sacrifice, and the Epilogue. Contrasting with the washed-out live-action cinematography, these images are peaceful and colour-saturated, although they are not completely still images; there are subtle movements, such as a rainbow forming in (4). Von Trier describes them as a 'God's-eye view' over the unfurling narrative.[39] Dubbed over the chapter images are 1970s tracks by the likes of David Bowie, T-Rex, Jethro Tull, Leonard Cohen and Elton John. In the rest of the film, however, music is largely diegetic – one of several respects in which *Breaking the Waves* prefigures Dogme 95, although the period setting, widescreen format and post-production manipulation are all against Dogme rules.

Von Trier claims that his film is about 'goodness'.[40] The film contrasts the elders' rigid, puritanical, life-denying conception of goodness with Bess's apparently spontaneous goodness. This is why feminists have accused von Trier of glorifying female passivity and sexual slavery.[41] Although the film criticises the patriarchal community which forbids women to speak in church or attend funerals, it elevates Bess's obedience to her husband into an act of goodness, thereby reaffirming patriarchy. It nonetheless avoids stereotypical male-gaze voyeurism and has Bess's sister-in-law Dodo and Dr Richardson both accuse Jan of 'playing Peeping Tom'. Yet, by the end of the film, Jan is exonerated, if not exactly forgiven, for the humiliation and degradation to which he submits Bess. Bess breaks her body so that Jan may live.

Festen (Thomas Vinterberg, 1998)

Shot on digital video, the first Dogme movie *Festen* takes place at a country mansion where Helge Klingenfeldt invites his family to his sixtieth-birthday celebration. Offering a toast at the banqueting table, Helge's eldest son Christian reveals why his twin sister Linda committed suicide: their father sexually abused them both when they were children. *Festen* astounded audiences when it premièred at Cannes – as much because what looked like a home video seemed to have 'wandered onto the screen' as for the narrative's shocking revelations.[42] By awarding *Festen* the Special Jury Prize, Martin Scorsese and his jury legitimated digital video and low-budget filmmaking in the eyes of the film world. Thereafter, *Festen* was Oscar-nominated for Best Foreign Film. It became the most popular of the first Dogme wave, hailed as the kind of success that could break Hollywood's grip on Europe's cinema-goers. Its story of 'repressed family secrets' coming to the surface is 'universally recognisable' and made it eminently exportable; but it is the Dogme style, which complements the story, that distinguishes the film from countless others.[43]

When Christian reveals the family secret in the guise of a celebratory toast, the guests attempt to take it for what it pretends to be and carry on with the festivities. The effectiveness of these scenes is due partly to the casting of Henning Moritz, a well-known Danish star, against type as Helge. The extras playing the guests were not told about his role as child-abuser in this film, so they reveal genuine surprise, or fail to register Christian's news altogether. This establishes the pattern of response to his revelations: as Christian opens up cracks in the polite dinner-party façade, the rest of the family and the 'German' Toastmaster use dinner-party rituals – further toasts, coffee, after-dinner cigarettes, music and dancing next door – to reseal the façade and sustain appearances. When Christian makes his second charge that his father murdered his sister, his brother Michael and some other guests forcibly eject him from the house. Vinterberg understands that, in this respect (of keeping a lid on things), his film has 'really touched something Danish, and that people have felt . . . provoked by it'.[44] The ritual of manners only ceases to work when Christian's other sister Helene agrees to read Linda's suicide note, which she had hidden in her pill case.

When Gbatokai, Helene's African-American boyfriend, arrives at the party – in a taxi driven by Vinterberg playing a cameo role – we learn more about the family's insularity by their attitudes to him. Michael starts up a racist Danish song to taunt him – a children's song, which everybody knows – evoking the swing towards the xenophobic far right in Denmark's contemporary political climate. In addition to race, *Festen* foregrounds class issues. The impetus for change comes from the servants, who steal the guests' car keys to prevent them from leaving and to ensure that they hear Christian out.

With its country-house and upper middle-class dinner party, *Festen* contains more than shades of Bergman (*Smiles of a Summer Night* [1955] and *Fanny and Alexander* [1982]) as well as Luis Buñuel's satire of bourgeois dinner rituals *Discreet Charm of the Bourgeoisie* (1972). It also draws heavily on Scandinavian *Kammerspiel* traditions. However, *Festen*'s handheld home-camcorder style, with its restless, jerky camerawork, gives it an edgy quality, introducing an amateurish desperation into the scrutiny of intimate lives. The dizzy camerawork underlines the sense of disorientation, unease and moral chaos – the loss of control in a setting where behaviour is supposed to be controlled. Operating a small digital camera, cameraman Anthony Dod Mantle mingles with the actors like an extra guest at the party, sometimes physically intervening in the action. This explains the first scene when Michael orders his wife Mette and his children out of the car to make room for Christian; there would indeed not be enough room with the cameraman too. Moreover, the cameraman's knowledge of narrative events appears to be just as restricted as ours – he is often taken by surprise, as when the angry Mette jostles the camera.

Festen's style is very confrontational. Shock cuts abound, as in the abrupt sound cut when Helene screams, hits the wall and then is sick in the bathroom after her quiet decorum at the table. Vinterberg comments that, in the absence of other means such as dramatic music or lighting effects, 'you just have your actors, so you have to make them faint, or puke, or fight – something, to express what it is that you want to get out'.[45] *Festen* is widely accredited as an acting triumph, but that doesn't mean other stylistic devices are redundant. For example, Dod Mantle's cinematography makes use of available light to convey the story's darkening mood. As the evening wears on and light diminishes, the pixels become increasingly visible, suggesting that the image is disintegrating just as the family falls apart. The interior scenes after Christian is ejected from the house are all shot in low-light conditions – as is the film's psychological nadir, when Michael beats up his father. Michael reacts to news of his father's incest in the only way he knows – by assaulting him and thereby assuming his legacy.

The film also manages to tell a ghost story within the confines of the rules, thereby exceeding narrow conceptions of 'realism'. When Helene finds Linda's suicide note, the film cuts to shots of Christian's girlfriend Pia submerged in the bath, suggesting the drowned sister's ghostly presence. Slow-motion shots and static overhead shots indicate that we are now outside the agitated viewpoint of the cameraman/guest who dominates the rest of the film. Slow motion announces Linda's presence again when Christian collapses and hallucinates. Yet, because Dogme rules forbid special effects and flashbacks, we actually never leave the here-and-now. A persistently ringing phone punctuates this hallucinating sequence, existing both as a reality within the hallucination – Linda's 'call' to Christian from the spirit world – and as the reality that wakes him, an actual telephone call from Helene. Dogme does not allow superimposed titles, hence opening and closing credits must be conveyed by other means. *Festen* uses pieces of paper floating in water, another allusion to Linda's presence outside the film.

Together (Lukas Moodysson, 2000)

Together is set in the idealistic heyday of 1970s Sweden, where battered housewife Elisabeth leaves her alcoholic husband Rolf and takes refuge with her children Eva and Stefan in her brother Göran's hippie commune, named 'Together'. In Sweden, admissions for the film narrowly beat those for *Show Me Love* – and it also did well abroad. Searching for alternatives to nuclear parenting and capitalist society's growing consumption, the communal living movement flourished during the 1970s and was particularly popular in Denmark and Sweden. Some critics have accused Moodysson of travestying communal living and affirming conservative values – this is how Tom Paulin and Germaine Greer reacted on BBC TV's *Late Review* on 13 July 2001. However, *Together* is not a straightforward satire and looks back at the 1970s with both nostalgia and distance.

Its style is similar to Dogme 95 but works against Dogme in significant ways. Like *Festen*, it is shot with available light on location in houses rather than in studios. Its music is mostly diegetic: characters put on their favourite records and illustrate their eclectic tastes. An exception is the over-dubbed Abba song *SOS*. First heard as Elisabeth leaves Rolf, the song (like many Abba songs) appropriately deals with relationship breakdowns. Abba's presence on the soundtrack is ironic as well as nostalgic. The band, associated for people of Moodysson's generation with their childhood, was very popular among working-class people, yet 1970s commune ideologues – who were so eager to win over the working class – hated the band.

As a period drama, the film is, of course, unDogme-like. The use of fades to red, which close and open segments of the film, emphasises that this is a bygone era. The colour red itself stands for warmth, and is associated with the commune, its warm colours contrasting with the dull browns in the strait-laced neighbours' house.

Handheld camera is only used in scenes entailing fast action through several rooms. Dogme dissolved the barriers between cast and crew with its stripped-down technical approach and physical intimacy with actors. Moodysson, on the other hand, gives actors space for free expression, allowing them to decide what to do and making the camera follow in Cassavetes-like fashion; but mostly he places the camera on a tripod, away from the actors, crash zooming into medium close-ups.[46] Any movie-camera manual will tell you not to over-use zooms, as they can be intrusive. Here, the zoom acknowledges the presence of the audience as distant observers, but without breaking the naturalistic illusion.

We first encounter the communards joyfully hugging each other upon hearing news of the Spanish dictator Franco's death. They are Göran, Lena, Lasse, Lasse's ex-wife Anna and their son Tet, a gay man Klas, Signe and Sigvard and their child Moon, and militant communist Erik. The character who most champions the commune's value of togetherness is Göran, who cheers even when the opposing football team scores. In his homely homily, we start life alone like little oatflakes, but when we're cooked we all join together like porridge, no longer as isolated individuals. *Together* nostalgically reaffirms communal values felt to have been lost in the transition from welfare states to market individualism; it brings together nearly all the characters for a joyful football finale. The film also endorses the ideal of solidarity in its narrative construction. There is no 'central' character whose individual viewpoint is definitive. Instead, the film opts for a collective portrait where everyone is given their due: ensemble acting rather than individual 'star' turns.

However, the children have a slightly privileged perspective, enabling us to view the commune through their eyes. An argument over washing-up takes a bizarre turn when Lasse notices Anna standing there exposing her genitals, and proceeds to undo his own trousers. Eva and Stefan arrive just at this moment, setting the tone for their response to their new home. Eva complains to her friend Fredrik that people in the commune always take the opposite view from everyone else. They wear ugly clothes and listen to bad music. They don't have a TV and they don't celebrate Christmas. But when the film contrasts the commune with the conservative nuclear family in Fredrik's house, there is really no contest. Fredrik's parents pruriently disapprove of the commune's free values; yet they both spy on it, and Fredrik's dad Ragnar regularly retires to the basement in order to mastur-bate under the pretext of 'woodworking'.

The characters' roles are not 'fixed' at the outset, but unfold and change in the course of the film. For example, Rolf starts out as a drunken, abusive and negligent father but then reforms and stops drinking. What steels his resolve is his encounter with the lonely Birger, who shows Rolf what he might become and persuades him to try to win back Elisabeth. Birger appears in Moodysson's short film *Talk* (1997), where, left with nobody to talk to, he ends up killing a Hare Krishna devotee who visits his flat. In *Together*, Birger deliberately unscrews a pipe that Rolf, a plumber by trade, has fixed just so that he can have Rolf's company again.

People in the commune change, too. Lasse, relentlessly pursued by Klas, finally lets down his heterosexual barriers and accepts that a man can turn him on. In fact, those who won't change leave, including Signe and Sigvard, who object to Pippi Longstocking on the grounds that she is a capitalist-materialist involved in 'the eternal search for things'; it is the last straw for them when Göran buys the children a second-hand TV. Elisabeth changes through her friendship with feminist Anna. Some of this is played for comedy, as when she and Anna raise their arms in mock-revolutionary salute in the mirror, vowing never again to shave their armpits. But when Elisabeth passes this news on to Rolf, she adds that she will no longer be a housewife who waits on a man. Therefore when she accepts him back it is on a totally different footing. Far from a return to the traditional nuclear family, it implies a new beginning shaped by the values of communal living. The film moves towards an ideologically progressive ending in which the collective and the family redefine each other. Sick of vegetarianism, the children successfully picket for meat. One might balk at the film's levity in turning political protest to these ends. However, anti-capitalist principles are kept alive. The commune accepts hot dogs and pork cutlets but not Coca-Cola – as Lasse puts it, they draw the line at 'multinational pigs'.

Notes

1. Cowie, *Scandinavian Cinema*, p. 7.
2. Schrader, *Transcendental Style*, p. 116.
3. Soila et al., *Nordic National Cinemas*, p. 239.
4. Cowie, *Scandinavian Cinema*, p. 7; Soila et al., *Nordic National Cinemas*, p. 241.
5. Soila et al., *Nordic National Cinemas*, p. 234.
6. Ibid., p. 2.
7. Jäckel, *European Film Industries*, p. 85.
8. Hjort and MacKenzie, *Purity and Provocation*, pp. 199–200.
9. Hjort and Bondebjerg, *Danish Directors*, p. 221.
10. Stevenson, *von Trier*, p. 180.
11. Orr, 'Out of Dreyer's Shadow?', p. 70.
12. Hjort and MacKenzie, *Purity and Provocation*, p. 199.
13. Stevenson, *Uncut*, p. 43.
14. Hjort and MacKenzie, *Purity and Provocation*, p. 200.
15. Stevenson, *Uncut*, p. 18.
16. Hjort and MacKenzie, *Purity and Provocation*, p. 40.
17. Kelly, *Name of this Book*, p. 146.
18. Danish Film Institute, 'Success for Danish Cinema'.
19. Jäckel, *European Film Industries*, p. 120.

20. Stevenson, *von Trier*, p. 68.
21. Ibid., p. 78.
22. Hjort, 'Themes of Nation', p. 116.
23. De Castella, 'Way out West', p. 9.
24. Soila et al., *Nordic National Cinemas*, p. 231.
25. De Castella, 'Way out West', p. 8.
26. Moodysson, *Together*, DVD Notes, Metrodome 2001.
27. Soila et al., *Nordic National Cinemas*, p. 231.
28. Ibid., p. 231.
29. Finnish Film Foundation, 'Cinema Statistics / Finland 1990–1999'.
30. Siegel, *Baby It's Cold Outside*, p. 10.
31. Ibid., p. 10.
32. Von Bagh, *Drifting Shadows*, p. 106.
33. Soila et al., *Nordic National Cinemas*, p. 96.
34. Petrie, *Screening Scotland*, p. 207.
35. Žižek, 'Death and the Maiden', p. 215.
36. Ibid., p. 216.
37. Björkman, 'Naked Miracles', p. 12.
38. Heath, 'God, Faith and Film', p. 98.
39. Ibid., p. 104.
40. Björkman, 'Naked Miracles', p. 12.
41. Collins, 'Against the Tide', p. 47.
42. Kelly, *Name of this Film*.
43. Stevenson, *Uncut*, p. 86.
44. Kelly, *Name of this Book*, p. 118.
45. Ibid., p. 114.
46. Macnab, 'House Rules', p. 34.

CHAPTER 3

Middle Eastern Cinema

As discussed in the Introduction, the 'Middle East' is a Western term, denoting a region stretching from North Africa to the rest of the Arab world in South-West Asia, but also including largely non-Arab nations such as Israel, Turkey, Iran and Afghanistan. In 1978, Edward Said pointed out that the Middle East is more susceptible to being grasped under 'the imaginative demonology of the "mysterious Orient"' than any other region in the world.[1] This tendency has, if anything, increased in today's Western media images of Arabs and Muslims as terrorists. European and Hollywood films, moreover, have long drawn on 'exotic' Middle Eastern settings to portray 'Oriental' sensuality.[2] The urgency of regional or national self-representation is therefore heavily inscribed in Middle Eastern cinematic production, which has often evolved in order to challenge European or Hollywood images. Egypt, Israel, Turkey and Iran all have long filmmaking traditions. The Egyptian film industry started in the 1930s and, until recently, dominated regional filmmaking, exporting films across Africa and South-West and Central Asia. Now, under completely different circumstances, Iran has become the region's most internationally renowned film-producing centre and has refocused world attention on the cinema of the Middle East. This chapter selects trends from Egypt, Lebanon, Israel/Palestine, Tunisia and Turkey, saving a detailed discussion of Iranian cinema for Chapter 4. It will argue that Middle Eastern filmmakers have used film to mediate international attitudes to their societies and cultures, offering a counterpoint to Western mass-media representations.

Historically the birthplace of Judaism, Christianity and Islam, the Middle East is significantly diverse, but its territories have historical and cultural commonalities that validate cross-cultural comparisons. Israel, a Jewish homeland established in 1948 with a large European immigrant community, appears to be a foreign 'Western' presence; yet over half the Jews living in Israel originate from the region. This territory is also the homeland of Palestinians, many of whom the Israelis drove off their lands, forcing them to live in refugee camps or in exile, stateless and homeless. This unresolved Israeli–Palestinian conflict has had repercussions throughout the region, with the Arab nations generally hostile to Israel, leading to a series of wars since 1948. The other major nationality in the region without their own state is the Kurds, who reside on the borders of Iran, Iraq and Turkey.

Most of the Arab Middle East was under the Turkish Ottoman empire until the end of the First World War, then passed into the hands of European colonisers. The British controlled Palestine, Jordan, Iraq and Kuwait (to add to their existing imperial possessions Egypt and Afghanistan) while France gained Lebanon and Syria, having previously annexed Algeria and taken possession of Tunisia and Morocco. As the European colonial powers departed in the two decades after the Second World War, their influence was replaced by the two superpowers who competed in the region as part of their Cold War strategy. The USA is now the only remaining superpower, its presence in the region representing both 'an alluring model and a new imperialism', although that allure is fast disappearing since the USA occupied Afghanistan and Iraq.[3]

A number of factors – including war, colonialism, neocolonial dependency, Islamic moral restrictions, Hollywood domination and censorship – have hampered film production in the region. The colonial powers restricted and devalued local culture in the territories they ruled; this was particularly true of the French, who upheld their language and education system as superior. These colonies had to wait until independence in the 1950s and 1960s before they could use the cinematic medium to narrate their own stories. Even after independence, technical training, funding and facilities for film production were difficult to obtain, creating a long-standing dependency on the West and the former Soviet Union. The scarcity of exhibition venues is another persistent problem in Muslim states. As it emerged from a break with pagan idolatry, Islam traditionally forbids images of any beings with souls (human or animal), yet this has not prevented representational arts – not only decorative arts – from flourishing in the Islamic world. However, traditionalists view cinema as a corrupting influence. In several countries, including Iran and Saudi Arabia, state policies geared towards Islamicisation have drastically impacted on, and restricted, film production; in Taliban-era Afghanistan, filmmaking was banned altogether. Throughout the region, there is strict censorship prohibiting any film from showing its country and its people in what is deemed to be a poor light. In Arab and Muslim states, censorship revolves around the depiction of sex, religion and politics. Most are one-party states in which direct criticism of political rulers or official policy is forbidden, as is criticism of Islam. Usually, projects have to be approved by a censorship committee before filming starts; and, once the film is completed, filmmakers must obtain an official licence for commercial exhibition.[4] Many films, including foreign co-productions, encounter censorship at this stage.

Traditional cultural motifs in Middle Eastern films include oral story-telling, calligraphy, textile arts and musical theatre (which arrived in the twentieth century). Films also incorporate influences from the region's contemporary performing and visual arts such as dance, music and TV. These influences are locally determined, often mixing centuries-old tradi-tions with diverse international influences. For example, contemporary music often draws on traditional religious music, such as the call to prayer, and Arabic, Persian, Berber and Hellenic influences, using instruments such as the lute and the zither together with imported or adapted Western instruments.[5] Middle Eastern dance, a key element in film, is inseparable from music and has its own rhythmic vocabulary involving 'isolations' of the hips, abdomen and other body parts.[6] Dance existed in the region before the Islamic conquest, and some aspects of female dancing may have originated in fertility cults of pre-Islamic deities; women had important roles in pagan Arab societies, which were matrilinear and endorsed poly-andry – pagan practices that Islam reversed, along with idolatry.[7] In the Islamic world, dancing – especially solo dancing performed for money – is seen as sinful, as it involves publicly revealing the body, raising questions of 'honour' for female performers, whether performing live or on film. For these reasons, performers in Middle Eastern societies are regarded as having a low social status – except those who attain transcendent stardom like the famous Egyptian singer Umm Kulthum, who died in 1975; many contemporary films pay homages to her.

The importance of dance, music and oral storytelling often means that sound is generally not as subordinated to image and diegesis as it is in Western cinema. Although Hollywood dominates the box office now, Indian, Egyptian and Turkish films have traditionally enjoyed popularity across the region; and there are many similarities between their popular forms (see also Chapter 7). The most popular local genres are melodrama and comedy farce, linking the popular cinemas of Egypt, Lebanon, Turkey, Iran and even Israel – where the *Bourekas* genre, 'a product of conflicts between European and Mizrahi (Oriental) Jews featured within the framework of melodrama or comedy', is a syncretic meld of Arab–Jewish influences.[8]

In the wake of Egypt's 1952 revolution which overthrew the British and brought Gamal Abdel Nasser to power, revolutionary Arab films were made in Egypt, Algeria and Syria celebrating anti-colonial struggle and expressing support for Palestinians. Inspired by new movements in Europe such as Italian neorealism and *cinéma-vérité*, these films departed from both Hollywood and the region's own commercial traditions. This was a politicised cinema energised by anti-imperial pan-Arab nationalism and socialism. The neorealist model which it adopted mixed documentary and fiction; the best-known example is the Italian–Algerian collaboration *The Battle of Algiers* (1965), which utilises a naturalistic street-level shooting style to recreate the Algerian war for independence from France (1954–62). These films come under the category of what Fernando Solanas and Octavio Getino call 'Third Cinema'. However, more recent manifestations of 'Third Cinema' from the region display a shift in perspective from the public realm of nationalist revolution to the more private realms of gender relationships and social institutions like the family, using these to interrogate the fulfilment of nationalist goals. The realist impulse in these films is modified by 'a more subjective, self-critical, and pluralist' approach.[9] In style, they often turn to satire or comedy, seen to be more flexible for critiques of the nation.

Shohat and Stam remark that 'the allegorical tendency available to all art becomes exaggerated in the case of repressive regimes'.[10] Due to censorship, this certainly seems to be the case in Middle Eastern 'Third Cinema' – allegory serves as 'a form of protective camouflage' enabling filmmakers to 'speak for and about the nation as a whole'.[11] In these films, gender is often linked to issues of nation, with images of women creating 'metaphors for the loss of individualism, national rights and political suppression'.[12] Since the 1990s, there has been a rush of films dealing with the oppression of women in Islamic societies, often as a covert critique of political regimes that oppress men as well as women. Other prevalent themes include: politics; imagining the nation; religious extremism; war and occupation; exile and loss of 'belonging'.

As in Europe, co-productions are becoming a common strategy. Co-productions are primarily French-backed, creating another site of tensions between France and its ex-colonies. Audiences and critics often question the 'authenticity' of these films, alleging that they are tailored for the West, as if there were any 'pure' indigenous elements not already modified by 'Western' influences. Filmmakers themselves are understandably hurt by such charges, yet the style and ideological content of their films have, unavoidably, been influenced by their close contact with France and French culture. Also, many contemporary Middle Eastern filmmakers are diasporic or exilic filmmakers who live abroad in Europe and America. This, too, has shaped the style and thematic content of their work, just as emigration within the region – especially to Cairo – had a decisive impact on cross-cultural flows in Middle Eastern filmmaking in the past.

Egyptian and Lebanese Cinema

By the time Egypt began making its own films, the country was relatively autonomous and more politically stable than other Arab states, although it remained a British colony until 1952. Its film industry was aided by a flourishing cosmopolitan culture and native capital from other local industries. In 1959, the Ministry of Culture set up the Higher Film Institute for training film professionals, a breeding ground for subsequent generations of Egyptian directors. At this time, Egypt was the most influential power in the region, politically as well as culturally – the centre of pan-Arab nationalism under Nasser's leadership.

The Egyptian film industry became known as the 'Hollywood on the Nile' and established the standards for commercial film production in the region. It exploited the commercial potential of popular Egyptian songs which were broadcast on the radio throughout the region, familiarising Arabic-speaking audiences with the Egyptian dialect. This gave Egyptian cinema an advantage over other Arab cinemas. Song, music and dance – especially belly-dance – became staples in Egyptian films.[13] Hollywood musicals were another key influence. Early films containing *Arabian Nights*-style tales, verbal comedy and sentimental love stories crystallised into a popular star-driven multi-genre formula which combined farce and melodrama and had an 'obligatory happy ending'.[14] This popular formula did not change when President Nasser nationalised the film industry, although production faltered. Nasser's successor Anwar Sadat partially reprivatised the film industry in 1971, launching in the same year an Open Door policy which increased Egypt's relations with Western capitalism. With the arrival of TV in the 1970s, Egyptian films became more popular in the Gulf States, where cinema-going is more rare. This affected the Egyptian film industry substantially, as it made it dependent on Gulf State distribution companies, who set the selling price and hence the budget of a given film on the basis of the stars' popularity. Actors' salaries rocketed, comprising the lion's share of the total budget, while the content of Egyptian films had to comply with Saudi Arabia's strict censorship. With the balance of political power in the region shifting to Israel and the Arab Gulf States, both in close alliance with the USA, the Egyptian film industry also waned, suffering from a 'chronic lack of investment'.[15]

Youssef Chahine, whose career as a film director stretches from the 1950s to the present, is the international figurehead of Egyptian cinema. His films are central to the mainstream Egyptian film industry but also ambivalently positioned towards it, inaugurating a new kind of cinema which is 'entertaining but not frivolous'.[16] Genre-mixing and the dramatic use of song-and-dance inserts are key traits, but his films add eclectic influences, including neorealism, Hollywood musicals, Douglas Sirk's melodramas, historical epic and surrealism. Initially, Chahine relied on small independent producers; then he established his own production company Misr International Films and inclined towards co-productions with other Arab countries such as Lebanon and Algeria. But since the mid-1980s his co-production deals have been with French cultural associations and TV stations, especially the French TV channel TFI. During the 1990s, Chahine's international stature rose, but his films *The Emigrant* (1994), *Destiny* (1997) and *The Other* (1999) provoked controversy at home for their portrayal of Islamic extremism (he himself is a Christian). His French co-production deals increased suspicion that Chahine was collaborating 'at Egypt's expense'.[17]

In *The Emigrant*, Chahine depicted the prophet Joseph, a 'blasphemy' for which he was taken to court. Around the same time, the Nobel Prize-winning writer Naguib Mahfouz was stabbed by Islamic militants. In *Destiny*, Chahine transposes these two incidents to twelfth-century Arab Spain, focusing on the historical philosopher and judge Ibn Rushd (known in the West as Averroës), a contributor to the Renaissance who was denounced as a heretic, and a gypsy singer, Morwan, whose poetry, song and merriment are anathema to a radical Islamic sect, who plot to stab him. Morwan's wife, Manuela, uses music and dance to try to bring the Caliph's son Abdullah, who has become a sectarian, back to his senses. When he tells her that she will dance in hell, Manuela pointedly replies: 'Maybe, but you have made hell on earth.'

Chahine won a lifetime achievement prize at Cannes in 1997 for *Destiny*, which also became his first film to be picked up for US distribution. This accolade attracted criticism from the Arab press, where Chahine's attack on Islamic fundamentalism appeared to be simplistic, designed to 'please' French co-producers and serve the West.[18] Actually, Chahine reverses received ideas about Western influences in *Destiny* through his use of the figure of Ibn Rushd, whose free-thinking ideas did not come from the West but went to the West, enabling it to emerge from its Dark Ages – a time that was a Golden Age for Arab civilisations. Chahine thus warns that the rise of Islamic fundamentalism has brought the Middle East to a sorry state, threatening to mire it in its own Dark Ages.[19]

Of all the region's film industries, the Lebanese film industry has the closest ties to the Hollywood on the Nile. It exported its stars to Egypt and produced many Egyptian-dialect films during its brief boom before the Lebanese civil war (1975–90), when Beirut was divided into two by warring Christians and Muslims, adding to existing frays on Lebanese soil involving Palestinians, Israelis and Syrians. Lebanon had the region's best technical facilities and sold the most cinema tickets per inhabitant before the outbreak of the war, which destroyed the film infrastructure, forcing Lebanese filmmakers to move elsewhere.[20] Numerous Lebanese filmmakers have made films about returning to war-torn Beirut, making the ruined city a persistent feature of Lebanese cinema. They include Jocelyn Saab (*Once Upon a Time, Beirut* [1995]), who lives in France and is the best-known of Lebanon's many female directors, and the Los Angeles-based Ziad Doueiri, former cameraman to Quentin Tarantino. Doueiri leads a younger generation of Lebanese directors whose work is marked by the trauma of the long civil war.

Doueiri's debut feature, *West Beirut* (1998), revisits the start of the civil war from the perspective of teenagers Tarek and Omar. Accompanied by a Christian girl, May, they roam around the bombed-out city, treating it like a playground, after the war forces their school to close. Tarek stumbles across a brothel belonging to Madame Oum Walid which is situated in No Man's Land between the Christian-controlled East and the Muslim-controlled West. Frequented by both Muslims and Christians, the brothel acknowledges neither West nor East, while in No Man's Land bras are used for white flags enabling one to avoid snipers and go anywhere one likes. The brothel is a political and sexual utopia for the adolescent Tarek, but ultimately signifies a failed utopia – although ostensibly a 'free' zone, it cannot but represent exploitation. The film keeps up its light humour – Tarek and Omar find Oum Walid unreceptive to their plans for organising Middle East peace here in her house – but after this the tone becomes increasingly bleak.

Despite the war, Doueiri strives to represent the Middle East as a 'normal' place – part of a strategy of self-representation to counter Western media images. His story of youths on the streets moreover belongs to neo-noir territory already pinpointed in relation to *La Haine* (see Chapter 1 and, for more examples, Chapter 5). It also has affinities with the naturalistic, handheld, street-level shooting style of Italian neorealism and the region's Third Cinema traditions. *West Beirut* was banned in several Arab countries for its frank discussion of sex and religion, but became a smash hit when released in Lebanon, beating top American films at the box office for several months.[21] Funded by the French production company La Sept-Arte after a number of Middle Eastern financiers rejected his script, Doueiri claims: 'Without the French, my film would not have been made.'[22] This post-colonial irony is reinforced in several scenes in the film showing how the French imposed their language and schooling system on the Lebanese, including the opening where Tarek interrupts the French national anthem at school assembly by singing the Lebanese national song over a loud-hailer.

Palestinian/Israeli Chronicles

In the Balfour Declaration of 1917, the British pledged support to the Zionist movement seeking to create a Jewish homeland in Palestine. The British, however, also tried to appease the Palestinians by promising to limit Jewish immigration, leading to a Zionist terrorist campaign against the British. In the 1948 War of Israeli Independence, many Palestinians were killed and over half of them were displaced from their homes to refugee camps in Gaza and the West Bank. The Israeli state requisitioned their property and has never allowed them back.

Israeli filmmaking began as early as 1918, with films made for the Zionist project, promoting and justifying Jewish immigration to Palestine. They continued to be made until 1970, when Israeli state television became the main organ of propaganda. Throughout the twentieth century, Israeli film-making has closely followed the mood of the nation. From the 1980s onwards, the optimism of early Zionism and the heroic nationalism of the 1950s and 1960s subsided to interrogations of national ideals and apoca-lyptic despair at the prospect of perpetual war. One of the defining events was the 1967 Six-Day War, when Israel destroyed Egypt's entire military fleet and seized control of the Sin'ai desert and Gaza from Egypt, East Jerusalem and the West Bank from Jordan, and the Golan Heights from Syria – a euphoric victory for Israel just as it was a humiliating defeat for the Arabs. In the longer term, however, the war resulted in deadlock, with Israel refusing to relinquish its occupied territories.

The Palestinians who remained within Israeli state borders, including in Gaza and the West Bank, found themselves being exploited in low-paid jobs, occupied and curfewed, their homes and livelihoods constantly over-turned by Israeli bombardment and bulldozed for the building of new Jewish settlements. In 1987, a Palestinian *intifada* (uprising) began, ending with Israeli Prime Minister Yitzhak Rabin and the Palestinian Liberation Organisation (PLO) signing the Oslo Accords in 1993, marking the start of the peace process. Trust, however, quickly broke down: Rabin was assas-sinated in 1995 by an Israeli hardliner. When the right-wing Likud Party returned to power, it reversed his policy and encouraged settlements in occupied territories. By 2000, the *intifada* had restarted, responding with suicide bombings to Israeli attacks on Gaza and the West Bank. Western (especially US) interests have further jeopardised the peace.

The Holocaust and other Judeocides were naturally the main reason for supporting the foundation of a Jewish homeland. Zionist propaganda created the myth of Palestine as a 'land without people' for the Jews, 'people without a land'.[23] It either caricatured the Palestinians or pretended they did not exist, erasing them from the picture in favour of panoramas of the 'Promised Land'. Israeli state ideology proceeded to relate a one-sided history which suppressed the expulsion of Palestinians and tried to erase it from collective memory. Palestinians refer to the traumatic loss of their lands since 1948 as the *Nakba*, which literally means 'disaster'. The Holocaust and the Nakba have been subject to historical and political forgetting on both sides, with Arabs denying or expressing apathy towards the Holocaust as well as the Jews erasing the Palestinian Nakba.[24] However, some recent Israeli and Palestinian films have dealt with these suppressed events, showing how the exile of Jews and the exile of Palestinians are bound to each other, intersecting on the same land. The work of Israel's internationally best-known filmmaker, Amos Gitai, exemplifies this trend.

Gitai started out making documentaries about the Israeli–Palestinian conflict in the early 1980s, including *House* (1980), which is about the Nakba. These films were banned for their sympathy towards Palestinians. Gitai left Israel in 1982 due to lack of support for his films and moved to France, before returning to Israel in 1993. His recent films include the fictional dramas *Yom Yom* (1999), a story of a mixed Arab–Jewish marriage; *Kadosh* (1999), which shows the oppression of women in the orthodox Jewish community living in Jerusalem's Me'a She'arim quarter; *Kippur* (2000), an apocalyptic rendering of the 1973 October (Yom Kippur) war, which bred disillusionment about Israeli state ideology and institutions among many Israeli liberals and was a formative event for Gitai; and *Kedma* (2002), which interrogates Israeli state ideals and British imperialism through a story about the arrival of European Jewish immigrants in 1948.

At its beginnings, Palestinian filmmaking was keen to alert the world to the situation of Palestinian refugees and the loss of their homeland. In the aftermath of the 1967 war, documentaries were made by film units attached to Palestinian armed resistance organisations such as the PLO (established in 1964), the Popular Front for the Liberation of Palestine (PFLP) and the Popular Democratic Front for the Liberation of Palestine (PDFLP). The realist paradigm is paramount for this early stage of Palestinian filmmaking. Palestinian filmmakers trusted in the 'veracity' of documentary images to record the plight of those who had been bereft of their image in Zionist propaganda. However, they lacked access to equipment and expertise, having to depend on regional facilities such as those in Lebanon, where the PLO went after being expelled from Jordan in 1970–1. In 1982, Israelis invaded Beirut, displacing the PLO to Tunis. Since then, the PLO has changed its policy to supporting Western films sympathetic to the Palestinian cause. Alongside the documentaries, there sprang up revolutionary fiction films, which presented the Palestinian–Israeli conflict in Manichean terms (heroic nationalist versus occupying villain), often through genderised iconography figuring Palestine as a raped woman.

Recent Palestinian cinema is a cinema of *auteurs* rather than collective filmmakers. The best-known directors are Michel Khleifi (who, with his *Wedding in Galilee* [1987], was the first to receive international acclaim), Rashid Mashawari, Ali Nassar and Elia Suleiman. All of them deal with the psychological effects of Israeli occupation, with its bureaucratic rules, raids and mobility restrictions. They use stylistic forms such as magic realism and parable as well as documentary realism to express themes of exile, disappearance and resistance. Co-productions with European TV stations are their major source of funding, although Nassar's *Milky Way* (1997) was financed by the Israeli Film Fund, created in 1979 for the promotion of 'quality' Israeli films.[25]

Current international attention is focused on Suleiman, who was born in Nazareth, grew up as a Christian in Israel, studied film in London and New York (where he lived for over a decade) and currently lives in Paris. Suleiman's films use absurdist strategies and deadpan humour to encapsulate the psychological toll of Israeli occupation – the experiences of stasis, interminable waiting, internal exile and civil disputes. They closely engage with Zionist discourses that misrepresent Palestinians and their situation, particularly strategies consigning Palestinians to silence and invisibility. The diary-like form of the narratives fuses the personal with the political, with Suleiman figuring his own displacement through a thinly disguised fictional version of himself, among other self-reflexive devices. In his debut feature *Chronicle of a Disappearance* (1997), for example, he retells Palestine's disappearance through a story about a returning émigré filmmaker, played by himself. At a public gathering, he is asked to discuss the film he is making, but problems with the microphone prevent him from communicating. Throughout the film, he is mute; and, when the Israeli police raid and make an inventory of his house, they brush past him without acknowledging his presence. A woman, Adan, becomes his vocal alter ego, who turns her enemies' weapons against them. Over the police CB radio, she recites the Israeli national anthem, making it signify its 'original' meaning as 'an anthem of the oppressed who have lost Jerusalem' on behalf on the Palestinians.[26]

Suleiman's use of comic timing has been compared to the French director-comedian Jacques Tati.[27] Like Tati, he also uses static long shots and wide-angle framings to maximise his deadpan visual comedy. This is exemplified in a scene in *Chronicle of a Disappearance* which satirises the bureaucratic functionality of the Israeli police: a police van skids urgently to a halt for the policemen to line up against the wall in perfect unison and then pile back into the van, leaving as abruptly as they came. In *Divine Intervention* (2002), a winner of the Grand Jury Prize at Cannes, humour takes the form of 'slapstick provocation' – from the opening where Santa Claus gets mugged to the cartoon-like revenge fantasy where Israeli troops engaged in target practice with a cardboard Palestinian are dispatched by a single female warrior, referred to in the credits as 'the Woman'.[28] The film figures exile through restricted traffic at the Ramallah–Jerusalem checkpoint, where E.S. (played by Suleiman), coming from Jerusalem, meets the Woman, who drives from Ramallah. They hold hands and exchange looks, confined in their cars. Anchoring audience identification with the lovers, the film evokes subversive delight as they release a balloon printed with the face of PLO leader Yasser Arafat. The balloon sails freely past the checkpoint in defiance of the confinement which Palestinians daily endure and flies over the rooftops until Arafat's smiling face finally nestles against Jerusalem's Dome of the Rock.

New Tunisian Cinema

Tunisia's film culture benefited from thriving film societies, which began a decade before independence in 1956. Since then, two state organisations have been important. One is the Société Anonyme Tunisienne de Production et d'Expansion Cinématographique (SATPEC), set up in 1957 to handle film production, import, distribution and exhibition. It went bankrupt in 1994 and was incorporated into Canal Horizon. The other is the Secrétariat Etat aux Affaires Culturelles et à l'Information (SEACI), which initiated rural film distribution and founded the Carthage Film Festival, a biennial Arab festival, in 1966. State support also came in the form of a 1981 law, which provided financial assistance to film-producers in return for 6 per cent of box-office takings. However, Tunisia has only seventy cinema theatres.[29] Such a small distribution base cannot sustain a local film industry, even with state support. Therefore, since the mid-1980s, international co-productions have been increasing. Many filmmakers pre-sell rights to European film or TV companies, particularly Germany's ZDF, France's La Sept and UK's Channel 4, both to finance their films and to obtain further distribution outlets. Co-production has had a significant impact on the content and style of Tunisian films, encouraging defiance of censorship regulations as well as – according to some views – Oriental exoticisation.[30]

Although critically acclaimed in Europe and America, New Tunisian films generally receive lukewarm, even hostile, responses at home. The filmmakers themselves have pointed out that in terms of style and moral ideology their films are vastly different from the Egyptian commercial films and soap operas that Tunisian audiences are accustomed to watching on TV.[31] In comparison to the high melodrama of Egyptian commercial cinema, the Tunisian films appear understated and de-dramatised to Tunisian audiences. Moreover, the leading directors of New Tunisian Cinema – Férid Boughedir, Nouri Bouzid and Moufida Tlatli – are generally considered to belong to 'a westernized elite that is "out of touch" with the social realities and morality of the average Tunisian'.[32]

However, contrary to this view, the films do engage with the realities of contemporary Tunisian society in a number of respects. In the post-colonial period, Tunisia was the only Middle Eastern country apart from Turkey which significantly challenged the *sharia* code of Islamic law. This law governs many aspects of life from dress code to forms of punishment and is interpreted and enforced differently in each Muslim country. Habib Bourguiba, the first president of independent Tunisia (1957–87), who set about modernising and secularising Tunisian society, introduced the Code of Personal Status, which overturned aspects of *sharia* law, abolishing polygamy and child marriage; it also legalised divorce, replacing a former practice whereby a man could repudiate his wife purely by public declaration. These measures, together with the country's geographical and cultural affinities with Western Europe, have made Tunisia the most westernised country in the Arab world. Despite this, Tunisian society remains one in which the sexes are rigidly segregated and governed by patriarchal family structures. This tension between tradition and modernising trends, particularly in relation to gender, is a key theme in New Tunisian Cinema.

Nouri Bouzid's work offers some of the best examples. Like several other Tunisian filmmakers, Bouzid studied film abroad (at Insas, Brussels) and gained practical experience on foreign productions shot on Tunisian locations. Following a lively, socially committed realist approach, he is known for confronting controversial subject matter rarely broached in Arab cinemas. His first three films, *Man of Ashes* (1986), *Golden Horseshoes* (1989) and *Business* (1992), deal with themes of damaged masculinity, child abuse, male prostitution, sex tourism and relationships between Jewish and Muslim communities. In *Man of Ashes*, his protagonists Farfat and Hachemi refuse their society's definition of what it means to be male – dominant, sexist, heterosexual and married – aware that there are other possibilities, including the possibility of being gay.[33]

In *Clay Dolls* (2002), Bouzid turns to the situation of poor rural girls who are recruited as maidservants for Tunis's *nouveaux riches*. He uses associative, thematic editing and staging within given shots to link the stories of Rebeh, a former maidservant, and a young arrival, Fedhah. Both break out of their masters' homes to enjoy the city's exhilarating freedoms. Yet, in a sex-segregated society, these freedoms are compromised; when Rebeh enters a public café, a typically all-male social space, her presence is viewed as shameful and scandalous. Another interesting treatment is of the man who recruits the girls, Omrane, who spends much of the film in tortured drunkenness, or battered on the floor after fights – one of Bouzid's damaged men. An abusive homosexual relationship with his former master, Baba Jâafra, is also hinted at. The film further treats the conflict between traditional norms of gender behaviour and modern expectations in a scene, where Rebeh describes to Omrane the type of man she wants: kind, affectionate, attentive, not a drunkard. Omrane jokingly replies: 'Call that a man? Get yourself a woman!'

Moufida Tlatli is Tunisia's foremost female director. She trained at the IDHEC in Paris and worked as a film-editor on Tunisian, Palestinian, Algerian and Moroccan films. She achieved instant international recognition for her directorial debut *Silences of the Palace* (1994). Structured as a flashback to the childhood of a singer, Alia, who was a servant of the Beys (Tunisia's one-time monarchy) during the 1950s when the nationalist struggle was at its height, this film focuses on the private rather than the public realm. Through images of the female servants cloistered in the palace, it portrays women as the colonised of the colonised; subject to the proprietorship (and sexual advances) of male aristocrats, they do not even own their own bodies and are sworn to silence about palace incidents. However, Tlatli's film also shows how women in patriarchal Islamic societies subverted their restrictions within the private sphere in which they were confined. Through mutual support, they create 'a non-patriarchal family within a patriarchal context'.[34] Lofti, her middle-class nationalist lover, likens Alia to her country, and helps her to find her voice. Yet nationalist hopes ultimately fail her, signalled by the opening where the sad-looking Alia sings Umm Kulthum's song 'Amal Hayati' ('The Hope of My Life'). In post-colonial Tunisia, Alia's life has improved, but her low status as a singer exposes her to gendered insults and also prevents Lofti from marrying her. She concludes the film by admitting that revolutionary Lofti could not save her – and neither could her voice.

Many filmmakers have capitalised on the unprecedented focus on the region in the wake of the attacks of 11 September 2001 in order to make comparisons with their own countries' predicaments (see also Chapter 4).

In *Clay Dolls*, for example, there is a brief reference (on a car radio) to America's war against the Taliban in Afghanistan; Bouzid thereby situates his own story in relation to burning contemporary topics. Like many other Middle Eastern countries, Tunisia is a one-party state, where free speech is absent and artistic expression is fraught with censorship and repression. Robert Lang has argued that it is to this that 'the silences' in the title of Tlatli's film ultimately refer.[35] Tlatli allows the censors to believe that her story is about the oppression of women, yet through allegory the situation she portrays in her film is pertinent to everyone living in present-day Tunisia – not merely to servants in the Beys' palace in the 1950s.

New Turkish Cinema

Turkey's former incarnation as the Ottoman empire made it a rich cultural thoroughfare between Europe and the Middle East. However, Kemal Atatürk, the founder of the Turkish Republic in 1923, instituted westernising reforms aiming to wipe out the Ottoman legacy and to orientate Turkey towards Europe. These reforms included the creation of a secular state and the removal of Islamic practices from public life, the introduction of the Latin alphabet and the exclusion of Arabic and Persian influences. Kemalist measures also suppressed the empire's multicultural identity, most notably the Kurds, who form the largest of Turkey's many minorities.

Kemalist ideology created an 'authoritarian context of production', introducing strict censorship regulations that were on a par with the rest of the region.[36] These lasted from 1939 to 1986. Although Turkish narrative cinema goes back to 1916, popular entertainment films did not emerge until the 1950s. The 1960s and 1970s were the golden age of popular Turkish cinema, when the average annual turnover was 200 films, making Turkey one of the world's most prolific film-producing nations after the USA, India and Egypt.[37] This cinema, known as 'Yeşilçam cinema', declined after the mid-1970s due to rising production costs for colour photography, the spread of TV, and political upheaval which led ultimately to the 1980s military dictatorship.

Turkey also has strong traditions of social-realist filmmaking, as exemplified in the work of its most internationally celebrated director, Yilmaz Güney – a major influence on New Turkish Cinema. *Yol* (1982), Güney's penultimate film before his death in exile in France in 1984, received the Palme d'Or at Cannes. It follows five prisoners on a week's leave from prison, employing '"prison" as a metaphor for the state of Turkish society under military rule'.[38] Güney wrote its screenplay in 1979 while he himself was in prison (from which he escaped during a leave of absence like that depicted in the film), and he edited and released the film abroad. Like his other works, *Yol* was banned in Turkey.

The dictatorship implemented neoliberal economic policies designed to integrate Turkey into the global economy but which widened the gap between rich and poor in the midst of extreme recession and crisis. These events, together with civil war which flared up in the 1990s between the Turkish army and Kurdish separatists and the tension between the rising popularity of nationalist discourses and a growing distrust of homogenising notions of nation implicit in Kemalist ideals, form the immediate backdrop to New Turkish Cinema.

Kevin Robins and Asu Aksoy argue that the story of Turkish cinema 'can be told in terms of the progressive disordering of the ideal of the Kemalist nation, which may be regarded as a productive disordering'.[39] This disordering has actually taken place in the very forms of popular culture. Kemalist ideals are seen as belonging to the culture of the urban elite, as opposed to the Anatolian countryside, where people continue to abide by 'traditional, usually folk-Islamic, values'.[40] However, migrants from the countryside living in urban squatter settlements, known as *gecekondu*, fostered the music and culture of *arabesk* – the antithesis to Kemalist values – unleashing it as an 'unofficial' force in the new popular culture which flourished in commercial television and New Turkish Cinema, both of which arose in the 1990s. Consequently, key themes in New Turkish Cinema include the urban/rural dialectic and class conflict, as well as issues of national and regional 'belonging'.

The Bandit (Yavuz Turgul, 1996), a major box-office success, set the precedent for a swathe of new popular Turkish films which mixed action-driven narratives and polished production values with 'an ironic handling of Yeşilçam themes'.[41] The directors of the new popular Turkish cinema came from backgrounds in TV and advertising, generating their high budgets from these sectors. However, the films of Nuri Bilge Ceylan (*The Small Town* [1998], *Clouds of May* [1999] and *Uzak* [2003]) and Zeki Demirkubuz (*Block C* [1994], *Innocence* [1997], *Third Page* [2000], *Fate* [2001] and *Confession* [2001]) testify to another side of New Turkish Cinema, labelled by critics as a new, introspective and psychological strain.[42] Demirkubuz and Ceylan prefer to make low-budget films, participating in their own films as writers, cinematographers, editors and occasionally also as actors. Their films are highly praised at international and national film festivals but are not widely promoted or distributed and have not been commercially successful. In 'Horror of a Different Kind: Dissonant Voices of the New Turkish Cinema', Asuman Suner claims that these directors approach the themes of belonging in a non-essentialist fashion – in contrast to their popular counterparts – by rendering 'home' a site of the uncanny (in German, *unheimlich*, 'unhomely').[43] The uncanny is a psychoanalytical category, shown by Sigmund Freud to be etymologically linked its opposite – what is homely (*heimlich*) is also uncanny (*unheimlich*) and vice versa.

Ceylan's films have been compared to those of Abbas Kiarostami (see Chapter 4). He utilises a minimalist, documentary-like style, depicting everyday situations that 'seem to be both all too real and at the same time somewhat skewed and bizarre'.[44] Ceylan often casts his own family and friends in his films, which are all autobiographical, referring to his profession as photographer and director, if not directly referring to his life. At Cannes in 2003, *Uzak* received the Grand Jury Prize and the Best Actor Award for its two leads, Mehmet Emin Toprak (1974–2002) and Muzaffer Özdemir. In the film, Mahmut, a divorcé and a photographer living in Istanbul (a figure of intellectual urban alienation reflecting aspects of Ceylan's own life), is visited by his country cousin Yusef, searching for a job at a time of recession. *Uzak* means 'distant': the film explores themes of estrangement within the home where the two men uneasily cohabit. In shot compositions, the characters are divided by bars, doors and window-panes, or placed into different spatial planes, as when Mahmut is shown in focus in the foreground while his part-time lover undresses out of focus in the background. The home becomes further estranged – an uncanny place – through the use of magnified sounds that do not match images but act as an overbearing discordant element, particularly in the night-time scene where the mouse in Mahmut's kitchen is caught in his glue trap; its pitiful squeaks reverberate throughout the house, intermingling with Yusuf's hallucinatory dreams.

Notes

1. Said, *Orientalism*, p. 26.
2. Zuhur, *Enchantment*, p. 16.
3. Shohat and Stam, *Unthinking Eurocentrism*, p. 285.
4. Shafik, *Arab Cinema*, p. 34.
5. Zuhur, *Enchantment*, p. 8.
6. Ibid., p. 6.
7. Ibid., p. 6; Ali, *Fundamentalisms*, p. 63.
8. Shohat and Stam, *Unthinking Eurocentrism*, p. 315.
9. Shafik, *Arab Cinema*, p. 212.
10. Shohat and Stam, *Unthinking Eurocentrism*, p. 272.
11. Ibid., p. 272.
12. Zuhur, *Enchantment*, p. 13.

13. Shafik, *Arab Cinema*, p. 24.
14. Ibid., p. 24.
15. Ibid., p. 43.
16. Fawal, *Chahine*, p. 39.
17. Ibid., p. 49.
18. Hammond, 'The Incoherence of Destiny'.
19. Fawal, *Chahine*, p. 182.
20. Kennedy-Day, 'Cinema in Lebanon, Syria, Iraq and Kuwait', p. 365.
21. Asfour, 'Politics of Arab Cinema', p. 47.
22. Ibid., p. 47.
23. Ali, *Fundamentalisms*, p. 90.
24. Bresheeth, 'Telling Stories of *Heim*', p. 36.
25. Kronish, *Israel*, p. 3.
26. Bresheeth, 'Telling Stories of *Heim*', p. 33.
27. Rich, 'Divine Comedy'.
28. Ibid.
29. Armes, 'Cinema in the Maghreb', p. 427.
30. Shafik, *Arab Cinema*, p. 42.
31. Lang, 'Choosing to be "Not a Man"', p. 91.
32. Lang, 'Tunisian Cinema' e-mail, 17 November 2003.
33. Lang, 'Choosing to be "Not a Man"', p. 92.
34. Shohat, 'Post-Third-Worldist Culture, pp. 59–60.
35. See Lang, 'Le colonisé et le colonisateur', pp. 189–204.
36. Robins and Aksoy, 'Deep Nation', p. 212.
37. Suner, 'Horror of a Different Kind', p. 1.
38. Suner, 'Yilmaz Güney's *Yol*', p. 283.
39. Robins and Aksoy, 'Deep Nation', p. 215.
40. Ibid., p. 209.
41. Suner, 'Horror of a Different Kind', p. 2.
42. Romney, 'A Silky Sadness', p. 23.
43. Suner, 'Horror of a Different Kind', p. 5.
44. Ibid., p. 8.

CHAPTER 4

Iranian Cinema

Since the late 1980s, Iranian films have been screening to critical acclaim at film festivals around the world. These are largely 'art' films belonging to what is known as the 'New Iranian Cinema', which accounts for only 15 per cent of Iran's total annual film output. New Iranian Cinema was preceded by the Iranian New Wave which began in the decade prior to the 1978–9 Islamic Revolution. Although these earlier films also won international recognition, the post-revolutionary films have stunned audiences and critics alike, as a repressive Islamic republic existing in relative cultural isolation seemed a most unlikely quarter for a cinematic renaissance.

New Iranian Cinema used to be entirely state-sponsored but now increasingly relies on foreign (especially French) investors. In connection with this, some critics – both from within Iran and abroad – have attacked the films for bearing little relation to Iranian social or political reality and thereby indirectly legitimating a regime keen to transform its reputation abroad.[1] This chapter focuses on New Iranian Cinema, situating this controversy in the context of post-revolutionary Iran and offering the other case – that many New Iranian films communicate social realities through a subtle negotiation of censorship constraints but also through open and passionate engagement. It will explain certain aspects of Iran's filmmaking climate before going on to explore general themes and characteristics of New Iranian Cinema, including the films of Abbas Kiarostami and Mohsen Makhmalbaf, ending with case studies of *Through the Olive Trees* (1994), *A Moment of Innocence* (1996) and *The Apple* (1998).

Iran had no direct experience of colonisation, but during the Pahlavi Dynasty it became an arena of neocolonial struggle between the superpowers, with the USA safeguarding its strategic and economic interests in the region by ensuring that the Shah (the Iranian monarch) remained in power. The last Shah was an autocratic ruler, whose secret police, the Savak, became notorious for their torture and execution of political prisoners. A growing backlash against Americanisation and the Shah's corruptions culminated in the 1978–9 Revolution in which the Shah was overthrown. His opponents, who included secular forces as well as Islamic militants, hoped for freedom and independence.[2] The clergy, led by

Ayatollah Khomeini, won majority support to form an Islamic Republic with promises to bring social justice and end corruption. However, when they took control, they eliminated all opposition, utilising the same methods of execution and torture as the old regime. Khomeini moreover issued an edict making the veil compulsory – allowing women to show only their hands and faces in public – and enforced this and other civil restrictions through the religious police (a branch of the Revolutionary Guards) and their network of informers.

Under Khomeini (1979–89), Iran's slogan became 'neither East nor West', opposing the capitalism of the USA (the 'Great Satan') and Soviet communism, and emphasising Islam as a third alternative.[3] In the 1979 hostage crisis, clerics mobilised the masses to demand the exiled Shah's return for trial and took over the US embassy. This event helped to define Iran's sinister image for the West. The USA supported the Iraqi leader Saddam Hussein during the Iran–Iraq war (1980–8). This was a traumatic conflict involving trench warfare, poison gas and over a million lost lives, and ended with neither side achieving its aims. In Iran, the dictatorship remained intact albeit with dissent emerging within its ranks. When Khomeini died, Ayatollah Ali Khameini (the former president) replaced him as supreme leader, and limited reforms allowed a new president, Hojjat-ol-Eslam Rafsanjani, to be elected. Rafsanjani made several U-turns on Khomeini's policies, including opening Iran to 'friendly' international capital.[4] As in China (see Chapter 5), the regime found a way to 'co-exist with the international community' by creating an ideological façade of moderation and reform.[5] Following student protests, reformist cleric Mohammed Khatami was elected president in 1997. Since then, however, there have been continued demonstrations, strikes and skirmishes against religious police and clerics, testifying to cracks in the regime's new reformist image.

Initially, cinema was denounced by Islamic revolutionaries, who perceived it as an agent of the Shah's corrupt policies and set about burning and destroying film theatres, bringing film production to a halt. Khomeini nonetheless declared that he was not opposed to cinema or other media – only the 'misuse' of such media to promote 'vice'. He advocated using cinema for teaching so-called 'Islamic values', including traditionalism, monotheism, theocracy and anti-imperialism.[6] His authorities reversed Pahlavi policy by restricting Western imports and permitting hitherto banned anti-colonial revolutionary films like *The Battle of Algiers* (1965). While strict censorship had been operative in the Shah's era also, the clerics ordered a drastic purging of the film industry. Pre-revolutionary films were re-edited and retitled; images of unveiled women were censored by applying black ink directly to the frames.[7] Many filmmakers and entertainers were forced into exile, threatened with imprisonment and confiscation of their property.

The Ministry of Culture and Islamic Guidance (MCIG) supervises Iran's film industry. Its censorship regulations include rules of *hejab* (women's veiling and modesty). Films undergo multiple stages of inspection, in addition to synopsis and screenplay stages. The precise rules are always changing, due to debates between government agencies and filmmakers, film critics and audiences – but not always to filmmakers' benefit. Mohammed Khatami, who was appointed Minister of the MCIG when it began in 1982, was known as a supporter of controversial filmmakers like Mohsen Makhmalbaf – one of the reasons why he was removed from his post in 1992. His election as president in 1997 owes partly to his reputation as a defender of artistic expression (and his support for women's rights).

Two other important film organisations are the Institute for Intellectual Development of Children and Young Adults (established before the Revolution), which funds the production, distribution, exhibition and archiving of films, and the Farabi Cinema Foundation, which the MCIG formed in 1983 to support local industry, and which was a major force behind the international visibility of New Iranian Cinema until the mid-1990s.[8] Around this point, in tandem with its U-turn towards 'friendly' international capital, the state founded local companies to invest in Iranian films and manage foreign co-production deals. Also, despite the appearance of Iran's cultural isolation, international film festivals have been held in the country since the 1960s, giving Iranian filmmakers valuable contact with foreign films and filmmakers.

Yet, regular cinema-going in Iran has been decreasing since the Shah's era, due to factors such as censorship, shortage of exhibition sites and poor facilities in existing theatres.[9] Iranian audiences know that foreign films are censored, so they prefer to watch them on video and satellite, both of which undermine the regime's attempts to control cultural flows. Video, previously banned, is now approved; but the 1994 *fatwa* on satellite dishes remains, although the police have found it almost impossible to enforce.

Despite these difficulties, low production budgets and a large national market make it relatively easy for Iranian films to recoup their costs. This has increased critics' suspicions about New Iranian Cinema: these films are said to be 'simple', cheap to make, so the ratio of investment to revenue is favourable for foreign producers and distributors. However, to call the films 'simple' is to misjudge them, as will be seen below.

New Iranian Cinema

Some New Iranian Cinema filmmakers started work before the Revolution, including Dariush Mehrjui, Abbas Kiarostami, Amir Naderi and Bahram Beizai. Mohsen Makhmalbaf, Rakshan Bani-Etamed, Majid Majidi, Jafar Panahi, Abolfazl Jalili, Tahmineh Milani, Samira Makhmalbaf, Marzieh Meshkini and Bahman Ghobadi are among those who emerged after the Revolution.

Although their stylistic range is much wider than this, the directors of New Iranian Cinema became associated with neorealist films characterised by natural (usually rural) locations, the use of non-actors (especially children, with boys predominating during the 1980s and girls during the 1990s), the blurring of documentary and fiction, a meandering journey or quest, approximate real-time duration, a repetitive or cyclical structure, symbols inspired by Persian culture, and closing freeze-frames – an influence from *400 Blows* (1959), a French New Wave film close in sensibility to New Iranian Cinema. There are also many continuities with the 1960s Iranian New Wave whose highlights include Dariush Mehrjui's *The Cow* (1969) and Forugh Farrokhzad's *The House Is Black* (1963).

Thematically, New Iranian films are united by preoccupations with the psychological effects of the Iran–Iraq war (*Bashu* [1989], *Blackboards* [2000]), the relationship between life and art (nearly all of Kiarostami's films, *A Moment of Innocence*, *The Apple*), the representation of women in society and on screen (*Two Women* [1999], *Leila* [1996], *The Apple*, *The Day I Became a Woman* [2000] and countless others), and the situation of minorities such as the Kurds (*Blackboards*, *A Time for Drunken Horses* [2000]) and Afghans, who were displaced into Iran when the Soviets invaded Afghanistan (*Baran* [2001], *Delbaran* [2001]). At the turn of the millennium, cross-currents between filmmaking in Iran and Afghanistan emerged. A number of Iranian films are set in Afghanistan, drawing parallels between the two neighbouring states (*Kandahar* [2001], *At Five in the Afternoon* [2003]). The MCIG and Mohsen Makhmalbaf's production house have also trained and equipped Afghan filmmakers.

The rise of women-themed films since the mid-1980s is a major trend. Previously, women generally occupied background roles, partly due to filmmakers wanting to avoid complicated censorship rules, which forbid cross-gender contact between actors who are unrelated, and which stipulate that women wear a *chador* (a head-to-toe cloak), scarf, wig or hat on screen at all times, even at home, where most Iranian women would not veil themselves. These censorship rules have motivated the use of children in New Iranian Cinema, although this is also attributable to the role of the

Institute for the Intellectual Development of Children and Young Adults (discussed below, in relation to Kiarostami).

Emphasis on women's modesty led to a tendency to use long shots in the 1980s, or shots showing women with their gaze averted.[10] New Iranian films tend to keep spectators observing on the outside rather than 'stitching' them into narratives through classical (Hollywood) shot structures such as point-of-view and shot/reverse-shot. However, when point-of-view shots are used, it is often with startling effects (discussed below). Censorship regulations also create interesting implications for the use of cinematic space. Some films gesture to off-screen space by means of doors and other internal frames in order to emphasise the limits of what can be shown.

The foregrounding of women's issues has led to allegorical uses of the veil to address other aspects of society that are repressed by censorship. A pioneer in this respect is Rakshan Bani-Etamed, one of several female directors emerging since the mid-1980s who were instrumental in highlighting women and women's issues, inspiring a number of male directors including Jafar Panahi (*The Circle* [2000]), Dariush Mehrjui (*Leila*), Mohsen Makhmalbaf (*Kandahar*) and Kiarostami (*Ten* [2002]). The ideology of veiling ostensibly protects women from the male gaze, yet comes from a tradition of equating women with sin; their sexuality is seen as harmful to men and therefore to be restricted and controlled by men. In *Off the Limit* (1987), Bani-Etamed creates an 'aesthetics of veiling' through her use of visual and jurisdictional barriers showing how the veil 'marks women' and 'sets them apart from men'.[11] In *Nargess*, a film about a female thief Afagh and her younger lover Adel, she treads a fine line with censorship rules which forbid female 'bad guys' and restrict the representation of women to chaste and modest homemakers. Afagh and her rival Nargess (the chaste, law-abiding woman whom Adel marries) moreover refute the stereotype of the subjected Muslim woman, both being more determined and independent-spirited than either Adel himself or his male cronies.

Over the past two decades, women in Iran have gained a few rights, including voting in elections and holding political office. However, many aspects of Islamic *sharia* law remain strictly interpreted. In her book *Persian Mirrors*, Elaine Sciolino includes the following among her list:

> adultery is still punishable by stoning to death. Polygamy is legal . . . Men can divorce their wives at will, but women need to prove that their spouses are insane, impotent, violent, or unable to support the family . . . A woman's testimony in court has half the weight of a man's. Women can be arrested for jogging or bicycling or swimming in sexually segregated places, and for exposing their heads and necks and the curves of their bodies in public.[12]

Some of these issues are taken up in Tahmineh Milani's work, which, like Bani-Etamed's, differs stylistically from the dominant variety of New Iranian Cinema shown abroad. Milani's films are characterised by melodrama rather than neorealism. They belong to a group of films looking at issues like women's education, divorce and topics that are taboo in Iran, like extramarital pregnancy and prostitution. In *Two Women*, Milani confronts the ideal and actual conditions for women in marriage through the friendship between two women. Fereshteh escapes from the torments of a dangerous stalker, Hassan, and marries Ahmad, who immediately reneges on his promises to allow her to continue her university studies. Within the first few months of marriage, Ahmad locks her up in the house, hides the telephone and forbids her from having company or seeing her college friend Roya who, in the meantime, has embarked on a happy marriage on equal terms with her partner. Fereshteh is imprisoned in her marriage: the law courts refuse to consider her petition for divorce because her husband shelters her, pays the bills and does not physically abuse her. Milani is one of the most controversial filmmakers in contemporary Iran. She was jailed for her subsequent film *The Hidden Half* (2001), which sympathetically portrays leftist rebels in the aftermath of the Revolution.

Kiarostami and His Protégés

Kiarostami is Iran's most internationally celebrated director, and it is his success that propelled Iranian cinema into the global arena. Kiarostami is a graphic arts graduate who began his film career making credit titles and commercials. From 1969, he worked at the Institute for the Intellectual Development of Children and Young Adults and established a film department there, directing his first film, a short called *Bread and Alley*, in 1970. Kiarostami's earliest films (shorts and features) were educational films for children which regularly won prizes at Iran's Fajr Film Festival, and he made his first big international impact with *Where Is the Friend's Home?* (1987). The Institute supported his films up to and including *And Life Goes On* (1991), after which he has tended to collaborate with the French company MK2 who co-produced *A Taste of Cherry* (1997) (Kiarostami's Cannes Palme d'Or winner), *The Wind Will Carry Us* (1999) and *Ten* (2002).

Kiarostami's films are elliptical and minimalist. The idea of the 'halffinished' film, inviting creative input from viewers, and the principle of uncertainty, which plays with viewers' expectations, are distinctive aspects.[13] He works without a script, using mostly non-professional actors (including children) and largely rural or outskirt locations; landscape is an important feature of his post-revolutionary films, as is repetition.

Kiarostami's signature shots are of zigzagging roads. These reflect broad existential statements as well as the particular predicament of his characters. For example, in *Where's Is the Friend's Home?*, the zigzag path – constructed specifically for the film – signifies the 'hurrying around' of modern life as well as its child protagonist's tortuous quest to find his friend Mohammed's house so he can return his homework book, knowing that his schoolteacher will expel Mohammed if he does not do so. In this and many other Iranian films, the tyranny of adults over children fulfils an allegorical function, hinting at wider societal oppressions.

Kiarostami's later films turn increasingly self-reflexive. In these, the blend of documentary and fiction, a characteristic of all his work, is extremely complex. In the earlier works, he often appears as an interviewer; in the later films, he recedes from view, deploying a stand-in, representing a director or producer whose motives we question, filming a film-within-the-film. This self-reflexive trait has roots in Persian storytelling traditions but resonates internationally with European modernist forms (especially Godard and the French New Wave). Moreover, Kiarostami's brand of self-reflexivity is inflected by the conditions of Third World filmmaking: the films-within-the-films raise questions about the ethics of middle-class urban outsiders, like Kiarostami himself, who go to remote rural locations in order to film villagers and tribal folk. They highlight the potential for exploiting and exoticising their rural subjects, activating anxiety about replicating the Orientalist gaze.

In Kiarostami's work, this trend begins with *And Life Goes On*, the second part in a trilogy including *Where Is the Friend's Home?* and *Through the Olive Trees*. The trilogy is set in Rostamabad, a region in northern Iran devastated by an earthquake which killed almost 50,000 people in 1990. In *And Life Goes On*, a character representing the director of the first film returns to the region looking for the two boys who starred in his film. The director and his son Puya view the rural location and its people through car windows, emphasising their outsider status. Kiarostami takes the theme further in *The Wind Will Carry Us*, where film-producer Behzad visits a Kurdish village, Siah Dareh, and discovers that the old woman whose funeral rites he hoped to film has not yet died, jeopardising his plans. In both films, Kiarostami alludes to the thin line separating life and death and to life's arbitrary character. The earthquake, Puya philosophises, is like a mad dog that ravages people indiscriminately. The philosophical stance in both cases is focalised through characters alienated from the natural tragedy by their urban, middle-class existence. *The Wind Will Carry Us*, especially, encourages a critical attitude towards the protagonist, who is blatantly insensitive, selfish and irresponsible in his attempt to find the meaning of life and death through exploiting villagers; yet the film ultimately leaves its existential 'lessons' open to the viewer.

There is an 'ongoing dialectic' in Kiarostami's work where 'a film he makes reflects on and partially demystifies an earlier film he has made, a subsequent film demystifies that film, and so on'.[14] We can see this characteristic developing through the Rostamabad trilogy (see the discussion of *Through the Olive Trees*, below). Another important trait emerging in these films is use of the car as a kind of camera, especially in shots giving the car's point-of-view in place of the driver's point-of-view. Windscreen shots are a staple of *A Taste of Cherry*, where a middle-class man, Badiei, drives around Tehran's outskirts asking three men in turn to bury him after his suicide.

As a zone which is both public and private, the car enables Kiarostami to avoid censorship restrictions on the depiction of private space, which can result in unrealistic portrayals as we have seen with the compulsory wearing of *hejab*.[15] The treatment of suicide, an Islamic taboo, led to the temporary banning of *A Taste of Cherry*, but generally Kiarostami has been seen to abide by censorship regulations. He is also known to value the creative limitations they impose. This has entailed a near-absence of women in his work, for which he has been criticised. *Ten* displays a conscious attempt to rectify this. It is divided into ten episodes, all taking place inside a car and focusing on a female driver and her passengers. It demonstrates Kiarostami's awareness of feminist issues in Iran; for example, we hear the driver reveal her problems in getting a divorce. At another point, one passenger removes her headscarf to reveal that she has shaved all her hair off, a daring and illegal act for an Iranian woman.[16]

Many Iranian directors have been influenced by Kiarostami, including Majid Majidi (*Children of Heaven* [1997], *Colour of Paradise* [1999], *Baran*), Samira Makhmalbaf (*The Apple*) and Jafar Panahi (*The White Balloon* [1995], *The Mirror* [1997], *Crimson Gold* [2003]). Along with Kiarostami, these directors bore the brunt of attacks from critics alleging that their innocent child protagonists helped to give the Islamic regime an acceptable face in the aftermath of the hostage crisis and the Iran–Iraq war. A particular target was Panahi's debut feature *The White Balloon*, a story written by Kiarostami about a seven-year-old girl, Razieh, who loses her money in Tehran's streets on her way to buy a goldfish for New Year celebrations. *The White Balloon* won the Caméra d'Or at Cannes in 1995 and became the most lucrative foreign-language film in the USA and Europe the following year. In *Sight and Sound*, Simon Louvish slated the film for shielding the regime's harshness, horror and despair, calling it a 'sentimental piece of slush [which] has had wide distribution in the West at the expense of far better Iranian films'.[17]

However, the film's sombre ending belies this reading. Razieh retrieves her banknote, which disappeared down a grating, with the help of an Afghan balloon-seller. She departs without thanking him, buys the gold-fish and returns home. The film concludes with off-screen sounds of a clock ticking down to New Year and fireworks – and finally, a long-held freeze-frame of the Afghan refugee boy with his white balloon. Although both he and the white balloon have scarcely entered the film, this final, unexpected freeze-frame claims our attention and 'feeds back into and modifies the whole preceding "charming" narrative'.[18] The Afghan is left alone; he has no home to go to. A harsh absent reality is rendered present – namely Afghan refugees, Iran's most mistreated minority.

Whereas Kiarostami's films tend to move from concrete particulars to abstract universals, Panahi's work zooms in; yet, paradoxically, this is how he gives us the broader picture which, in his films, is primarily social rather than philosophical.[19] Although his films work allegorically as well, Panahi treats socio-political topics more overtly than Kiarostami. This is reflected in his interest in the immediacies of the inner city and its inhabitants and his focus on girl protagonists rather than boys in *The White Balloon* and *The Mirror*.

Panahi's approach in these two films is very subtle, eluding Iranian censors, but *The Circle* is more explicit and was banned. *The Circle* follows several Tehran women, including a jail-breaker, a prostitute and a woman seeking an abortion, passing the narrative 'baton' from one woman to another. The circle motif symbolises the regime's restrictions on both men and women (but of course especially on women). Panahi's subsequent film *Crimson Gold*, also banned, follows a schizophrenic pizza-vendor from south Tehran (the poorer part of the city) who enters the homes of Tehran's bourgeoisie. It is based on Kiarostami's script and echoes aspects of Kiarostami's earlier film *Close Up* (1990).

Film House of Makhmalbaf

In *Close Up*, a poor unemployed man, Ali Sabzian, pretends to be the film-director Mohsen Makhmalbaf and gains access to the home of a middle-class family who believe that he is location-hunting for his next film. *Close Up* is based on a real-life case – Kiarostami heard about it from the news-papers when the family took Sabzian to court for his imposture. In the film, actors play themselves, including the real Makhmalbaf who appears at the end to support Sabzian when he apologises to the family. This Kiarostami method – involving the fictional transformation of a documentary base – has stylistically impacted on Makhmalbaf's own films and those of his daughter Samira Makhmalbaf.

Ali Sabzian's great admiration for Makhmalbaf points to the broad mass appeal that Makhmalbaf's films enjoyed in Iran at the time. Makhmalbaf himself comes from a poor background; men like him formed the vanguard of the Islamic Revolution. A founder of an underground Islamic militia group at the age of fifteen, Makhmalbaf was put in a Pahlavi jail when he was seventeen for stabbing a policeman. He was released four and a half years later, just after the Revolution. It was at this point that he became interested in film; prior to this, he claims he had never watched films, perhaps because his grandmother told him that anyone who went to the cinema would burn in hell.[20]

Makhmalbaf's body of work is filled with abrupt changes in style, tone and ideology. His earliest films were dedicated to the revolutionary cause. However, from the mid- to late 1980s he made social-realist films that register his disillusionment with the revolutionary regime, which failed to tackle the condition of the deprived classes. In the 1990s, his ideological convictions continued to shatter, engendering more poetic and self-reflexive films concerned with the multiplicity of truth, freedom of speech and democracy. He has said that their ethos is similar to the saying by the thirteenth-century Persian poet Rumi: 'Truth is a mirror that falls from the hand of God and shatters into pieces. Everyone picks up a piece and believes that that piece contains the whole truth, even though the truth is left sown about in each fragment.'[21]

These later films are undoubtedly influenced by Kiarostami, but continue to address socio-political concerns more or less overtly. Makhmalbaf's use of self-reflexivity also differs from Kiarostami's insofar as it contains greater reference to his personal life – with Makhmalbaf frequently appearing in his own films as his own representative, contrasting with Kiarostami's increasing use of fictional stand-ins. Like Kiarostami's early films, Makhmalbaf's films often have a parable-like quality, but they are distinguished by their surrealist humour and their more ornate visual style. Makhmalbaf's 1990s movies mark his renunciation of revolutionary fervour. They also brought him into conflict with the regime's conservative factions, who often banned them, including *Time of Love* (1990) (for its morally relative view of adultery), *Gabbeh* (1996) (for its close-ups of the heroine) and *A Moment of Innocence*.

Makhmalbaf offers his own skit on censorship, past and present, in *Once Upon a Time, Cinema* (1992), which rolls back and forth in time. Characters from celebrated Iranian films sashay into the main story about a cinematographer at the sultan's court during the nineteenth-century Qajar Dynasty. In one scene, the sultan orders the cinematographer's scripts to be chopped up on the gallows. When the sultan falls in love with Golnar, an early film heroine, his jealous eighty-four wives cut off her plaits, which metamorphose into strips of celluloid. In another scene, the entire royal court falls asleep watching a film so heavily censored that all it contains is an old woman trying to thread a needle.

Makhmalbaf's first film to obtain wide international distribution was the nomadic pastoral *Gabbeh*, an Iranian–French (MK2) co-production. It has a magic-realist style and follows the Ghashgh'ai tribe who weave carpets known as *gabbeh*, also the name of the female protagonist. In the film, the figure in the carpet – a horseman spiriting away his lover – crystallises its themes of forbidden intertribal love and patriarchal control. It also makes analogies between rugmaking and filmmaking. The nomads extract dyes for their colourful carpets from herbs, flowers and fruit rinds. At school, children chant 'Life is colour', 'love is colour', 'man is colour', 'woman is colour' – subversive slogans in a regime which has effectively abolished colour in public life, regulating women's clothing to uniform black.

Makhmalbaf achieved big international success again with *Kandahar*, produced by Makhmalbaf Productions with French companies Bac Films and Studio Canal. *Kandahar* premièred at Cannes in 2001 and drew sell-out crowds in Europe and the USA in the immediate aftermath of September 11th. Its general release could not have been more timely: America was preparing to go to war; names of Afghan locations like Kandahar were on everyone's lips. It was even rumoured that President Bush wished to see it. In *Kandahar*, as in Makhmalbaf's other recent films, actors play roles that approximate their own lives. Nelofer Paizira, an Afghan expatriate and writer of the story on which the film is based, plays Nafas. She returns to Afghanistan to save a sister, who is threatening to commit suicide before a solar eclipse, symbolising the impending eclipse of Afghan women's lives. As Nafas travels towards Kandahar, a destination she never reaches, she witnesses multifarious ills plaguing Afghan society under the Taliban following decades of intertribal warfare and the Great Powers' imperial exploits. Bandits, fraudsters and scavengers seize advantage of the breakdown in law and order. Innocent lives are wrecked by landmines: in a typically surreal image, Makhmalbaf shows a horde of landmine-maimed amputees hopping on crutches towards a supply of artificial limbs parachuting down from a Red Cross helicopter. In other remarkable images, women clothed head to foot in brightly coloured *burkas* move in groups across the desert. 'The burka gives a beautiful form and it's very simple, but at the same time it's the worst dress for women in the world', Samira Makhmalbaf has remarked in the context of her own Afghanistan film, *At Five in the Afternoon*.[22] *Kandahar* and *At Five in the Afternoon* both acknowledge this paradox. *Kandahar* contains point-of-view shots through a *burka*, emphasising its physical restriction on its wearers.

In 1996, Makhmalbaf temporarily stopped filmmaking to teach. The MCIG rejected his initial proposal to enrol 100 students in a four-year course, so he set up the Makhmalbaf Film School in his own house with eight family members and friends as pupils, including his daughters Samira and Hana, his son Maysam and his wife Marzieh Meshkini.[23] The Film House of Makhmalbaf also formed a production arm, Makhmalbaf Productions. All films made during the four years of schooling were collaboratively produced by the students together with Makhmalbaf. Although some of their films involve foreign co-producers such as MK2, the Film House of Makhmalbaf is largely an artisanal, family mode of production – the like of which has rarely been witnessed.

This collaborative form of filmmaking has produced a stylistic consistency in their films – a Makhmalbaf 'house style'. Mohsen Makhmalbaf has contributed to his students' films in the form of storylines, scripts and editing, and his influence on them as 'teacher, mentor and aesthetic model' is undeniable.[24] However, *they* (especially Marzieh, Samira and Hana) have also influenced *him* – and this is evident in the more urgent attention to gendered injustices in Mohsen's post-1996 films, including *Kandahar*. The use of symbolic props with multiple associations is a defining aspect of the Makhmalbaf house style. Also striking is the use of space. Not only do doorways function as barriers to vision – an allegory of censorship restrictions found in many Iranian films – but the House of Makhmalbaf films often emphasise disconnected portions of space, another way of indicating the selectiveness of what we see, as in shots of disembodied women's hands handing out food or watering flowers in *A Moment of Innocence* and *The Apple*.[25]

Samira Makhmalbaf made her debut feature, *The Apple*, when she was seventeen years old. Her work since then includes *Blackboards*, which won the Jury Prize at Cannes 2000, and *At Five in the Afternoon*. Initially, there was much speculation as to whether this work was really Samira's or her father's, despite their significantly different outlooks. Ironically, a uniting theme in these films is a constraining father–daughter relationship: in *The Apple*, a father imprisons his daughters; in *Blackboards*, Halaleh's father marries her off, barely asking her consent; and Noqreh struggles with a father whose mindset still belongs to the Taliban in *At Five in the Afternoon*. Samira uses the motif of parental tyranny to comment on wider gender oppressions in Iran and elsewhere. According to critics, what distinguishes her filmmaking style is her 'strategic naivety' and the 'anthropological eye' that she casts over her subjects.[26] In *Blackboards*, she focuses on the situation of the Kurds, particularly boys earning their livelihood by smuggling contraband across the Iran–Iraq border. Itinerant teachers come searching for pupils, carrying their blackboards on their backs, looking like ungainly blackbirds, out of place in the barren mountainous landscape. The blackboards are symbolic props with multiple functions in the film, serving as a refuge from possible chemical attack (a reference to the Iraqi mustard-gas attack against Kurds in Halabcheh during the Iran–Iraq war), a private wall for a man and his wife, and a splint for a wound. The film uses off-screen sound to suggest menacing helicopter surveillance and border patrols.

Borders also form a key motif in *A Time for Drunken Horses*, directed by Bahman Ghobadi, himself a Kurd, who plays one of the teachers in *Blackboards*. So too in this film is smuggling the means by which child protagonists survive, taking inebriated mules across mine-infested snow-covered mountains into Iraq. Both films emphasise how the Kurds are always crossing borders imposed on them by others, showing them displaced and lost in nightmarish liminal zones where 'inexplicable military atrocity' hangs over them.[27]

Samira's first 'Afghanistan' film is a short, *God, Construction and Destruction*, which she contributed to *11' 09" 01* (2002), a collection of short films by eleven filmmakers including Youssef Chahine (Egypt), Danis Tanovic (Bosnia-Hercegovina), Ken Loach (UK), Amos Gitai (Israel) and Mira Nair (India). Her film manages to be both irreverent and serious, underlining the incomprehensibility and distance of the World Trade Center attacks to those who are in a very real sense affected by their repercussions – Afghan refugees in a camp on the Iran–Afghanistan border, who only know that American bombs are about to fall. A teacher asks a group of schoolchildren to name the world-shattering incident that has just occurred. The children haphazardly guess – 'A man fell into a well and died', claims one, but the teacher insists the event is bigger than that. 'Two people fell down a well and one broke his leg', another offers. One girl mentions a woman being stoned to death in Afghanistan, but that is not big enough either. Finally, the teacher tries to make her pupils grasp the enormity of the event by making them stand in silence under a tall chimney, the closest thing the children know to a skyscraper.

In *At Five in the Afternoon*, again recruiting non-professional actors on location, Samira allows Afghan people to articulate their own tragic experiences under the Taliban within her story's fictional parameters. The film begins with much optimism. Women and girls attend school for the first time in years and are told that they can do anything they want – become doctors, lawyers, teachers, even presidents. But twenty-year-old Noqreh, who aspires to become Afghanistan's first female president, faces several obstacles – starting at home with her father. On the streets, men turn their faces to the wall whenever they see unveiled women, signalling that the Taliban's legacy is far from over. When her father is out of sight, Noqreh slips on some white shoes (the film's main symbol) to practise her steps to freedom. In one scene, she asks a French soldier about democracy in his country. Through his answer – 'I am a soldier. I don't interfere in politics' – Samira underlines the irony of soldiers who don't participate in their own democracy 'providing' democracy for other countries.

In *Joy of Madness* (2003), a behind-the-scenes documentary of *At Five in the Afternoon* made by Hana Makhmalbaf at the age of fourteen, we witness the obstacles Samira faced in making her film. So many fear to take part; the same fear keeps women wearing their *burkas* despite the Taliban's departure. However, neither Hana's nor Samira's film particularises the predicament of women in Afghanistan; instead, they invite self-recognition and comparison. Despite differences between Iran and Afghanistan (fundamentalist Iran opposed the Taliban), the similarities are sufficient for the Iranian government to be nervous about films critical of Afghanistan and/or endorsing moves towards 'democracy' in neighbouring countries (this applies to Iraq as well as Afghanistan). This is why, Hana believes, her film is banned in Iran.[28] In Iran, women are also treated as third-class citizens, forced to cover themselves (although, unlike *burka*-clad Afghan women, they are permitted to show their faces and hands), and there is no right of public assembly. However, the relevance of the Makhmalbafs' critiques of gender oppression in Afghanistan goes even wider. Asked what she personally thought of the *burka*, Hana replied that in Afghanistan there is the *burka*, and in Iran the *chador* version of it, but elsewhere there is 'a subjective veil' – for how many female directors, let alone female presidents, are there?

Close Analysis

Through the Olive Trees (Abbas Kiarostami, 1994)

Through the Olive Trees is the last film in Kiarostami's Rostamabad trilogy, co-produced with CiBy (France), the Farabi Film Foundation (Iran) and Miramax Films (USA). It crystallises many aspects of his approach, especially his notion of the 'half-finished' film. In it, a film-director (a Kiarostami stand-in) casts non-professional actors to play a couple who marry after the earthquake. The first actor to play the husband stammers whenever he speaks to the female lead, Tahereh, so a runner at the film unit, Hossein, replaces him in the role. Hossein is in love with Tahereh in real life and wishes to marry her, although her family have rejected him because he is illiterate and has no house. The film director, acting like a matchmaker, gives Hossein a second chance, potentially enabling life to imitate art.

The film begins with the actor playing the director, Mohammed Ali Keshavaz, directly addressing the camera in front of a crowd of young, *chador*-clad village women auditioning for the film. One woman asks if the film will be shown in her village and whether there is any point in making the film if it is not shown: 'Your last film went out on Channel 2, which we can't get here.' At the outset, the film activates self-reflexive anxiety, not only about the construction of the film artefact but also about who its main audiences are – not rural inhabitants whose earthquake tragedy the crew has come to film, but 'cultural consumers back in Tehran and in cities around the world'.[29]

The film continually refers back to previous Trilogy films, as when Mrs Shiva gives a lift to the teacher from *Where Is the Friend's Home?*, although we hardly see him because Kiarostami keeps the camera on the road (one of his car point-of-view shots) throughout the journey. In *And Life Goes On*, the director figure, Farhad, stands at the porch of a newlywed's house and questions him about his motives for marrying so soon after the earthquake. This marginal episode from the previous film becomes the dramatic centrepiece of *Through the Olive Trees*, both its film-within-the-film and the film as a whole. Farhad appears in *Through the Olive Trees* to recreate his role, asking the newlywed how many relatives he lost in the earthquake. Playing the newlywed, Hossein claims that he lost twenty-five relatives because the scripted response, sixty-five, contradicts his real experience. In numerous retakes, Hossein repeatedly fluffs his line, displaying the complexities involved when art tries to imitate life. The repetition breaks the naturalistic illusion, together with clapperboards announcing the start of each take and bleeps calling for retakes.

The tension between the film and the film-within-the-film creates a subtly non-linear narrative, with events being referred to before they happen. This begins in the prologue, where the fictional director, talking direct to camera, relates that 'actors were hired on location'. Past tense shifts into present tense as we see the actors being hired before our eyes. In another instance, Hossein reports his visit to the cemetery where he sees Tahereh at her parents' grave (they perished in the earthquake), then the scene is dramatised (and filmed).

For Hossein, Tahereh's losses are a 'heaven-sent opportunity', levelling their class differences.[30] Neither of them now has a house. Hossein identifies with the newlywed in the film-within-the-film, whose motto is to seize the day before another earthquake comes. Tahereh, however, remains caught in her society's conventions, which prescribe 'how a married woman should behave or how an unmarried girl must conduct herself, but may not furnish guidelines on the comportment of people in Tahereh's rather complicated position'.[31] Within these limitations, she cannot convey her 'true' feelings to Hossein nor to the viewer, whose access to Tahereh's subjectivity is further restricted by censorship regulations; Kiarostami rarely gives us Tahereh's 'reaction shots'.

Through the Olive Trees is totally shaped by these regulations and is aware of the problems they impose. The first actor's stammering whenever he speaks to girls can be seen as symptomatic of taboos relating to cross-gender contact. Given censorship restrictions on private spaces, Kiarostami uses sets which are simultaneously public and private, as already mentioned. Here, a balcony and porch serve as the main set.[32] Most of the film-within-the-film is shot at ground-floor level, the conversation between the newlyweds taking place off camera, with Tahereh on the upstairs balcony. The camera is positioned perpendicular to the house, creating a deliberately 'flat' image.

Tahereh and other young women in the film avoid the camera's gaze and the gaze of male admirers. A peasant girl turns her face away from the director, who expresses an interest in her; on set, Tahereh resolutely looks away from Hossein. As noted above, point-of-view shots are rare in New Iranian Cinema; but there is a startling instance of one here in the cemetery, where the camera takes Tahereh's position and shows Hossein as the point of her glance. Later, Hossein reveals, 'Since [you gave me] that look, I've been following you . . .'.

Towards the end of the film, Hossein follows Tahereh again, with the director's encouragement. In a four-minute take, we see the two figures in wide long shot walking up a zigzag path (constructed for *Where Is the Friend's Home?*), through an olive grove and into a valley. Like the director, watching from the hill, we want to know whether Tahereh will turn around and give Hossein the sign of acceptance; but the exchange takes place outside our earshot and almost outside our vision. All we see is one distant white speck catching up with the other and then returning (whether in joy or despair) before the credits start to roll. This conclusion exemplifies the notion of the 'half-finished' film which gives viewers creative space for interpretation. Kiarostami states: 'The filmmaker has carried the film up to here, and now it is given up to the audience to think about it and watch these characters from very far away.'[33]

A Moment of Innocence (Mohsen Makhmalbaf, 1996)

When he was seventeen, Makhmalbaf, then an Islamic militant, tried to attack a policeman in order to steal his gun, rob a bank and blow up the Pahlavi regime. The policeman shot him, and Makhmalbaf ended up in jail. In *A Moment of Innocence*, his personal favourite film, he revisits this incident, trying to imagine the policeman's perspective as well as reflecting in hindsight on his own firebrand youth. He plays himself as a director of the film-within-the-film, which re-enacts the event. The Iranian title, *Nun Va Goldoon*, means 'The bread and the vase', but Makhmalbaf's French co-producer MK2 preferred *A Moment of Innocence*. The film won the Special Jury Award at the Locarno Film Festival in 1996.

Kiarostami's influence is evident in the film's minimalist style and formal organisation, with title cards and clapperboards opening and ending scenes. But, more significantly, in the blurring between reality and its staged remake, *A Moment of Innocence* embodies the multiplicity of truth through 'a quiet erosion of the dead certainties, that separates the real from the make-belief, and that is precisely the trade-mark of the best of the post-revolutionary Iranian cinema'.[34] These 'dead certainties' include the single-mindedness of terrorists who believe that there is no other course of action.

In the film, the former policeman (or rather, his fictional representative), knowing that the rascal who tried to kill him is now a famous film-director, visits his home to ask him for a part in a film and is greeted by Makhmalbaf's daughter (Hana, starring as herself). Having chosen their topic, Makhmalbaf and the ex-policeman separately audition and coach actors to play their younger selves. We follow the Ex-Policeman and his protégé first, and learn that when he was on his beat, a woman kept asking him for the time. He fell in love with her, convinced that she must love him also, although he never saw her again after the Makhmalbaf incident.

Cutting to Makhmalbaf's perspective, we discover that this woman was Makhmalbaf's cousin and accomplice, who flirted with the policeman just to distract him so that Makhmalbaf could stab him with his knife. Makhmalbaf and his cousin were in love with each other and determined to save the world by using violence. Makhmalbaf instructs his younger self to re-enact this version of the past; but, although the young actor is happy to embody the youthful ideal of robbing a royalist bank and using the money to plant flowers in Africa, he refuses to use violence, insisting that there must be some other way. On set, the Young Makhmalbaf sobs and discards the knife with which he is supposed to attack the policeman. When the Ex-Policeman discovers that the rendezvous he was expecting with the woman he loved is actually part of the assault plot, he becomes furious, realising that the love he cherished for twenty years is a delusion. Whereas before he had coached the Young Policeman to offer the woman a flower in a pot (or vase), he now instructs him to draw his gun. But, in the climactic concluding scene, when the assault is finally filmed, the Young Policeman does not draw his gun and impulsively offers the woman the flower, and the Young Makhmalbaf, in turn, presents the policeman with a flatbread, under which he had hitherto concealed his knife. This exchange, with the *chador*-clad woman caught in between, is arrested in the film's ending freeze-frame.

Into his fictional reimagining of events, Makhmalbaf adds these elements: (1) the policeman in love, (2) the revolutionaries in love who want to save the world by any means, including violence, and (3) the younger generation's refusal of violence and desire to save the world by other means, including love. Just as the Ex-Policeman finds his twenty-year-long delusion shattered, so are Makhmalbaf's former ideological convictions also called into question.

As the narrative progresses, more and more alternative realities are negotiated and put into contact with the past 'as it happened'. As in Rumi's broken mirror, all the narrative shards are connected to each other, even when they appear not to be, resulting in the surreal encounter between the Young Makhmalbaf and the daughter of Makhmalbaf's 'real' cousin – two characters who do not know each other yet behave as if they were already lovers, cousins and co-conspirators. The narrative has an overlapping structure, with two scenes which are shown twice, but each time from a different perspective. For example, just after the Ex-Policeman reveals his love during a rehearsal with his younger self, a woman asks the Young Policeman the time. 'It happened just like that!' exclaims the Ex-Policeman. But, when the scene is repeated, we have learnt that the woman is the Young Makhmalbaf's cousin. We realise that the two sequences have not taken place in chronological order, as we thought, but simultaneously. The repeated scene is imbued with a different point of view, as it is now no longer inserted within the strand dealing with the Ex-Policeman but in the strand dealing with Makhmalbaf. The repetition gives the words 'It happened just like that!' an ambiguity they did not have before.

What such scenes underline is that there is no absolute reality, but one that always changes, depending on the angle at which one views it (or, in terms of the second repeated scene, involving the lost flowerpot, 'sunlight never stays in the same place'). Now Makhmalbaf believes that the reason why people resort to violence is that 'Firstly [they say] we are absolutists, and the truth is with us. Secondly, in order to carry out this [they say that] no other way exists except violence.'[35] In his film, Makhmalbaf defies these and other dogmas of contemporary Iranian culture, which he sees as 'a culture that closes doors' – doors are shut by 'patriarchal power' and 'absolutist worldviews'.[36] Not coincidentally, several scenes take place in front of closed (or partially closed) doors, including some showing disembodied women's hands giving directions or handing out soup.

In the final freeze-frame, the veiled woman (representative of Iran's revolutionary Islamicisation) and the Young Policeman (emblem of the despised Pahlavi regime) are the astonished recipients of peace offerings. The image 'arrests' the moment where the past – Makhmalbaf's original terrorist act – is transfigured by the present – the young actors' spontaneous refusal of violence. But the 'moment of innocence' of the film's title could refer to numerous other meanings embedded in this image: Islamic militancy, revolutionary idealism, terrorism, law and order, adolescent romance, unrequited love, revenge and pacifism, and so on. This freeze-frame, which holds multiple competing ideologies within the same image, succinctly expresses Makhmalbaf's revised stance on his past: 'I no longer believe in absolutes and have accepted that I don't have all the right answers.'[37] The film was banned in Iran until 1997.

The Apple (Samira Makhmalbaf, 1998)

A co-production between Makhmalbaf Productions and MK2, *The Apple* is an astonishing work, the debut of a major new talent in world cinema. It is based on the true story of eleven-year-old twins Zahra and Massoumeh Naderi, whose elderly father and blind mother locked them up at home and never let them out. Their neighbours complained about the girls' treatment to the authorities – the twins could not speak properly and had not had a bath for years. Samira was inspired to make the film when she saw the twins at a welfare centre on television. She went there herself and asked the family members and Azizeh Mohamadi, the social worker involved in their case, to act as themselves.

Because she did not initially have a 35mm film camera, Samira used a video camera to record the twins at the welfare centre and inserted this footage near the beginning of the film. The video stock signals to us that events were captured in their immediacy, as they were happening. The rest of the film is shot using a 35mm camera, which Samira obtained three days after the television broadcast. The shooting took place over eleven days. It reconstructs the twins' return to their house, where the father promptly locks them up again, and their re-release into the outside world, largely filming in continuity (but also at times interfering with the temporality for symbolic resonance). The fictional reconstruction of events that took place only a few days previously gives *The Apple* its extraordinary quality, although it has an important precedent in Kiarostami's *Close Up*, which was also inspired by a news story and was filmed four days after actual events. Mohsen Makhmalbaf, who has *The Apple*'s script credit, has revealed that 'Most of the film was improvised and its dialogue spoken verbally prior to being written down.'[38] Mohsen himself stayed away from filming, getting ideas for the script on the basis of what Samira told him was happening.

The film opens with an image of a girl's outstretched hand watering a withered flower through the bars of a door. This image is lifted from *Advice to Fathers*, from which the twins' father, Ghorban, reads: 'A girl is like a flower. If the sun shines on her she will fade. A man's gaze is like the sun and a girl is like a flower.' The story of a father locking up his daughters is, for Samira and Mohsen Makhmalbaf, 'the story of our nation'.[39] However, Samira seeks to understand rather than condemn in *The Apple*. She chooses to focus not on the twins' incarceration but on their liberation – and therefore, for critics such as Hamid Dabashi, she embodies the hopes for a more open society common to Iran's post-revolutionary youth generation who voted for Mohammed Khatami.

The two key symbolic props which Samira uses in her fictional reconstruction of events are the apple and the mirror. These 'directly materialize the twins' process of coming to terms with the outside world'.[40] The mirror can be discussed in terms of the French psychoanalyst Jacques Lacan's theory of the Mirror Stage. According to Lacan, an infant identifies with its image in the mirror – or with another infant – between the ages of six and eighteen months, that is, at a time when it is speechless and lacking bodily co-ordination.[41] The mirror stage marks the beginnings of the infant's self-awareness and its recognition that it inhabits a world with others, forming a prelude to its acquisition of language and other social conventions. Upon their release from their house, the twins can barely walk or talk; they had no mirror except each other. When they examine themselves in the mirror presented to them by the social worker, we witness them undergoing a delayed Mirror Stage, the mirror in part signifying their transition into the world of others and their growing self-awareness.

The film emphasises these processes of socialisation. When the social worker releases the twins from the house, they have no grasp of the conventions of social behaviour. Lacking the concept of money and commerce, they help themselves to ice-cream bars and apples without paying. Playing hopscotch with two girls whom they meet at a park, Massoumeh hits one of her new friends with an apple, apologises, then hits her again, and finally gives her the apple. But it is through these games that the twins learn how to orientate themselves through established axes – literally by mounting a climbing frame (mastery of space) and admiring a girl's watch (mastery of time).

The apple configures the girls' curiosity about the world. As in the story of Adam and Eve, common to Judaeo-Islamic-Christian cultural inheritance, the apple signifies desire, knowledge and temptation – hence the boy dangling an apple on a stick. The twins endlessly try to grab the apple from him. The boy leads the twins to the market, and takes them back to their father to get money to buy goods, ushering a fall from innocence into the perils of consumerism; the twins demand apples, ice-creams, watches. But, on the other hand, this brings new freedoms and opportunities. Previously, only their father went to the market and determined what goods the girls should have; now the girls can go and choose their own goods.

When the social worker imprisons Ghorban in the house, leaving him with a saw to hack his own way out, it is ostensibly to give him a taste of his own medicine. But then she gives the key to the twins, saying that he will be released if they can open the door. Massoumeh eventually does work out how to use the key, and her knowledge is his release. *The Apple* can be read as a feminist allegory about women seizing opportunities, disguising its wider socio-political implications through the figure of childhood for the censors' benefit.

In the concluding scene, the twins' blind mother wanders out of the house. Throughout the film, she has been as housebound as the twins, and moreover covered from head to toe by her *chador*. She is perhaps the film's most imprisoned figure, having internalised her society's patriarchal beliefs and meted out her own oppression on her daughters. On her way out into the street, she passes a mirror, affixed to the door. She cannot see her reflection; but, once in the street outside, she reaches for the dangling apple, holding it firmly in her grasp in the film's final freeze-frame.

Images such as these are rich with allegorical associations yet also resist fixed meanings. Dabashi writes, '*The Apple* . . . becomes a devastating condemnation of the mind-numbing oppression of women, not just in Iran, but anywhere.' It is, he rightly puts it, 'an allegory of global relevance'.[42]

Notes

1. See Dabashi, *Close Up*, p. 277; also Farahmand, 'Perspectives on Recent (International Acclaim for) Iranian Cinema', pp. 86–108.
2. Ehteshami, *After Khomeini*, p. 215.
3. Ibid., p. 203.
4. Ibid., p. 209.
5. Payami, 'Necessary Illusions', p. 29.

6. Naficy, 'Under the Islamic Republic', p. 230.
7. Ibid., p. 231.
8. Naficy, 'Iranian Cinema', p. 155.
9. Naficy, 'Under the Islamic Republic', p. 231.
10. Naficy, 'Veiled Vision', pp. 132–3.
11. Naficy, 'Under the Islamic Republic', p. 234.
12. Sciolini, *Persian Mirrors*, p. 269.
13. See Laura Mulvey, 'Kiarostami's Uncertainty Principle', pp. 24–7.
14. Bransford, 'Days in the Country'.
15. Ibid.
16. Ibid.
17. Louvish, 'Letters', p. 64. For the original review, see Louvish, 'The White Balloon'.
18. Chaudhuri and Finn, 'Open Image', p. 56.
19. Rapfogel, 'Don't Look at the Camera'.
20. Ridgeon, *Makhmalbaf's Broken Mirror*, p. 9.
21. Ibid., p. 12.
22. Macnab, 'A Woman's Place', p. 10.
23. Fatemah Meshkini, Mohsen Makhmalbaf's first wife and mother of Samira, Maysam and Hana, died in 1992. Marzieh Meshkini is her sister.
24. Danks, 'The House that Mohsen Built'.
25. Chaudhuri and Finn, 'Open Image', p. 48.
26. Hebron, 'At Five in the Afternoon', p. 19; Danks, 'The House that Mohsen Built'.
27. Chaudhuri and Finn, 'Open Image', p. 48.
28. Hana Makhmalbaf, Q&A following her film's screening at the London Film Festival, 27 October 2003.
29. Bransford, 'Days in the Country'.
30. Raghavendra, 'An Unmarried Woman', p. 80.
31. Ibid., p. 81.
32. Bransford, 'Days in the Country'.
33. Hamid, 'Near and Far', p. 23.
34. Dabashi, 'Mohsen Makhmalbaf's *A Moment of Innocence*', p. 123.
35. Ridgeon, *Makhmalbaf's Broken Mirror*, p.16.
36. Ibid., p. 12.
37. Ibid., p.17.
38. Pusan, *Salaam Cinema*, p. 44.
39. Dabashi, *Close Up*, p. 269.
40. Chaudhuri and Finn, 'Open Image', p. 53.
41. Lacan, *Écrits*, pp. 1–2.
42. Dabashi, *Close Up*, p. 271.

CHAPTER 5

East Asian Cinema

This chapter will explore recent trends in Chinese Mainland, Taiwanese, Japanese, South Korean and Thai cinema, leaving a fuller discussion of Hong Kong cinema for Chapter 6. It will focus on the genres of family saga/melodrama, urban youth film, supernatural horror, apocalyptic fantasy/science fiction and evolving blockbuster forms, arguing that these constitute exemplary responses to the region's historical particularities and the conditions of cinema under globalisation.

These East Asian territories were mostly late to modernise, resulting in converging patterns of rapid and drastic societal change. Their overlapping histories, which films negotiate from various 'national' viewpoints, also encompass the impact of Japanese colonisation before and during the Second World War, the Communist Party's victory in China in 1949, and American economic and military presence in the region.

The territories are highly distinctive and different from each other in numerous respects. However, they share many centuries-old cultural traditions: Confucian ethics, based on filial obligations and loyalty between rulers and their subjects, and between family members and friends; Buddhism; supernatural beliefs; classical theatre, including Peking Opera in China and Japanese Kabuki theatre, both involving male actors playing female roles; and Chinese classical painting, characterised by the subordination of figures to landscape and the absence of the illusion of depth. These do not apply uniformly across the region; for example, Buddhism is more central to Thailand than to other territories.

In East Asia, the influence of American consumerism and Western modernisation has been mediated by Japanese variations on the American model. Japan modernised well before other Asian territories: an agrarian, feudal nation until the mid-nineteenth century, it rose to become an industrial market economy and, despite sustaining large-scale destruction during the Second World War, it almost overtook the West in its massive post-war economic expansion – an attractive model for the East Asian 'Tiger' economies, including Taiwan, South Korea and Hong Kong. Ironically, not long after it became known as the second richest country in the world, Japan entered economic decline, following a devastating stock-market collapse in

1989. The ensuing economic malaise produced moral uncertainty for the Japanese about their emphasis on materialism and economic success. The financial crisis that hit the Tiger economies in 1997 formed a similarly defining moment for the rest of the region.

The commonalities produced by this pan-East Asian economy are frequently articulated in the region's popular culture, especially film, TV, music and comic-books (known in Japan and across East Asia as *manga*). As David Desser has argued, the transnational distribution of regional popular culture through means such as the Internet, digital media and communications (including video games, cellphones and VCDs) and the growing importance of regional film festivals (Tokyo, Hong Kong, Pusan, Bangkok) have facilitated an unprecedented cross-fertilisation and convergence of styles and themes in contemporary East Asian films.[1] For Desser, one major phenomenon resulting from this is the 'explosion' of films about people who are marginalised or left morally directionless by the economic boom and bust. Such films emphasise disaffected youth, generational conflict, unstable families, rebellion, crime, violence and sexuality and revolve around locations such as video arcades, street corners, nightclubs and small restaurants.[2] They resonate with international neo-noir paradigms as well as regional cinematic antecedents such as the 1950s Japanese 'suntribe' films dealing with 'middle-class youth running amok in newly economically resurgent Japan'.[3]

The *manga* aesthetic forms one stylistic pole of contemporary East Asian cinema. This aesthetic alternates hyper-kinetic exaggerated violence with moments of contemplative stasis that freeze the action in the manner of a comic-book panel. The *manga* style has free-flowing, dynamic, conflictual rhythms and compositions, yet it is also economically compressed. Like traditional Japanese and Chinese art – for example, scrolls, prints and calligraphy – it purposefully repudiates realism (the word *manga* literally means 'caricature'). In Japan, there are strong aesthetic affinities between *manga*, video games and animated films (the latter known as *anime*). Although video games were invented in America, it is the Japanese who have 'perfected' the form; *manga*, *anime* and video games have evolved together.[4] Recently, live-action cinema has become a fourth element in this mix. Visually laconic, *manga* springs from Japan's minimalist and formalist visual traditions, which have taken different forms in the past. The formalist tradition is exemplified by the work of Japanese modernist director Yasujiro Ozu (*Tokyo Story* [1953]), known for his 'empty shots' of objects and settings, and low-angle 'tatami' shots, named after the floor mats on which the Japanese sit and eat.

There has been a resurgence of modernist aesthetics across the region –

including Ozu-like formalism in works by Taiwanese director Hou Hsiao-Hsien and (via Hou's influence) Japanese filmmaker Hirokazu Koreeda. Other modernist influences include Akira Kurosawa's 'Samurai' films portraying warriors-for-hire bound by codes of honour and loyalty to their master. Kurosawa's *Rashomon* (1950), which retells the same episode from different perspectives to show how all narratives or 'truths' are necessarily subjective, is a major inspiration for non-linear narratives worldwide and circular storytelling techniques (also inherited from oral traditions) in some contemporary East Asian films.

In addition, melodrama – a genre typically centring on the family, marriage and motherhood – has been adapted to express the region's cultural particularities and to deal with issues of memory and history. While Hollywood melodrama dwells on individual will and desire in conflict with the family, following a moral value system based on individual agency, personal choice and self-expression (values historically entwined with either Protestantism or capitalism), Asian melodramas traditionally focus on 'the family as a unity'.[5] As Chris Berry has argued in the context of Chinese cinema, a Confucian emphasis on behaviour – namely, filial obligation – replaces the Western emphasis on morality and self-expression.[6] (There are similarities with South Asian films discussed in Chapters 7 and 8, although their ethical basis is different.) The tension between changes wrought by rapid societal modernisation and traditional Confucian values and expectations is a major theme in contemporary East Asian family melodramas. One urgent site at which this tension has emerged is the issue of gay and lesbian sexuality – namely, the problems of being gay in a family-centred society where parents make demands on their children for grandchildren to continue the patrilineal family line.

In the rest of this chapter, I have selected certain tendencies in each of the territories: melodrama and urban youth films by the Chinese Fifth and Sixth Generation filmmakers; Taiwanese family sagas; apocalyptic fantasy/science fiction and horror in Japanese live action and animation; Korean art films and blockbusters; and Thai 'nostalgia' films.

Chinese Fifth Generation

The so-called 'Fifth Generation' Chinese directors were the first to graduate from the Beijing Film Academy since it reopened in 1978 after the Chinese Cultural Revolution (1966–76), during which film production halted. The defining event for the Fifth Generation, the Cultural Revolution was led by Communist Party Chairman Mao Zedong and was an attempt to bring all aspects of Chinese life under official Communist

Party ideology. It began idealistically but was ultimately disastrous. The principal leader in post-Mao China was Deng Xiaoping, whose catch-phrase was 'to get rich is glorious'. Since 1979, he and his successors have allowed foreign investment and domestic private enterprise to co-exist alongside the state-run sector, resulting in rapid economic modernisation without much political liberalisation.

Upon leaving film school, the Fifth Generation directors were assigned to China's regional studios. New levels of state support and the help of Wu Tianming, head of Xi'an studio, were major factors behind their ascendance. Among the best-known Fifth Generation directors are Chen Kaige, Tian Zhuangzhuang and Zhang Yimou. Others include Huang Jianxin, Sun Zhou, Zhang Zeming, Zhou Xiaowen and female directors Hu Mei, Li Shaohong, Ning Ying and Peng Xiaolian. They were the first Chinese filmmakers exposed to the influence of European modernist cinema. Their own films combine a modernist film aesthetic – with strong formalist tendencies, including long takes – with a colour palette and shot composition reminiscent of both classical and folk Chinese painting. This visually spectacular aesthetic was part of their challenge to the hitherto dominant socialist-realist style, which was intended to reflect socialist dogma in an unembellished manner.

Some Fifth Generation directors were active in the Cultural Revolution as 'Red Guards', revolutionary emissaries sent to rural outposts. Their films critically reflect on this era, often delving into the pre-socialist, feudal past to critique the recent socialist past or post-socialist present. Many films have rural settings, featuring a stubborn female protagonist on a quest or migrating to the city (*The Story of Qiu Ju* [1992], *Ermo* [1994], *Not One Less* [1999], *The Road Home* [1999]). Historical epics such as *To Live* (1994), *Blue Kite* (1993) or *Farewell My Concubine* (1993) use melodrama to juxtapose moments of national and familial crisis, while melodramas centring on female protagonists such as *Ju Dou* (1990), *Raise the Red Lantern* (1991) and *Ermo* present the woman's suffering as a symbol for the nation's suffering.

The reform of the socialist state-owned economy was slow to impact on film, as the authorities viewed cinema as a form of pedagogy rather than commerce. A fixed budget was allocated to each film, with studios receiving fixed returns.[7] In the early 1990s, however, the state allowed private investment and let film studios manage their own distribution; commercial success then began to matter. Yet, filmmakers still had to obtain permits to make films and had to submit their films for censorship to the Film Bureau, just as under the old system – risking bans if films were not approved. The film authorities imposed tougher censorship constraints in the aftermath of the June 1989 Tiananmen Square massacre, when the army killed hundreds of students and workers demonstrating for democratic reforms. Although most Fifth Generation films were made with permits, many of them were temporarily banned.

As a condition of China's entry into the World Trade Organisation, the annual import quota on foreign films was raised from ten to twenty films. The increasing success of Hollywood imports has been a setback for the local industry, compounding the drastically falling cinema attendances occasioned by VCD piracy, cable and satellite, increased leisure options, the breakdown of state distribution and haphazard production schedules due to censorship bureaucracy.

Increasingly, Fifth Generation filmmakers have relied on foreign investment. While some have hailed them for creating a truly 'transnational' cinema, shaped and determined by myriad global socio-cultural and economic forces, others believe that the need to make films commercially acceptable to foreign financiers and audiences has made it harder to be stylistically and thematically adventurous – a line of attack particularly aimed at Zhang Yimou's films. With their sensuous, colour-saturated *mise en scène*, victimised heroines played by Gong Li (who became the most famous Chinese actress worldwide as a result of these performances and her off-screen love affair with Zhang) and allegedly 'invented' feudal rituals (such as the lighting of lanterns in *Raise the Red Lantern*), Zhang's films are said to pander to Orientalist tastes. Contesting this kind of critical reception, Rey Chow proposes that they might be better understood in terms of a self-reflexive or 'autoethnographic' gaze.[8] Ethnography is a sociological methodology, involving the mapping of a regional group's social practices and customs, traditionally undertaken by colonial or 'Western' outsiders. Chow suggests that filmmakers like Zhang Yimou have undertaken the role of 'autoethnographers', allowing the Chinese to gaze at themselves at the moment of their international emergence.

Zhang's filmmaking strategies have constantly shifted according to changing filmmaking pressures in globalising China. Since *The Story of Qiu Ju*, which made him the 'toast' of the Beijing authorities with his favourable portrait of officials and led to the lifting of bans on his other films, Zhang has been seeking to avoid bans in order to enter the now openly commercial arena of film-going in China.[9] In *The Road Home*, the debut for Gong Li's successor Zhang Ziyi – shortly afterwards to be catapulted to international stardom with *Crouching Tiger, Hidden Dragon* (2000) (see Chapter 6) – Zhang provides a self-reflexive comment on relations between American and Chinese films in the global market, carefully framing posters of *Titanic*, China's most popular film import, hanging on two facing walls in a North China village.

With his next film, *Hero* (2002), Zhang outperformed *Titanic* at the Chinese box office and in August 2004 reached number one in the USA. A martial-arts epic in *Crouching Tiger*'s mould and starring Hong Kong actors Jet Li, Tony Leung and Maggie Cheung alongside Zhang Ziyi, *Hero* is the most expensive Chinese film to date and heralds a new breed of film – the Chinese blockbuster – and yet another new direction for its director. In *Rashomon*-like fashion, it retells the story of four assassins' failed attempts on the life of the King of Qin from different perspectives – finally, from the king's own perspective. In breathtaking fight scenes, combatants dressed in lushly coloured, flowing robes fly through the air like calligraphic flourishes. Their swords trail in lakes like ink-brushes, extending an analogy between calligraphy and swordplay. Like Zhang's former films, *Hero* has come under attack from critics arguing that the film's prettified landscapes and martial-arts choreography serve up an eminently exportable Orientalist fantasy, while its narrative gives implicit ideological endorsement to China's ambitions to unify regional territories, as the historical King Qin did in 221 BC, when China was divided into different kingdoms – a matter that alarms audiences in post-handover Hong Kong and Taiwan.[10] Chosen as China's 2002 Oscar entry, there is no doubt that the film pleased Chinese authorities; yet, from another view, the film might be seen as Zhang's ambivalent response both to the demands of censorship and to the global challenge of Hollywood, an allegory not only of how all narration is necessarily subjective, but also of how all narratives are shaped by contingencies of power.

Chinese Sixth Generation and Beyond

In contrast to the Fifth Generation, the directors who graduated from film schools as part of the Sixth Generation – Zhang Yuan, Wang Xiaoshuai, Emily Tang, Li Yu, Jia Zhangke and others – tend to favour urban, contemporary stories, focusing on ordinary characters (usually alienated, disaffected youths), using a realist 'stream of life' style rather than melodrama, often giving the feeling that characters are 'trapped in an intense present'.[11] These directors make underground films on low budgets, outside the official studio system. As a result, their films are considered 'illegal', and few have been publicly screened in China to date. Like Fifth Generation directors, they seek private funding, but they depend even more on networking and winning prizes at international festivals to obtain distribution and secure funding for subsequent films. Even though some of them handle topics that conflict with official agendas, for example, gay cottaging in *East Palace, West Palace* (1996) and lesbian sexuality in *Fish and Elephant* (2001), they are not 'dissident' filmmakers as such. Rather, Jenny Lau suggests, what most confounds the Chinese Film Bureau is the Sixth Generation's 'disengagement from the official political discourse'.[12] Too young to experience the idealism and disillusion of the Cultural Revolution, these directors grew up during the years when China was opened up to the West and gradually transformed into a semi-market economy, so their indifference to socialist discourse is not surprising. Characters in Sixth Generation films often display a split or schizophrenic subjectivity, apathetically registering the shocks of historic reversals demanded by the 'architects of one new China after another' – before, Maoist revolution, now modernisation, the WTO and globalisation, but then what?[13]

Jia Zhangke's *Unknown Pleasures* (2002) is an exemplary treatment of youth in globalising China. Unlike his previous film *Platform* (2000), which was an unauthorised production, *Unknown Pleasures* was chosen as China's official 2003 Oscar entry – a sign of the Chinese authorities' changing attitudes to independent filmmakers. In *Unknown Pleasures*, TV news from distant places – including the mass suicide of members of the religious sect Falun Gong (outlawed in secular China) and Beijing's triumphant bid for the 2008 Olympics, promising to mark China's arrival as a world economic power – permeates the protagonists' homes, while brand new highways connect all places. Despite this, the overwhelming sense is of directionlessness, underlined by the recurring motif of the highway. In Zhangke's earlier film, the metaphor of the platform describes the characters' perpetual state of waiting for promised miracles that never happen. By contrast, characters in *Unknown Pleasures* seem to have everything they want, but they don't know what to do with it. Boredom defines their lives, but they express defiant attitudes in their movements, dancing and dress, saving them from utter nihilism. As in other Sixth Generation films, music and dance – rock, techno and 'modern Chinese' – play an important role. The Chinese rock star Cui Jian, who appears in Zhang Yuan's *Beijing Bastards* (1993), is virtually the movement's mascot.

Split identity is the focus of Lou Ye's Shanghai-set *Suzhou River* (2000). With its doubling of two women, Moudan and Meimi, who blend into one in the protagonist Mardar's unstable mind, the film recalls Madeleine and Judy in Alfred Hitchcock's *Vertigo* (1958): one threatens to commit suicide and come back to haunt Mardar as a mermaid, while the other performs as a mermaid in a nightclub. With Moudan as the socialist past and Meimi as the capitalist present, *Suzhou River* depicts the schizophrenia of a

society in uneasy transition.[14] Its pleasurably chic style and emotional tone
have set a precedent for the current crop of commercial films produced
through official channels by a younger generation of Chinese directors and
some former Sixth Generation directors.[15] These films shun the Sixth
Generation's realist aesthetic, adding elements of the marvellous, and
mixing references to high and low culture, American popular culture and
European art cinema, signalling the full-blown arrival of postmodern
culture in China hand-in-hand with its cities' consumer lifestyles boom.
These films display further detachment still from the Fifth Generation's
political critique, reflecting perhaps, Chris Berry suggests, young Chinese
people's rejection of what they view as 'the excessive politicisation of life
in China in the past' and the government's refusal to countenance 'any
direct and honest engagement with social issues' through its censorship of
the media.[16]

Taiwanese New Wave

The Chinese Nationalist Party, the Kuomintang (KMT), fled to Taiwan
after the Communist Party's victory in China and established a dictatorship there. With help from American and multinational investors, the
KMT oversaw Taiwan's rapid passage to post-industrial society. Until
martial law was lifted in 1987, prompting some democratic reforms, film
production was strictly controlled by the government. Nonetheless, alongside officially promoted films, a commercial Taiwanese cinema flourished,
producing films on Hong Kong models, and it was common for Hong
Kong films to be shot in Taiwan (see Chapter 6). The Taiwanese New
Wave directors emerged in the early 1980s. Hou Hsiao-Hsien's *City of
Sadness* (1989) won the Golden Lion trophy at Venice in 1990 and was the
first film to deal with the controversial 1947 'February 28 Incident', when
the Kuomintang army brutally suppressed supporters of the Taiwanese
Independence movement. The urgent concern with history and issues of
historical representation in this film, and subsequent films dealing with the
fifty-year Japanese occupation (Hou's *Puppetmaster* [1993]) and the
KMT's anti-communist 'White Terror' purge in the 1950s (Edward Yang's
A Brighter Summer Day [1991]), springs from the need for a collective
history to be addressed. Until the lifting of martial law, these topics had
been suppressed. The other major tendency in New Taiwanese Cinema,
especially films by Edward Yang and Tsai Ming-Liang, studies the effects
of Taiwan's swift modernisation, urban alienation and dependency as 'a
post-Third World country' whose geo-political status remains 'a structu-
ral satellite of Japan or the US'.[17]

Taiwanese New Wave films have generally been unpopular at home while celebrated abroad. Some people have, unjustifiably, blamed them for the drop in local production during the 1990s. The shortfall can be explained by other factors: as with Mainland China, Taiwan's entry into the World Trade Organisation relaxed import quotas, increasing competition from Hollywood and Hong Kong cinema; consequently, Taiwanese investors preferred to fund Hong Kong films, which were more certain to be regional successes, as well as mainland films targeted at international art-house audiences (*Raise the Red Lantern*, *To Live*, *Farewell My Concubine*). Lack of support for local film production has led New Taiwanese Cinema directors to seek French and Japanese investment.

New Taiwanese Cinema is formally very intriguing, and this seems to be behind its enthusiastic international reception. Hou's cinema is characterised by detached cinematography, long takes, elliptical editing, elaborate *mises en scène* and oblique narration. According to Yeh Yueh-Yu, Hou's films have a certain Orientalist allure to foreign cineastes, offering as they do 'a precious option outside the norms of Western cinema'.[18] I would argue, however, that the pleasures which they offer lie in their innovative interpretation of modernist film aesthetics. Hou, like the Chinese Fifth Generation, deals with history through the perspective of the family, yet his use of family saga is non-melodramatic and his emphasis is on quotidian lives that have been brushed by historical events – all with the purpose of contesting the KMT's version of history. In *City of Sadness*, which traces the period 1945–9, there are direct citations from official history – such as KMT radio broadcasts – but these are muffled into the background, thus diminishing their power to influence our interpretations. In *The Puppetmaster*, Hou shows goodwill between the Taiwanese and their Japanese colonisers, which the KMT would never countenance.

Edward Yang's films explore the social and psychic consequences of modernisation on ordinary Taiwanese. His film *Yi Yi: A One and A Two* (2000), which won Best Director Award at Cannes, is set in Taipei and Tokyo. It portrays an extended family and their neighbours, friends and business partners in a 'world of jet travel, bullet trains and instant electronic transfer of money, image and information'.[19] *Yi Yi* displays Yang's characteristic visual style – long takes and wide shots depicting characters in their socio-spatial context. For example, when NJ's ex-girlfriend weeps alone in her Tokyo hotel room, the scene is entirely shot in one take, in reflection, looking out of the window into a densely built-up metropolitan night sky. Throughout the film, glass reflections convey the permeability of space – space without borders appropriate to the age of transnational capitalism.[20] The characters' identities, relationships and affective states fuse with the cartography of global cities, teeming with anonymous trans-national spaces, ambivalent signifiers of aspiration and alienation.

The Taiwanese lesbian and gay movement is one of the many popular movements emerging after the lifting of martial law.[21] The films of Taiwanese Second Wave director Tsai Ming Liang add a gay/camp poli-tics to their portraits of alienated city-dwellers. *Vive l'amour* (1994), a film popular with Taiwanese lesbian and gay audiences, takes place against a contemporary Taiwan which is 'bulldozing its various pasts – social, archi-tectural, spiritual'.[22] In an empty apartment, estate agent May engages in wordless sex with travelling salesman Ah-jung. A gay man, Hsiao-kang, who works in the funeral-urn business, gains a key to the apartment and secretly cohabits with the couple. This affords opportunities for subtle visual comedy, with characters nearly missing or colliding together. Fran Martin has interpreted Hsiao-kang's ghost-like presence in the flat as alluding to the trope of the gay/lesbian as 'a ghostly counterpart to repro-ductive heterosexuality' in dominant Taiwanese discourse; homosexuality is held to be 'unreal' because it does not produce children.[23] Hsiao-kang renounces his original suicide plan and playfully transforms the flat, turning cartwheels while wearing May's suspenders, pouring washing powder into the Jacuzzi to wash his clothes, and falling in love with Ah-jung. Ironically, in terms of dominant discourse, it is the gay man who is the transformative agent in a world where traditional social bonds are rapidly eroding.

Japanese Live Action and *Anime*

The base for Japan's prolific production until the 1970s was its studio system, run along similar lines (oligopoly and vertical integration) to the Hollywood studio system.[24] The Japanese majors include Toho, Shochiku, Nikkatsu, Toei, Daiei and Shin Toho.[25] Unlike Hollywood, where produc-ers invariably reign supreme, some Japanese studios gave directors and screenwriters more control. This created the conditions for the emergence of Japan's New Wave in the 1960s, including directors such as Nagisa Oshima and Shohei Imamura, who are still making films today. The studio system began to decline in the 1970s due to competition from Hollywood. The studios' attempts to win back audiences included the production of sex films, which come in two forms – 'Pink Eiga' and 'Roman Porno'.[26] Many contemporary Japanese directors, including Kiyoshi Kurosawa, were apprenticed in this medium, which gives them total creative freedom as long as they insert at least six sex scenes per film and stick to allocated running time and budget. Live-action features face competition from two fronts – from *anime* and Hollywood. *Anime* are a mass-media phenomenon in Japan, produced on a huge commercial scale within the studio system – with essential jobs like colouring assigned to low-paid workers in South Korea, Taiwan, Hong Kong and Thailand – and consumed in vast quantities by domestic and regional audiences. *Astro Boy* (1963) was the first influential *anime* export to the West, but it was the breakthrough *Akira* (1988) which announced *anime* as a huge cult phenomenon internationally.

Anime are sophisticated and complex, comprising an astonishing range of styles, genres and themes. Even *anime* intended for children contain mature themes rarely found in Western animation. *Anime* are produced not only as theatrical features but also as TV serials, straight-to-video (Original Video Animations, OVAs, or Original Animated Videos, OAVs) and multimedia spin-offs. These have all affected its narrative structures; the OVA medium in particular has enabled creators to experiment with fluid, open-ended episodic structures, benefiting theatrical features with their innovations. Thus, *anime* can have narrative strands that are only loosely connected, lacking the causality of Western storytelling. Narrative structures may be more circular than linear, with the same situations being negotiated, and characters playing similar roles, over and over again. Characters' goals are complex: 'villains' are not wholly evil; facile romantic conclusions are forestalled; closure is open-ended. Many *anime* films use mobile framings, sudden focal changes, varied and unusual 'camera' angles and distances, whereas Western animation usually deploys a uniform, middle distance.

This does not mean that *anime* has not borrowed Western influences, although these are never assimilated 'straight' – the process of assimilation transforms them. Stylistic influences include glam rock, with characters sporting hair of many colours for graphic variety and characterisation, and characters with 'Western' features – round, large eyes (often glistening with tears) indicating sensitive or sympathetic characters. The latter also derive from Japanese theatre traditions – the all-male Kabuki theatre (with female impersonators), and the all-female Takarazuka Revue (with male impersonators), where actors dress in Western clothes and perform Western stories.

Anime emerged as a distinctly post-war popular culture, expressing the concerns of post-war youth generations. Its imagery is often apocalyptic. The atom bomb is a recurring reference – sometimes explicitly, as in the *Hibakusha* nuclear-war survivor genre encompassing live action as well as *anime*. The live-action *Godzilla* (1954), where a prehistoric beast is awakened by radiation from nuclear tests and devastates Tokyo, could be considered the prototypical *Hibakusha* film. Apart from being the only nation to have suffered atomic attack, the Japanese are said to live under a number of other collective stresses, including the continual threat of earthquake, typhoon and fire on a volcanic island ridden with climatic extremes.[27] During the economic downturn of the 1990s, sporadic acts of violence, such as the cult Aum Shinrikyo's gas attack on a Tokyo subway, and the grisly murder by a teenager called Sakakibara (after whom the Japanese youth of the 1990s are named 'the Sakakibara generation'), reinforced a growing millenarian angst. Since *anime* generally do not offer respite from such unpalatable social realities, Japanese scholar Susan Napier has suggested that *anime* is a cinema of 'de-assurance', contrasting it with Robin Wood's characterisation of Reagan-era Hollywood as a cinema of 'reassurance'.[28]

The pessimistic tone of present-day *mecha*, a sub-genre dealing with futuristic machines – like the *Patlabor* series – partly derives from Western cyberpunk influences. Cyberpunk depicts dystopian worlds populated by virtual entities – Artificial Intelligences and other human–machine interfaces. Like a lot of science fiction, it portrays an intensification of present-day tendencies, namely the tendencies of post-industrial capitalist society. Japanese animation since *Akira* has imported Western cyberpunk elements, including films like *Videodrome* (1983), *Terminator* (1984) and *Blade Runner* (1982), and combined them with its own 'imagination of disaster' derived from centuries-old apocalyptic, elegiac forms and animist beliefs; Shinto, Japan's oldest religion, holds that inanimate entities such as rocks, trees and rivers are sacred and that gods (*kami*) dwell in them. Films such as *Ghost in the Shell* (1995) use these influences to comment on and reflect the unique circumstances of Japan's post-industrial society. Here, and in other recent *anime* showing bodies disintegrating, mutating or vaporising and then being reconstructed differently (*Akira*, *Rojin Z* [1991] and many more), there is unexpected promise in 'this mutant technological life'.[29]

Japan's most popular filmmaker is Hayao Miyazake, whose *anime* cross boundaries of age and gender in their mass appeal. *Princess Mononoke* (1997), an eco-fable about the destruction of the forests set in fourteenth-century Japan, was the best-selling film of all time in Japan until *Titanic*; but Miyazake's next film *Spirited Away* (2001), which traces ten-year-old Chihiro's adventures in a spirit realm where sorceress Yubaba transforms her parents into pigs, did better still. *Spirited Away* also won an Oscar for Best Animated Feature and the Golden Bear at the Berlin Film Festival. Miyazake's earlier animations *My Neighbour Totoro* (1988) and *Kiki's Delivery Service* (1989) are also extremely popular across East Asia.

Typical Miyazake traits include richly realised fantasy worlds, pre-industrial or futuristic settings, plucky girls and formidable matriarchs. The motifs of flight and empowering labour also unite his work.[30]

Miyazake's films are not alone among *anime* in portraying images of strong women. These have a long tradition in Japanese stories and legends, including Queen Himiko, legendary ruler of Japan, who has formed the basis of speculation that early Japan may have been a matriarchy.[31]

This complex attitude towards women is demonstrated in *Princess Mononoke*, where the eponymous heroine lives among wolves and is first seen with her visage smeared with red war-paint and blood, spitting out bullets from her 'mother' Moro's side and licking the wound. A hairy pelt hangs around her neck, connoting unbridled animality and, together with suggestions of menstrual blood, pointing to dangerous female sexuality beyond society's accepted norms. Yet Mononoke is not subjected to mechanisms of abjection or containment meted out to her type in patriarchal narratives; that is, she is neither destroyed nor domesticated by offer of marriage. There is an equally ambiguous villain: Lady Eboshi rules over a gun-manufacturing ironworks, heralding the arrival of iron-age technology and the destruction of the forests, but she also gives refuge to society's marginals, ex-prostitutes and lepers, providing them with a better life than they might have otherwise. The film charts the disappearance of the former ecological order and the shift away from pre-modern communion with the natural world and its spirits, as expressed in animistic beliefs and depicted in Mononoke's ability to interact with the host of nature's spirits. Lady Eboshi's actions epitomise the desire to make nature subservient to human will – the essence of modern technology – eradicating and repressing traditional animistic beliefs about nature's autonomous agency.

The 'New' New Wave

The leader of Japan's 'new' New Wave filmmakers is Takeshi Kitano. Otherwise known as 'Beat' Takeshi, Kitano was originally an actor and TV comedian. His breakthrough international success was *Hana-Bi* (1997), his seventh directorial effort, which won the Golden Lion at the Venice Film Festival. Kitano's films focus on *yakuza* (Japanese mafia), mixing violence with pathos and visual comedy. They are often compared to Tarantino's films, sharing swordplay and Hong Kong triad (gangster film) influences, although Kitano evolved his style first. Where Kitano particularly differs from Tarantino is his emphasis on pause over action: exaggerated bursts of movement punctuate long scenes of silence, waiting or stasis.

According to Chuck Stephens, what distinguishes the 'new' New Wave from the 'old' New Wave directors such as Oshima and Imamura is that the younger generation acknowledges Japan's multi-ethnic culture and is even keener to gain the West's attention.[32] Significantly, however, the new and old Japanese New Waves share a preoccupation with youth. The commonality between generations is shown in Kiyoshi Kurosawa's *Bright Future* (2003), which sympathetically portrays a relationship between twenty-year-old Yuji and his friend Mamoru's father, who belongs to the 1968 generation. Both are powerless against authority. Kiyoshi Kurosawa – no relation to Akira – broke through internationally with his film *Cure* (1997), and 'by popular and critical consensus' is 'the first major Japanese filmmaker to emerge since Takeshi Kitano'.[33] Kurosawa belongs to what has been called the 'new' New Wave's 'intellectual' stream, which also includes Hirokazu Koreeda and Shinji Aoyama. This distinguishes them from both the maverick director Takashi Miike and the explosive industrial punk aesthetic of filmmakers such as Shinya Tsukamoto (*Tetsuo* [1988]) and Sogo Ishii (*Electric Dragon 80,000 Volts* [2001]).

Kurosawa trained in experimental Super-8 filmmaking while working as assistant director to Shinji Somai. Although *Bright Future* is an independent film, shot on digital video, Kurosawa has also made films within the studio system and is known for weaving philosophical and environmental themes into genres such as police thrillers, ghost stories, family melodramas, dystopic science fiction and *yakuza* films. As well as recalling Japan's own cinematic allegories of nuclear radioactivity, especially *Godzilla*, his films are influenced by Hollywood directors such as Sam Peckinpah, Robert Aldrich and Don Siegel. Characteristic features in his films include the apocalyptic imagery of toxic pastures and streams, themes of industrial entropy, and 'celestial' high overhead shots reducing cityscapes to minimalistic geometric compositions. A concern with botany pervades throughout. At once tame and voracious, plants can sometimes survive for centuries by decimating life around them; they fascinate Kurosawa because they are 'so differently alive' from humans.[34]

In *Bright Future*, jellyfish rather than plants occupy this role. Released into Tokyo's canals after being acclimatised to fresh water, they glow luminous orange, poisonous yet mesmerising. Incandescence is a recurring motif – witness the youths wearing Che Guevara T-shirts and glowing headbands whom Yuji befriends in a video arcade. Despite sudden eruptions of violence, the bleak depiction of family relationships, Yuji's dead-end jobs and general purposelessness, allusions to Japan's worsening economic downturn and intimations of ecological disaster, the film's title is not ironic. The apocalyptic imagery in Kurosawa's films, as in many other Japanese films, implies not solely negation but also the hopeful possibility of 'starting again with nothing'.[35]

Japanese cinema got its biggest international breakthrough in the 1990s with a slew of visceral horror films. These are exemplary products of Japan's economic-downturn era, and their archetypal figure is the teenage girl, pre-eminent icon of Japan's bubble economy.[36] The films also cast teen pop idols to appeal to female teen audiences. The genre typically combines technology with the supernatural. Hideo Nakata's *The Ring* (1998), which stands at the forefront of the genre, revolves around a superstition regarding a certain videotape: if you watch it, you receive a telephone call; seven days later, you die. A single mother seeking to protect her son traces the videotape to the cabin where recorded events took place, uncovering the story of Sadako, buried alive in a well by her father, and whose psychic powers cause the violent deaths. The film makes implicit connections between Sadako's powers of telepathy and telekinesis and the malign influences of the telephone and television – all are technologies of influencing or 'touching' from afar. The film's terrifying climax brings together influences from *Video-drome* and Japanese legends, with Sadako clambering out of the well in the video image, then out of the television set itself. Since *The Ring*'s release, Sadako's name in Japan has become synonymous with technophobia.

In *The Ring*, the remedy for the curse is also the poison: to save oneself, one must play the tape to another, thereby ensuring the curse's perpetuation. *Ring 2* (1999) continues the first film's preoccupations with 'contaminating', possessed and possessive technology – with a new focus on survivors who have witnessed Sadako's terrible glance, and, as video images morph and mutate, so the curse evolves through yet different manifestations. In addition to sequels, *The Ring* spawned many spin-offs and remakes, including Kurosawa's ghost film *Pulse* (2001). The wave spread to Hong Kong, Korea, Thailand and Hollywood. In East Asia, it established a commercially viable trend for high-tension, low-budget horror films which worked with regional stars.[37] The company responsible for *The Ring*, Omega Project, marketed the film through the Internet, mobile phone dial-up entertainment and video-game licensing, 'creating marketing hype to rival Hollywood'.[38] In order to withstand the threat of Hollywood, the sequels and spin-offs have themselves morphed as they proliferate through interlocking media. In the Thai film *999–9999* (2002), for example, the mobile phone is the threatening technology, linking *The Ring*'s viral narrative motifs to stories circulating in the mid-1990s among Thai school teenagers about certain occult phone numbers.

The Ring qualifies as visceral horror – horror that proves itself on our pulses – for its techniques of high suspense. *Audition* (2000), another notorious Japanese horror film, adds the dimension of the body being opened up to its visceral horror characteristics. *Audition* is key to its director Takashi Miike's high international profile. *Audition* has solidified his maverick reputation – its slow-moving horror is quite unlike the string of yakuza films such as *Dead or Alive* (1999) for which he is otherwise known. In *Audition*, a middle-aged widower, Aoyama, seeks a spouse and interviews young women under the pretext of auditioning for a film. He instantly falls under the spell of demure, childlike Asami who, unknown to him, has a dreadfully abused past and plans to wreak revenge by sawing off his feet with piano wire. The film visualises Asami wearing a nurse's outfit with black leather apron and gloves, leaning over Aoyama's prone body with her sedative-oozing phallic syringe. The macabre sequence, initiated when Aoyama falls unconscious drugged with Asami's potion, is itself cut up into a series of flashbacks. Events which took place before are repeated, but subtly and disturbingly altered to accommodate Asami's different perspective, which Aoyama had previously elided, in his attempt to sustain his fantasy of her as 'the Woman', both beautiful and deferential, the two qualities he prizes most, and on whom he had decided, even before her 'audition'. At one point, the film flashes back to the couple's first time in bed, allowing us to think the foot-sawing may have been a dream, only then to jolt back to the narrative present.

Audition plays with the iconography of S&M porn to reveal pathologies of social relationships in Japan: the audition as courtship ritual results from loneliness and lack of interpersonal contact but culminates in personal torture, reflecting a society where 'male visions of women are increasingly blurred with violent images of domination and control'.[39] The image of the powerful, scary woman and castration anxiety is present in *The Ring*, too, where victims are found with identically frozen, terrified facial expressions; Sadako's terrible gaze recalls that of the Greek mythological gorgon, Medusa, who had the power to turn men to stone. The fascination with female castrators is not new to Japanese cinema. It is evident in attitudes to the 1936 legal case of a woman called Sada who strangled her lover to death and cut off his penis as a memento. Sada gained public sympathy in her trial and was acquitted of murder. Her story is told in Oshima's *In the Realm of the Senses* (1976) and retold in Nobuhiko Obayashi's *Sada* (1998). Australian feminist critic Barbara Creed has proposed that the trope of the monstrous-feminine is a misrepresentation of powerful female deities through centuries of patriarchal culture, but in Japanese cinema the 'monstrous-feminine' is rarely unequivocally monstrous.[40]

Thai Cinema

The Thai film industry has witnessed a revival since the late 1990s, with a series of films that smashed domestic box-office records, including *2499 Antaparn Krong Muang* (1997), *Nang Nak* (1999) and *Suriyothai* (2001).

Annual film production, which peaked at almost 200 films in the 1970s then slumped due to the onslaught of TV, video, cable and satellite, and rivalry from Hollywood, has been slowly recovering too, although still only a handful of films are released annually. Thai films are mostly funded through private companies and, increasingly, international co-production. The revival coincides with Thailand's rapid economic growth since the mid-1980s.

The growth of shopping-mall multiplexes since 1995 has also contributed, but during the early 1990s it was mainly teen audiences who watched Thai films, while Hollywood films drew young adults. Director Nonzee Nimibutr is credited with returning adult Thai audiences to the cinemas.[41] He belongs to a new generation of directors and producers who entered the film industry from former careers in TV commercials and music videos. His *Nang Nak* grossed $3.9 million in Thailand, selling more than *Titanic*. It was also acknowledged at international film festivals. It adapts a frequently filmed nineteenth-century rural legend – about a woman who dies in childbirth and returns as a ghost to haunt her husband – using striking lighting effects and polished camerawork. Nostalgic period films like these, which hark back to simpler and better times, sustained the Thai film industry through the Asian financial crisis, which actually started in Thailand and rippled out to the rest of the region. In fact, the Thai film industry flourished while other sectors of the economy floundered.

Directed by film veteran Prince Chatrichalerm Yukol and partly funded by Queen Sirikit of Thailand, the lavish historical epic *Suriyothai* surpassed *Nang Nak*'s box-office success, grossing $18 million. The most expensive Thai film ever made, employing a cast of superstars, thousands of extras and 160 elephants, it relates the story of a sixteenth-century queen who martyred herself in battle for her king and country during the Burmese invasion. *Suriyothai* caused a stir at Cannes and set a trend for big-budget Thai pictures, most of them aimed at international markets, with filmmakers seeking to capitalise on Thai cinema's rising profile. However, international acclaim for Thai cinema mostly rests on titles such as Wisit Sasanatieng's *Tears of the Black Tiger* (2000) and Yongyooth Thongkonthun's *Iron Ladies* (2000). Directors Pen-Ek Ratanaruang and Apichatpong Weerasethakul are also recognised abroad.

Wisit had been screenwriter for *Nang Nak* but was unable to repeat his popular success with *Tears of the Black Tiger* – a domestic flop, yet one of the most high-profile Thai films internationally. The story of cross-class love between a politician's daughter and a bandit, it too draws inspiration from the past – it is set in the 1950s and pays homage to films from that era, particularly the films of Thai director Rattana Pestonji. Its whirlwind romance and florid colours draw on classic Hollywood melodramas such as *Gone with the Wind* and appropriate the look of hand-painted Thai film posters. The other obvious influence is the Western, particularly Sergio Leone's Spaghetti Westerns: Wisit's bandits are outfitted as cowboys. *Tears of the Black Tiger* has been called a 'pad Thai Western'; a 'hybrid of a hybrid', it boldly displays its status as postmodern pastiche.[42] *Iron Ladies*, on the other hand, pleased crowds at home and at international film festivals, becoming the most popular Thai film that year. It recreates the real-life triumphs of an all-gay, transvestite and transsexual volleyball team who won the national championship in 1996. The film's focus on a small provincial community was a clear factor in its popularity during the financial-crisis recovery period.

South Korean Art Films and Blockbusters

Divided into the communist North and capitalist South after the Second World War, Korea was once known as the 'Hermit Kingdom', its cinema rarely seen beyond its national borders. Although the North is still isolated and its cinema still waiting to be 'discovered', that situation changed for South Korea after the mid-1980s with the success of widespread protests against its military regime, which had sped the country to full modernisation while suppressing basic political, civil and labour rights. Democratic reforms were initiated, leading to the deregulation of the film industry enabling private companies to finance films, the relaxing of foreign film imports, the partial lifting of censorship restrictions and the rebirth of film culture.

The Korean New Wave directors emerged as part of the underground movement against the military dictatorship. Although its heyday was 1983–94, the New Wave is still going today – often referred to in its present incarnation as 'New Korean Cinema'. Its directors include Im Kwok-Taek, Jang Sun-Woo, Hong Sang-Soo and Lee Myung-Se. Jang Sun-Woo was held as a political prisoner and tortured for distributing leaflets about the Kwangju Massacre in May 1980, when the military was accused of killing hundreds of protestors. The Kwangju Massacre provides the impetus for the political radicalism of early New Wave films. Jang's 1990s films tend to emphasise sexual politics but are no less political. His *Timeless, Bottomless Bad Movie* (1998) follows Seoul's street kids delving into sex, crime and drugs. It inspired a spate of Korean films dealing with delinquent youth and calling attention to violent undercurrents in Korean society, including Im Sang-Soo's digital film *Tears* (2000), which was also influenced by a Hong Kong film about teenagers on the street, *Made in Hong Kong* (1997) (see Chapter 6).

As elsewhere in the region, modernisation in Korea has destabilised traditional gender roles for both men and women.[43] This includes values stemming from Confucian beliefs which emphasise woman's subservience to her husband and family. In the new liberal climate of the 1980s, sexuality, particularly women's sexuality – hitherto a taboo topic – appeared on the cultural agenda. Jang's *Lies* (1999) belongs to a widespread trend emphasising the need for frankness in dealing with sex in contemporary Korean cinema. Here, a sadomasochistic affair develops between a sculptor named J and a schoolgirl named Y, both played by non-professional actors. Y enjoys being whipped, but halfway through the film she reverses the roles, taking control of the stick and, finally, leaving the relationship to start an independent life: she exits from the imprisoning dialectic of submission and domination. This has a clear political edge, referring to the residues of authoritarian power in Korean society, underlined by a scene where Y refuses to sign a political petition because of the country's lack of respect for its subjects. Based on a book *Tell Me a Lie* that was banned and burned in Korea for its 'pornographic' content, *Lies* deliberately sets out to provoke the censors. Released with cuts, the film caused a stir among Korean audiences. Despite, or perhaps because of, certain moral groups' attempts to close down screenings of the film, it became one of that year's top ten box-office hits. A self-reflexive sex film, *Lies* epitomises Jang's ability to appeal simultaneously to a modernist film aesthetic and to the box office. The struggle for power is enacted at the level of narrative in the form of a play with cinematic 'truth' and lies, utilising Brechtian alienation effects such as pseudo-documentary video footage where actors discuss their parts, voiceover narration hinting at the film's possible unfaithfulness to its source novel, and interruptions from the camera crew at moments of narrative intensity, breaking the naturalistic illusion.

Another New Wave director who has scored with the Korean public is Lee Myung-Se. *Nowhere to Hide* (1999), his sixth feature film, was a critical and commercial success, earning five times its $2 million production budget at the box office.[44] A detective noir/gangster/Western/martial-arts/action-comedy hybrid, *Nowhere to Hide* is peppered with eclectic references to film history, from *Battleship Potemkin* (1925) to *Dimensions of Dialogue* (1982). Critics have emphasised its formal innovativeness. Anne Rutherford, for example, refers to its marrying of a popular, fast-paced music-video and comic-strip aesthetic ('a cartoon with live actors') with 'an arthouse sensibility' and claims that it mixes its borrowed styles and genres in unpredictable ways: 'Any moment, any stylistic element, any generic clue or hook can become a point of departure for the film to take off into exuberant flights of fantasy and play, leapfrogging more conventional narrative transitions.'[45] Lee has stated that movement and kinetic energy are his main focus rather than story and characters. Certainly, the building of dynamic movement from pauses and stillness makes watching this film a sensual delight. But, for all its formal innovation, *Nowhere to Hide* offers familiar genre pleasures too. As in the films of John Woo and Jackie Chan (see Chapter 6), male violence is funny, slapstick, spectacular, sometimes elegiac and frequently brutal.

With the aid of a screen quota system which stipulates a minimum number of days for the screening of Korean films in Korean theatres, Korean films have been able to capture over 40 per cent of the national market share – one of the highest national market shares in the world. The screen quota has been an effective mechanism for regulating the US monopoly in the Korean film market and is widely supported by the Korean public. Although instituted in 1966, it was not strictly enforced until after the 1993 GATT negotiations.[46] The male buddy/gangster film *Friend* (2001) and the military thrillers *Shiri* (1999) and *Joint Security Area* (2000) are all Korean films that have smashed the Korean box-office record set by *Titanic*, each subsequent film outdoing the success of its predecessors. Blockbusters such as these have also transformed Korean cinema into a heavyweight contender in other East Asian markets, especially Hong Kong and Thailand.

Both *Shiri* and *Joint Security Area* deal with the burning topical issue of Korean reunification. International critics have generally preferred *Nowhere to Hide* to *Shiri* on the grounds of the former's formal innovation, but *Shiri* also has a daring style and cartoon violence. *Shiri* combines violent blockbuster spectacle with a love story and has superstar Han Suk-Kyu as the male lead. There is a long tradition of love stories between North and South Koreans in Korean cinema, but *Shiri* puts the formula in a gripping narrative with an urgent twist, given recent events. North Korea no longer disguises its possession of nuclear weapons and has earned the reputation of being the world's most unpredictable country, included in George W. Bush's so-called 'axis of evil'. *Shiri* touches South Korean audiences' fear of North Korea's military power which has made South Korea vulnerable in the event of nuclear attack. During the Cold War, especially after the 1950–3 Korean War between the Soviet-backed North and the US-assisted South, South Koreans were taught to view North Korea as the enemy. However, since the 1990s, North Koreans have been considered 'friends' whom South Koreans must help in order all to live together in the future, despite continuing ideological differences. The allure of the nation's enemy/friend or stranger/lover is at the emotional core of *Shiri*, evoking comparisons with the Indian film *Dil Se* (1998) (see Chapter 8). In

Shiri, Hee, a North Korean sniper fighting for a unified Korea, hides from the pursuit of South Korean special agent Ryu. She undergoes plastic surgery, takes on a new identity, Hyun, and gets engaged to Ryu's colleague Lee. Hee/Hyun's fractured identity becomes a metaphor for the division of North and South Korea. Described as a 'six-headed hydra', Hee/Hyun is at once sympathetic and monstrous. As the monstrous-feminine, she figures the general mistrust of women and the crisis of gender dynamics in contemporary society (as in *Audition*) as well as the monstrosity of the North Korean militia. Yet the film suggests that Hee/Hyun is a victim of history – really, she is just one entity, and it is because of partition that she has been forced to become many. Nostalgia for an imagined lost unity also drives the film's other main conceit, derived from the title: *shiri* are freshwater fish unique to Korea, apparently separated and longing to unite. In film reviews, they became the rallying cry for Korean cinema – little fishes that sank *Titanic*.

Notes

1. Desser, 'Pan-Asian Youth', p. 3.
2. Ibid., p. 1.
3. Ibid., p. 2.
4. Ibid., p. 11.
5. Dissanayake, *Melodrama and Asian Cinema*, p. 3.
6. Berry, *Chinese Films in Focus*, p. 183.
7. Lau, 'Globalization and Youthful Subculture', p. 15.
8. Chow, *Primitive Passions*, p. 13.
9. Rayns, 'Story of Qiu Ju', p. 55.
10. Berry, 'Hero', p. 24.
11. Xiaoping, 'New Chinese Cinema', p. 263.
12. Lau, 'Globalization and Youthful Subculture', p. 20.
13. Donald, '*Beijing Bicycle*', p. 192.
14. Xiaoping, 'New Chinese Cinema', p. 272.
15. Berry, 'Dazzling', p. 24.
16. Ibid., p. 25.
17. Jameson, *Geopolitical Aesthetic*, p. 145.
18. Yeh, 'Politics and Poetics of Hou Hsiao-Hsien's Films', p. 68.
19. Li, '*Yi Yi*', p. 204.
20. Ibid., p. 200.
21. Martin, 'Vive l'amour', p. 175.
22. Stephens, 'Intersection', p. 21.
23. Martin, 'Vive l'amour', p. 177.
24. Chapman, *Cinemas of the World*, p. 361.
25. Ibid., p. 365.

26. Möller, 'Shameless', p. 45.
27. Freidberg, '*Akira* and the Postnuclear Sublime', p. 97.
28. Napier, *Anime from Akira to Princess Mononoke*, p. 193.
29. Rutsky, *High Techne*, p. 138.
30. Osmond, 'Gods and Monsters', p. 34.
31. Lev, *Samurai from Outer Space*, p. 40.
32. Stephens, 'High and Low', p. 36.
33. Stephens, 'Another Green World', p. 68.
34. Ibid., p. 72.
35. Stephens, 'High and Low', p. 36.
36. Lu, 'Horror Japanese-style', p. 38.
37. Ibid., p. 38.
38. Ibid., p. 38.
39. Ward, 'Audition', p. 40.
40. Creed, *Monstrous-Feminine*, p. 21.
41. Kong, 'Cinematic Revival in Thailand', p. 12.
42. Stephens, 'Tears of the Black Tiger', p. 17.
43. For an argument about how this has affected men and masculinity in New Korean Cinema, see Kim, *The Remasculinization of Korean Cinema*.
44. Stephens, 'Kingdom Come', p. 38.
45. Rutherford, 'Arrested Motion'.
46. CDMI, 'Overview of the Screen Quota System in Korea'.

CHAPTER 6

Hong Kong Cinema

Hong Kong has had a commercially buoyant film industry for decades. In the 1970s, Hong Kong cinema commanded international attention through films such as *A Touch of Zen* (1969), but it was really during the 1990s that its international profile soared, partly through tastemakers such as Quentin Tarantino, who acknowledged influences from *City on Fire* (1987) in *Reservoir Dogs* (1992), presented an MTV Lifetime Achievement Award to Jackie Chan and secured US distribution for *Chungking Express* (1994). Ironically, just as Hong Kong cinema became internationally visible, its own commercial vitality started to drain due to the combined impact of uncertainty about Hong Kong's return to Mainland China in June 1997, the 1997–8 Asian financial crisis, increased video piracy and the success of Hollywood, South Korean and Thai blockbusters in regional markets. Hong Kong films used to be persistently more popular than Hollywood films in their home territory, with a domestic box-office share ranging between 50 and 70 per cent since the 1970s, but since the mid 1990s that share has decreased – to 38 per cent in 2002.[1]

Traditionally a port city at the intersection of various trading routes, Hong Kong was a British colony from the nineteenth century until it was handed back to China. Now it is officially a Special Administration Region (SAR) of China. Throughout its history, Hong Kong has been profoundly affected by the tumultuous events in the region – it was occupied by the Japanese during the Second World War and later inundated by refugees fleeing communist China. Mainland refugees helped generate Hong Kong's first economic boom in the 1950s and 1960s with their technical and manufacturing skills. As the city became a thriving capitalist outpost, multinational companies took their businesses there, encouraged by the colonial government's 'laissez faire' policies. Hong Kong has acquired an identity as a global city where goods, capital and people transit. The refugees who fled there saw it as a temporary home. Events such as the 1967 anti-colonial riots, fanned by the Cultural Revolution on the Mainland, and the 1989 Tiananmen Square massacre prompted Hong Kong residents fearing for the city's own fate to emigrate again – this time to places like the USA, Canada, Australia and Britain.

According to the terms of the bilateral handover treaty signed by Britain and China in 1984, China promises to leave Hong Kong's socio-economic structure unchanged for fifty years. Since the handover, however, there have been public demonstrations against the incoming government's encroachments on civil liberties. During British colonial rule, Hong Kong's cinema was subject to British censorship regulations, which forbade films that criticised the colonial government or harmed diplomatic relations with other countries, including China. Since the handover, Hong Kong films have been subject to censorship from the Chinese authorities, and this has affected the production of some films discussed in this chapter. Ambivalence towards China is a leitmotif in many contemporary films, which mingle nostalgia for the Chinese 'Motherland' with fears about China's territorial claims. In response to censorship constraints, some Hong Kong films have adopted allegorical positions, displacing fears for the city's current and future situation into past settings – the pre-modern Ching Dynasty era (the *Once Upon a Time in China* series), the 1920s (*Rouge* [1987]) or the 1960s (*In the Mood for Love* [2000]). During the late 1980s and 1990s, stories about ghosts, including *A Chinese Ghost Story* (1987) and *Rouge*, proliferated, registering anxieties about Hong Kong's 'disappearance'. Ackbar Abbas has given an influential account of these anxieties in his book *Hong Kong: Culture and the Politics of Disappearance*. Abbas refers to a sense of '*déjà disparu*' in Hong Kong culture – 'the feeling that what is new and unique about the situation is already gone'.[2] Given the traumatic impact of the Tiananmen Square massacre and the momentous nature of the handover, such readings have much validity; but other political perspectives, such as the global dynamics of Hong Kong's relationship with Hollywood as well as with other East Asian film industries, also need to be taken into account.

In Hong Kong, there is an unusually close relationship between 'commercial' productions and the 'art cinema' or New Wave, with the latter developing within, rather than outside, the commercial system. The industry's most sought-after actors during the 1990s – including Andy Lau, Tony Leung, Chow Yun-Fat, Michelle Yeoh, Maggie Cheung, Brigitte Lin and Leslie Cheung – regularly performed in both 'art-house' and commercial sectors. There is also a strong convergence between the film, TV and music industries. Cantonese TV fostered Canto-Pop, a hybrid of Western and Hong Kong popular music.[3] Canto-Pop singers perform in films; and many film stars are recording artists. For the sake of clarity in pinpointing how styles evolved, and to provide a context for the close analysis of *Hard-Boiled* (1992), *In the Mood for Love*, and *Crouching Tiger, Hidden Dragon* (2000) at the end of this chapter, the following sections treat commercial and art cinemas separately. For commercial cinema, I have focused on action genres, as these circulate the most globally.

Martial-Arts and Gangster Films

In a commercial cinema which relies on overseas and regional markets because its home market is too small to sustain production, genres are constructed for global appeal. Hong Kong's martial-arts genres are now familiar to many outside the traditional fan base through Yuen Woo-Ping's martial-arts choreography in *The Matrix* (1999), but it is worth remembering that they have always developed in conjunction with popular tastes for speed, sensation and spectacle cultivated partly by Hollywood. However, the martial-arts film (known in Chinese as *wuxia pian*; *wuxia* meaning 'sword and chivalry', *pian* meaning film) is also deeply entrenched in Chinese legends about chivalrous warriors, including female warriors such as Fa Mulan, who dressed in men's clothes in order to relieve her father from battle. The legends were adapted into Chinese opera and literature in the nineteenth century, then into films in the early twentieth century. *Wuxia pian* were set in a distant semi-fantastical past and used wires and other studio trickery to imitate flying. With the 1949 communist victory, the genre's development on the Mainland was curtailed; but émigré filmmakers continued the tradition in Hong Kong, combining it with generic influences from Hollywood and Japan, particularly the energetic style of masculine combat from Japanese Samurai films. As Mainland China was out of bounds, Hong Kong filmmakers often used Taiwan for spectacular scenery. The most successful films in the 1960s were produced in Mandarin (the dialect spoken in northern China and Taiwan, while the dialect of southern China and Hong Kong is Cantonese). These included films by King Hu – who preferred to work in Taiwan and whose *A Touch of Zen* is an importance influence on *Crouching Tiger, Hidden Dragon* – and by Chang Cheh, director of the *One-Armed Swordsman* films (1967, 1969, 1971) and mentor to John Woo. While Hu's films gave prominent roles to swordplay heroines, including Chang Pei Pei as Golden Swallow in *Come Drink With Me* (1966) and Hsu Feng in *A Touch of Zen*, Chang's films sidelined women in favour of male heroes, and display a ritual fascination with male mutilation – influences which can be seen in John Woo's films.

The Shaw Brothers Studio dominated the Hong Kong film industry during the 1950s and 1960s. Golden Harvest, founded in 1970 by former Shaw manager Raymond Chow, put an end to the Shaw Brothers' monopoly, eventually forcing their studio to cease production in 1986. Golden Harvest's first lucky strike was signing Bruce Lee, whose immigrant past

– he was originally an actor in the USA – shaped his vengeful star persona, embodying an empowering fantasy of Chinese masculinity 'that could take on the world'.[4] Lee's films were kung-fu films, using a southern Chinese style of fighting, in contrast to the swordplay film's northern fighting style. They emphasised authentic martial-arts skills. Lee's last film, *Enter the Dragon* (1973), was the first 'official' Hong Kong/US co-production.[5] After Lee's sudden death in 1973, Golden Harvest primed the next generation of kung-fu stars – Mainland actor Jet Li, Sammo Hung and Jackie Chan. Kung fu decisively marked the box-office ascendancy of male stars, whereas female stars had dominated previously, especially in Mandarin-dialect *wenyi pian* ('melodrama'), which was popular in the 1960s. However, Hong Kong's female stars retained a forceful presence – Michelle Yeoh, Cynthia Rothrock and Brigitte Lin all made their names in martial-arts genres.

Chan and Hung both trained in Peking Opera and performed as stuntmen before directing, choreographing and starring in their own martial-arts films. Chan's first success as an actor was in Yuen Woo-Ping's *Drunken Master* (1978). He became Golden Harvest's top box-office draw in the 1980s and 1990s. Also from an opera background, then a stuntman, Yuen Woo-Ping became director and choreographer for another studio, Seasonal Films, before joining Golden Harvest. Yuen's other Hong Kong films include, as director, *Iron Monkey* (1993) and *Wing Chun* (1994) and, as choreographer, the *Once Upon a Time in China* series. Northern acrobatics and an 'irreverent approach to fighting styles' inform Chan's, Hung's and Yuen's martial-arts choreography.[6] As his other influences, Chan cites Charlie Chaplin, Buster Keaton, Harold Lloyd, Fred Astaire and Gene Kelly – all Hollywood comedians or dance performers.[7] Chan brought slapstick comedy into the kung-fu genre as well as turning fighting into a form of choreographed dance spectacle. His films appeal largely because of their novel stunts – which Chan performs himself.

In the 1980s, the studio system gave way to 'a more flexible production-house system'.[8] Companies began packaging 'multi-genre' films, especially Cinema City Company (backed by Golden Princess), which mixed spectacular action with urban comedy and other elements such as ghost story and melodrama in order to win 'the largest possible audience'.[9] Other companies followed suit. The kung-fu film was relocated into contemporary urban settings, rather than historical or folk Chinese ones, and mixed with elements such as gunplay as well as comedy – Jackie Chan's *Police Story* (1985) exemplifies this shift. In *Police Story 3: Supercop* (1992), Chan stars alongside Michelle Yeoh, who trained in dance, first became famous as a beauty queen ('Miss Malaysia') and also performs her own stunts.

Set in contemporary urban settings, John Woo's films are renowned for their hyperbolic action sequences, extreme bloodletting, suspenseful gun-pointing standoffs, sentimentality, and heroes struggling to hold on to chivalric codes of honour, justice, loyalty, male friendship and brotherhood in a corrupt world. Woo also gives his 'knights-errant' Christian values such as 'victory through sacrifice'; he is himself a Protestant.[10] Woo worked his way through the studio system, serving as assistant to Chang Cheh at Shaw Brothers, then directing kung-fu films and comedies for Golden Harvest and Cinema City. His breakthrough film was *A Better Tomorrow* (1986), a huge domestic box-office success made in collaboration with New Wave director/producer Tsui Hark. The film made Woo's favourite leading man Chow Yun-Fat one of Hong Kong's most high-profile stars, his charismatic appeal based on his amiable self-confidence. Soon after, *The Killer* (1989) was shown at international festivals, winning Woo a cult following overseas. Woo later split paths with Tsui, teaming up with producer Terence Chang for his final Hong Kong films, including *Hard-Boiled*, before emigrating to Hollywood.

Woo's films bear a cross-cultural range of influences including Hollywood Westerns and gangster films (especially those by Sam Peckinpah and Martin Scorsese), Akira Kurosawa's *Seven Samurai* (1954), Chang Cheh's swordplay films and the works of Jean-Pierre Melville, 'father' of the French New Wave. Woo's style is visually flashy, characterised by a liberal use of freeze-frames, dramatic slow motion, rapid flashbacks, and extreme close-ups of retributive violence.[11] As a major influence, Woo acknowledges Melville's *Le Samurai* (1967), because it is a gangster film that shows how a gangster thinks and feels as well as how he behaves.[12] The signature theme in Woo's films is the *Doppelgänger* relationship between two men on different sides of the law, who discover 'kinship in their principled opposition to evil' right in the midst of confrontation.[13] These relationships, which emphasise intense male bonding to the exclusion of women, have often been described as homoerotic. In Woo's films, male friendship is portrayed romantically, although they always remain within traditions of Chinese patriarchy, and sexual feelings between men are never made explicit. Interestingly, in the documentary *Yang + Yin: Gender in Chinese Cinema* (1996) by gay Hong Kong director Stanley Kwan, Woo claims that he could not make films with such intense male bonding in Hollywood, implicitly because Hollywood heroes are even more obliged to 'prove' their heterosexuality.

Hong Kong New Waves

The Hong Kong New Wave started in 1979, led by directors such as Ann Hui and Tsui Hark. The New Wave directors attended film schools abroad and worked in Cantonese-language TV before entering the film industry. In the late 1980s, a second wave of directors emerged including Stanley Kwan, Clara Law and Wong Kar-Wai. The New Waves introduced a new technical and visual sophistication (particularly in films by Tsui Hark), combined popular genres with cosmopolitan art-cinema influences and explored aspects of Hong Kong's contemporary and historical social reality. Ann Hui studied at the London Film School, then returned to Hong Kong and worked as assistant to King Hu before directing for TV. Her films explore issues of history and exile, often through stories focusing on women. One of her early films, *The Boat People* (1982), deals with Vietnamese refugees (who fled from communist Vietnam to Hong Kong) but was widely interpreted as an allegory of handover anxieties. In her later, semi-autobiographical work *Song of the Exile* (1990), she looks at the psychological effects of exile through a female London graduate, Hueyin (Maggie Cheung). Hueyin is rejected for a job at the BBC – implicitly due to racial discrimination – and returns to Hong Kong to discover that her mother is Japanese, hitherto kept a secret because her parents met during the Japanese occupation of Manchuria. The film reassesses the past in flashback, as Hueyin undergoes a delayed recognition of her mother's oppression as a Japanese alien, reversing the customary image of the Japanese as oppressors.

Tsui Hark's trademark style is the vertiginous use of speed. His films are an eclectic combination of Chinese opera, Japanese *manga* and *anime*, MTV-style editing, and Hollywood-type special effects and production values.[14] Tsui is frequently credited as the 'author' of films in which he acted as producer, and is known for his shrewd commercial sense as well as his artistic inventiveness. He joined Cinema City Company, then formed his own company Film Workshop. His *Zu: Warriors of the Magic Mountain* (1983), a multi-genre film blending the supernatural with slapstick, is regarded as marking the transitional moment when he and the New Wave 'went commercial', clearing the path for the Second Wave, which includes Tsui's other revisionary martial-arts films, such as the *Swordsman* and *Once Upon a Time in China* franchises. Some of Tsui's films are concerned with gender-bending or gender-transformation and have attracted the interest of critics writing from the perspective of feminist and queer theory. In *Swordsman 2* (1991) and its sequel *The East Is Red* (1992), Brigitte Lin plays the male-to-female transsexual Invincible Asia who spears her enemies with deadly embroidery needles. The films revel in fluid conceptions of gender and impart homoerotic frisson in the playful attraction between Asia and Ling (Jet Li), who is unsure whether Asia is male or female.[15]

Gender-bending and drag both belong to Chinese traditions – female martial chivalry and Peking Opera – but the prevalence of these themes in contemporary Hong Kong cinema is partly related to the decriminalisation of homosexuality in 1989 and changing gender dynamics. However, the insistence on cultural conformity and claims that homosexuality is 'un-Chinese' or a 'Western' import still prevail. This is clear from subtexts underpinning the careers of director Stanley Kwan and actor Leslie Cheung, who committed suicide in 2003 reportedly due to depression (but, according to other accounts, a troubled love affair). Leslie Cheung's gay identity was kept a secret until *Happy Together* (1997), where he plays a gay character. But even before this, gay cultural stereotypes associating male homosexuality with femininity informed his roles. He plays an opium-addicted wastrel in *Rouge*, a mother-fixated delinquent in *Days of Being Wild* (1991), and a cross-dressing Chinese opera performer tragically killing himself for the love of another man in *Farewell My Concubine* (1993).

Kwan established his reputation with 'women's films', or *wenyi pian* ('melodrama'), making a closeted use of women to stand in for male homosexuality before he came out as gay in his documentary *Yang + Yin*. The women in his films are tragically misaligned with their milieu and times – *Rouge* features the ghost of a 1920s concubine encountering the unfamiliar streets and mores of present-day Hong Kong, while *Centre Stage* a.k.a. *Actress* (1992) is about 1930s Shanghai film star Ruan Lingyu, whose controversial life and career made her the victim of a sensation-hungry press, an uncanny repetition of her role in *New Woman* (1934). 'Life' and role-playing bleed into each other in the film through the jux-taposition of dramatic reconstruction with documentary and archival footage. In Bérénice Reynaud's 'queer' reading of the film, this points to the centrality of performance in the everyday lives of gay men seeking to 'pass' for being straight.[16] Financed by Jackie Chan's company Golden Way (a subsidiary of Golden Harvest), *Actress* was not a commercial success but garnered international prestige for Hong Kong cinema. It won lead actress Maggie Cheung the Silver Bear at the Berlin Film Festival. Another former beauty queen, Cheung is one of Hong Kong's most iconic female stars. From playing Jackie Chan's long-suffering girl-friend (who, however, does enjoy some jokes at *his* expense) in the *Police Story* series to swordplay queen in *Heroic Trio* (1993) and international idol in *Irma Vep* (1996), her star persona is radically inconsistent, yet many of her roles, according to Reynaud, reflect 'postcolonial dilemmas and displacement, racist misrepresentation and partial loss of cultural identity', chiming with certain aspects of Cheung's own life: born in Hong Kong, she grew up in Britain and has lived in Paris (once married to French director Olivier Assayas), and she can speak English better than she can read Chinese characters.[17]

Consistent with this profile, Clara Law, whose films specialise in themes of displacement and migration, cast Maggie Cheung in her film *Farewell China* (1990) as a Mainland Chinese immigrant to the USA who becomes a paranoid schizophrenic – switching between the Chinese and English languages, and recognising then not recognising her visiting husband, whom she finally stabs to death. Made in the shadow of the Tiananmen Square massacre, it indicts China for depriving its citizens of a home and presents migration as unrelenting trauma.[18] Law herself emigrated to Australia before the handover, together with her partner and scriptwriter Eddie Fong. Her other films include *Autumn Moon* (1992), *Floating Life* (1996) and *The Goddess of 1967* (2000), the latter two made in Australia. In *Floating Life*, a Hong Kong family tries to adapt to life in Sydney's suburbs. The film conveys their culture shock through disorientating low angles emphasising the huge Australian sky and harsh sunlight. The perils of migration are embodied in paranoid schizophrenic Bing, who arrives before her family and attempts to over-assimilate to her new environment. *Autumn Moon* and *Goddess of 1967*, on the other hand, refract themes of exile through a young male Japanese traveller who in both cases provides a defamiliarising perspective. For example, J.M. in *Goddess* travels to Australia and encounters people who have lived there all their lives yet are just as alienated and dispossessed as migrants who have left their homes behind.

Wong Kar-Wai's films narrate interwoven stories about young, lovelorn and regret-filled loners. His working methods, usually involving long production schedules and high budgets, are out of line with Hong Kong industry standards. Although he began as a TV scriptwriter, he is renowned for not pre-scripting his films. He works in a random, improvisatory manner, building stories as filming progresses, writing scenes and characters' lines just hours before each day's shoot. He tends to construct his films in the editing process, utilising voiceover and music to smooth over jarring cuts. Wong set up his own production company, Jet Tone, in order to have creative control. He has developed a distinctive visual style through his partnership with cinematographers Chris Doyle and Andrew Lau and art director/editor William Chang. Although Australian-born, Doyle's long-standing affiliation with Wong Kar-Wai has made him one of the foremost elaborators of visual style in contemporary East Asian film. Wong/Doyle/Lau's trademark style is 'smudge motion', achieved by shooting at slow shutter speed and 'step-printing' (repeating each frame two or more times in the printing process).

Wong won cult acclaim with the micro-budget *Chungking Express*, filmed during a two-month hiatus in the production of *Ashes of Time* (1994). *Happy Together*, which won the *Prix de la mise en scène* at Cannes in 1997, further solidified his international reputation. For some critics, Wong's 'effects'-driven style evokes the French New Wave films of Godard and Truffaut mixed together with a contemporary pop romantic, MTV aesthetic.[19] However, according to Ackbar Abbas, MTV is designed to hold the viewer's attention, whereas Wong's films demonstrate that attention cannot be held: ungraspable moments constantly slip away.[20] Images of clocks (especially in *Days of Being Wild*) and expiring food cans (*Chungking Express*) become staple motifs, drawing attention to the impending 1997 deadline, while variable film speeds – as when Cop 663 (Tony Leung) drinks his coffee very slowly while crowds whizz past in the background in *Chungking Express* – suggest constant mutations of space and time in the ever-changing cityscape, to which Wong's characters struggle to adapt. All Wong's films so far have been distinctively Hong Kong films, although they are not always shot there, and tourist sights of the city are conspicuously absent – except in *Happy Together*, which shows the Hong Kong island skyline upside down. Here, a gay couple travel to Argentina; Hong Kong is displaced into its antipodean double, Buenos Aires. The film implicitly shows Hong Kong as a British colony on the brink of handover to China with a shot of the protagonists' British overseas passports.

Intersection is a key device in Wong's work. This emphasises the spatial co-presence of characters who brush past each other, briefly sharing closeness without realising – as in the *Chungking Express* voiceover 'at our most intimate we were only 0.01cm apart' – or inhabiting each other's domestic spaces when the other is absent (a feature showing Wong's influence by Taiwanese director Tsai Ming-liang). This takes on a new meaning in *Happy Together*, which depicts men seeking same-sex intimacy in public places.[21] Gay audiences and critics have appreciated this frank portrayal of gay relationships from a non-gay director. The film, moreover, represents a different side to Hong Kong masculinity in the everyday tenderness of Yiu-fai to Po-Wing. Although his gender politics are more conservative than Tsui Hark's, Wong also refashions genre conventions, or pushes them to the limit – here the road movie/male-buddy film, and elsewhere the gangster film (*As Tears Go By* [1988]), martial-arts film (*Ashes of Time*, where melancholic characters prefer to brood in amorous longing rather than fight), and police thriller/film noir (*Chungking Express*, *Fallen Angels* [1995]). These popular genre roots, together with Wong's synthesis of the mood and movements of his characters with music – which, contra Abbas, *is* MTV-like – can be seen as the basis of his films' crossover appeal.[22]

The most internationally significant Hong Kong director to emerge after Wong is independent filmmaker Fruit Chan, whose films are about people in the backstreets of Mongkok, a district in Hong Kong's Kowloon peninsula. *Made in Hong Kong* (1997), *Little Cheung* (1999), *Durian Durian* (2000), *The Longest Summer* (1998) and *Hollywood Hong Kong* (2001) focus on Hong Kong's poor – volatile, disaffected youth and the new underclass of Mainland immigrants, especially those involved in the sex trade. They are good examples of what Desser calls the 'pan-Asian youth film', especially *Made in Hong Kong*, with its casual violence and apocalyptic ending.[23] This feature won the Hong Kong Best Film Award in 1996. It had the backing of star Andy Lau, an instance of how independent Hong Kong film production can get off the ground, while several of Chan's more recent films have been internationally funded. Chan's films combine documentary techniques (such as the use of non-professional actors) with international neo-noir-influenced fictional narratives. In *The Longest Summer*, fictional narrative is mixed with documentary footage of the handover. These films investigate social exploitation in post-handover Hong Kong, portraying places that other films rarely show: a typical shot vertiginously angles up or down crowded public housing estates, or winds down backstreet passageways.

Hong Kong into Hollywood

Against the backdrop of the handover and crisis in the film industry, a number of Hong Kong film personnel have been lured to Hollywood. Directors John Woo, Tsui Hark, Yuen Woo-Ping and Ringo Lam, and stars Michelle Yeoh, Jackie Chan, Jet Li and Chow Yun-Fat, have all been recruited to make Hollywood films. Terence Chang, who produced John Woo's last Hong Kong films, has become the main broker of Hong Kong's liaisons with Hollywood, securing *Replacement Killers* (1998) and *Anna and the King* (1999) for Chow Yun-Fat, and *Tomorrow Never Dies* (1997) for Michelle Yeoh. Hollywood producers realise the increasing importance of Asian markets and that casting proven Asian talent makes financial sense as a strategy of globalisation. *Tomorrow Never Dies* was a big success in East Asia due to Yeoh. However, Orientalising stereotypes – such as villainous Chinamen – have made it difficult for these actors to obtain appropriate Hollywood roles.[24] As Leon Hunt suggests, the absorption of Asian expertise into 'a cinema that continues to marginalise Asian performers' can be seen as a form of 'conquest' rather than a 'benign meeting'.[25]

Hollywood's appropriation of Hong Kong talent and action genres has consisted of three types: 'the high-octane gunplay of John Woo and Chow Yun-fat, the stunt-filled action-comedy of Jackie Chan and Sammo Hung, and the "wire fu" of Tsui Hark, Yuen Wo-Ping and Jet Li'.[26] In the wake of *The Matrix*, countless Hollywood films have been enlisting Hong Kong fight choreographers. Most in demand is Yuen Woo-Ping, now an international celebrity for his choreography of *The Matrix* trilogy, *Crouching Tiger* and *Kill Bill, Vols 1 and 2* (2003–4). *The Matrix*, moreover, set a precedent for 'authenticating' Hollywood stars by training them to perform their own fight scenes.[27] But while Hong Kong's fight scenes are not storyboarded or scripted and are more or less improvised on set, Hollywood shooting is rigorously planned. This has been a source of friction for Hong Kong directors in Hollywood. John Woo, for example, comments that 'In Hong Kong the director controls practically everything, but in Hollywood the producers and stars have an incredible amount of control'.[28]

The convergence between Hong Kong and Hollywood is two-way. In the new globalised climate, Hollywood is keen to invest in Hong Kong productions. In 1998, Columbia Pictures Asia was set up as the Hong Kong-based division of the Japanese conglomerate Sony, whose projects are vetted by Columbia Pictures in Hollywood. Its output includes *Crouching Tiger* and other Chinese-language films like *The Road Home* (1999). Meanwhile, local producers have incorporated Hollywood-style strategies, including bigger budgets and CGI, in order to win back domestic markets. Fast schedules, flexibility and impromptu decision-making, once key to the industry's productivity, are now thought to be partly responsible for its decline, leading to low-grade product which is unappealing to today's audiences accustomed to the standards of foreign imports.[29] The Hong Kong company MediaAsia, founded in the 1990s, now stipulates completed scripts and detailed budgets before shooting, and plans marketing months in advance.[30] Other new strategies include increased joint ventures with other East Asian countries such as Japan.[31]

These strategies were applied in Andrew Lau's and Alan Mak's recent success *Infernal Affairs* (2002), now expanded into a trilogy. Released at the end of a dismal box-office year, it grossed $7 million locally – a considerable amount in a territory whose population is about 7 million.[32] With a lower body count and less bloodshed than previous Hong Kong gangster films, *Infernal Affairs* generates narrative complexity by doubling the undercover motif found in films such as *Hard-Boiled*. It revolves around two men who are moles in their respective organisations: Yan (Tony Leung) is an undercover cop in a triad gang, while Ming (Andy Lau) is a triad mole among the police. The film emphasises metaphysical uncertainty bred by being trapped in long-term fake identities; both men undergo identity crises. In Woo tradition, there are mesmerising shots of two men locked in confrontation. This takes place on a rooftop, their disorientated, fractured identities reflected in Hong Kong's skyscrapers – suggesting that, several years after its return to China, Hong Kong itself is still struggling with its identity.

Close Analysis

Hard-Boiled (John Woo, 1992)

In *Hard-Boiled*, Woo collaborates with art directors James Leung and John Chong, and cinematographer Wong Wing-Heng, to produce one of his most visually stylish works, his last film before his departure to the USA. Some see it as his 'portfolio film for Hollywood'.[33] As neither purely Hong Kong nor yet Hollywood, *Hard-Boiled* can tell us a lot about the distinctive characteristics of Woo's filmmaking that make it hot property for the global marketplace. According to Desser, *Hard-Boiled* is 'the Asian entrée' to the 'international pulp genre', which draws its structures from 'combinations of film noir, gangster films and what used to be known as "pulp novels" or hard-boiled, violent thrillers'.[34] It is a particular outgrowth of 1980s Hollywood blockbusters such as *Die Hard* (1988), filled with 'high-powered explosions, special effects, and high body counts'.[35] In *Hard-Boiled*, Woo showcases his credentials as a director in this genre, particularly in the climactic hospital shoot-out.

The film, moreover, fuses Hollywood action blockbuster and the hard-boiled detective genre with the buddy film and martial-arts genre. Its violence must be understood in the socio-political context of the Tiananmen Square massacre and Hong Kong's return to China – a situation over which the Hong Kong population had no control, fuelling anxieties and pent-up frustrations. In Woo's work, handover insecurities generally trigger violent male heroics – both as a kind of catharsis and as a return of traditional male values – but *Hard-Boiled* sets out an additional response to Hong Kong's return to China, namely relocation, echoing Woo's own professional hopes of survival. This theme is announced in the early tea-house scene, where hard-boiled cop Tequila (Chow Yun-Fat) asks his partner Ah-Lung, 'Have you ever considered emigrating?' Immediately thereafter, a police code 'the invasion is about to begin' launches a raid.

Tequila loses his partner in this raid against a gun-smuggling ring headed by mobster Johnny Wong, who hides guns in birdcages and stashes his arsenal in a vault in the Maple Hospital morgue. Driven to avenge Ah-

Lung's death, Tequila encounters his *Doppelgänger* Tony (Tony Leung), who only wanted to be an ordinary cop yet is employed as an uncover triad killer. Tony mourns his lost identity. After confrontations where they nearly kill each other, Tony and Tequila finally work together to defeat Johnny.

The themes of justice, revenge and doubling are established in the teahouse fight. About to confront Ah-Lung's killer, Tequila rolls in flour, which whitens his face, making him look like 'a ghostly avenger out of Chinese opera'.[36] When Tequila shoots, the blood spurts over his own whitened face, underlining the viciousness of his own killing. Police chief Pang rebukes him for it – unknown to Tequila, the killer was an undercover cop. In this and other instances, Tequila shows his resentment at being a cog in a big organisation, expressing his own will against higher orders. Tequila's alienation from the 'system' is typical of Woo's heroes; however, as Kenneth Hall states, relationships of loyalty are crucial in Woo's films, as shown by the statue of ancient General Kwan Yi, who 'symbolizes loyalty', in the police station (Kwan Yi's statue appears in several Woo films).[37] Hence, Tequila learns in the course of the film to work as part of a team.

Appearances deceive in *Hard-Boiled*: there are images of melancholia and loss underneath the violent kinetic surface. Ostensibly a ruthless assassin, Tony grieves for the people he kills, especially his former gangland boss Mr Hoi, whom he respected. As a remorseful token for each killing, Tony makes paper cranes – symbols of transient life – which he hangs as mobiles in his yacht or drops into the water, where they are shown 'being borne off like little funeral barges'.[38] Meanwhile, his opposite number, Tequila, writes and plays a song for every cop who is killed. Even Johnny's ferocious henchman Mad Dog is guided by moral principles and challenges Johnny's senseless killing of innocent bystanders at the hospital, reminding him that he is only after the cops and that there are certain 'lines' one cannot cross.

The pairing of Tony and Tequila has an intimacy that goes beyond buddy genre norms. In a homoerotic gun-pointing sequence during a warehouse shoot-out, Tequila and Tony look into each other's eyes; their aggressive gazes give way to something more like brotherly tenderness. After this, the men only meet privately before they reunite for the hospital shoot-out. In a scene full of innuendo on Tony's yacht, Tequila has to hide before Johnny arrives – ostensibly lest he blow Tony's cover, yet the imagery suggests otherwise, as we see Tequila peeking out from under the pier, like a recondite lover.

In the hospital sequence, Woo uses a slow-motion Steadicam point-of-view shot when Tony takes Tequila hostage as a ruse to fool Johnny's men, underlining their teamwork – their 'double, yet unified vision'.[39] As Tony

and Tequila run down the hospital corridor, Woo positions them on opposite sides, making them continually cross places to underscore the doubling
motif.[40] At the climactic moment, Tony realises – like Tequila before him
– that he has killed a cop by mistake. Here, Woo's dramatic slow motion
emphasises Tony's shocked, belated reaction, with the camera dollying
towards his collapsing victim and then back to Tony.

The sidelining of women in these male-bonding relationships is shown
with Teresa, Tequila's colleague and estranged girlfriend, who forms triangular relationships with the men. In the beginning, much to Tequila's
bemusement, Teresa receives roses, apparently from a mysterious suitor.
The roses are really from Tony and contain messages in musical code (lines
from songs like 'I just called to say I love you') intended for Pang. Teresa
turns musical notes into numbers for decoding to Pang, who brusquely
shrugs aside her singing skills.

At the hospital, Teresa finds a single rose in her pocket, sent to her as a
message from Tequila, a 'trick' which he learnt from Tony. Hence, just as
Teresa is the medium of covert communication between Tony and Pang,
so she eventually becomes one between Tony and Tequila. Significantly,
the objects that circulate between the characters are associated with
romance, and particularly with women (love songs, roses). Despite sidelining female characters, Woo's films are known to appeal to (some)
women. This may be because they combine violent action with sentimentality and melodrama. This is not to say that women don't also enjoy undi-
luted violent spectacle, but that Woo's films offer certain pleasures to which
women traditionally have been known to respond. Additionally, Woo's
heroes have protective and caring attitudes to one another. This kind of
male 'mothering' also appears in the relationship between Mr White
(Harvey Keitel) and Mr Orange (Tim Roth) in *Reservoir Dogs*, a film
indebted to Woo.

In *Hard-Boiled*, the mothering motif culminates at the hospital, where
Tequila and Teresa try to save the countless babies left in the maternity
ward, a scene which creates opportunities for humour about men and
babies. Babies are the ultimate innocent hostages. Johnny's hostage-taking
and massacre of hospital patients therefore has a particular resonance with
the events of Tiananmen Square. The babies are Hong Kong's future population, and the blazing hospital a sign of apocalyptic despair at Hong
Kong's return to China.[41]

In contrast to the Hollywood films he makes now, heroes may die in
Woo's Hong Kong films. Tony redeems himself for his killings by sacrific-
ing himself for Tequila. He is 'resurrected' before the end credits. Tony's
resurrection and departure (his yacht sails off into the horizon, with a

voiceover repeating his wish to move to the North Pole) match the movement of spatial translation across the film – for example, the babies are relocated, one by one, 'to a safe place' – the motif of relocation laying down
future possibilities and conditions, including Woo's own emigration to the
USA and his subsequent redefinition of Hollywood action films.

In the Mood for Love (Wong Kar-Wai, 2000)

At Cannes in 2000, *In the Mood for Love* won Best Actor Prize for Tony
Leung and the Technical Achievement Award for cinematographers Chris
Doyle and Mark Li Ping-bing and editor/art-designer William Chang.
Tony Leung has performed in a range of East Asian films including *Hero*
(2002) and *City of Sadness* (1989) as well as appearing in previous Wong
films (including *Ashes of Time* and *Happy Together*) and Hong Kong thrillers like *Hard-Boiled* and *Infernal Affairs*. His tendency is to play solitary
and sorrowful characters, a persona exemplified in this film.

In the Mood for Love is made in a more restrained style than Wong's
earlier films, although links with his earlier work are clear. It was filmed
back-to-back with Wong's science-fiction feature *2046* (which premièred
at Cannes in 2004). Investors withdrawing due to the Asian financial crisis
and China's censorship laws delayed production for both films. *In the Mood
for Love* was eventually funded by French company Paradis-Orly Films.

Set in the 1960s, the film deals with the intimacy between two neighbours, Mr Chow (Tony Leung) and Mrs Chan (Maggie Cheung), who discover that their spouses are having an affair, but resolve not to be 'like
them'. According to Stephen Teo, it is a typical 'romance melodrama'
referring back to *wenyi pian* of that era; additionally, Teo says, its plot
echoes a 1940s Chinese film, *Springtime in a Small Town*.[42] But *In the Mood
for Love* draws on Western as well as Chinese melodramatic traditions. In
Wong's film, as in Douglas Sirk's melodramas, unarticulated emotions are
displaced into details of the *mise en scène*. Most of the action takes place in
enclosed spaces – apartments, restaurants, street corners – contrasting
with the film's 'coda' which opens onto a wider, geo-political space,
showing 1966 news footage of French President de Gaulle's arrival at
Pochentong airport, Cambodia (Chow, a journalist, is sent to cover it) and
a scene at Angkor Wat temple. Yet, throughout the film, geo-political
events exert a subtle pressure, testifying to the presence of an uncanny out-
of-field – a return of the repressed within its enclosed spaces.

Introducing episodes in the film are excerpts from Liu Yichang's 1972
novella, *Intersection*. These are 'restless times', they tell us at the start of
the film, gesturing to a wider but understated backdrop against which the

romance takes place – beginning in 1962, when the couples move into next-door apartments, coinciding with the tide of refugees from communist China into Hong Kong that caused housing shortages; and ending in 1966, the eve of the Cultural Revolution, when communist supporters provoked riots in the city, causing Hong Kong residents to move out. The film is set in the Shanghainese quarter, where Wong himself lived when he came to Hong Kong from Shanghai in 1963. For Wong, what is special about this period is that the immigrant families still retained local Chinese identities – dialects, food, popular music – believing Hong Kong to be a temporary residence away from China.[43] This, together with its Chinese title, *Huayang Nianhua*, which roughly translates as 'Full Bloom' or 'those wonderful varied years', might suggest that this is a nostalgia film.[44] Yet, if it is, it looks back at the past in order to use it to speculate about the future, as shots and ideas intended for *2046* – the title referring to the expiry date for Chinese promises to leave Hong Kong's socio-economic structure unchanged – migrate into the film, especially in sequences at the South Pacific Hotel, where Mr Chow rents a room, numbered 2046, ostensibly to write his martial-arts novels with Mrs Chan's help.

Throughout, as in other Wong films, there are no establishing shots of unified spaces. Instead there are repeated angles on certain spaces – including the red-curtained hotel corridor, the street corner and the stairs down to the noodle bar, where Mr Chow and Mrs Chan continually pass each other. Like Wong's other films, *In the Mood for Love* uses intersection as one of its structuring devices, as protagonists cross paths in ways determined by the spatial layout of their neighbourhood. These intersections moreover express the spatial status of Hong Kong itself as a place of migrants, a threshold at the intersection of other destinations, post-handover Hong Kong as much as Hong Kong of the 1960s. Thus, the enclosed spaces which the protagonists inhabit are shown as being produced by urbanisation and wider geo-historical mutations.

At the same time, the unseen becomes a guiding principle. The camera is secreted behind obstacles, filming from inside or underneath intimate, hidden-away spaces such as wardrobes, closets and beds. The frame is divided up with curtains, doorways, mirrors, vertical bars and diagonal stripes, ostensibly giving viewers the point-of-view of prying neighbours. We never see Mr Chow's and Mrs Chan's adulterous partners, except obliquely, usually from the back. This sets the stage for an elaborate game of doubling, which interrupts the narrative's linear flow, as Mr Chow and Mrs Chan wonder how their spouses' affair started – re-enacting who may have made the first move. Each time we begin to read their story purely as a chronicle of a romantic affair, the film catches us out with lines like 'you have my husband down pat', reminding us of the role-play. It also scuppers a platonic reading of their relationship with riddles, such as Mrs Chan's young son, who accompanies her at the end of the film, the identity of his father unknown. A number of narrative alternatives co-exist, subsisting in unseen, virtual dimensions, where Mrs Chan and Mr Chow are in fact just 'like' their unfaithful counterparts, contrary to their stated resolve.[45]

When Mrs Chan arrives at the South Pacific Hotel, she appears to turn on her heel and leave just as soon as she arrives, as overlapping shots show her ascending and descending the spiral stairway. As in a later scene, where Mr Chow discovers a lipstick-smudged cigarette in his Singapore hotel room *before* Mrs Chan has entered and smoked it, the shuffling of time makes Mrs Chan's sojourn in the room seem as if it were a virtual alternative to the one where she politely leaves – and the characters' selves and their 'others' multiply in mirrors strategically embedded in the *mise en scène*. 'What do you think they're doing now?' they wonder of their spouses, who are away, supposedly on business; the film abruptly flashes forwards to the red-curtained hotel corridor, and we see Mr Chow and Mrs Chan themselves in Room 2046 affecting stylised, coy poses, drenched in saturated colours.

Throughout the film, the setting – the ornate wallpaper in their flats and Mrs Chan's sensual, figure-hugging dresses – testifies to mechanisms of displacement, as does the music. A melancholy waltz, 'Yumeji's theme', accompanies their early passing encounters, mingling hints of passionate desire with the need for social conformity, while Nat King Cole's Spanish renditions drift in and out of their arranged rendezvous, and later his 'Quizas, Quizas, Quizas' ('Perhaps . . .') plays when Mr Chow leaves the hotel for Singapore, narrowly missing Mrs Chan, whom he invited to go with him. Room 2046 itself is set up as an erotic retreat, a repository of their secrets; but it subverts this function, refusing to remain closed and unconnected with the film's other, as yet unseen sets.

Room 2046 is always photographed ambiguously. The doors and red curtains which line the walls outside continually switch positions as shot-changes jump across the axis of action, giving the impression of a shifting, mutating space. Hotel corridors with their identical bedrooms could be seen as anonymous transnational spaces, but here the corridor is also a liminal space between endless virtual alternatives, or possible futures, the doorways leading to a number of other possible worlds. The room and the spatially distorted sequences surrounding it mark an osmosis between intimate and geo-political space, an index of shifting parameters in a complex, mutable, globalised world. When Mrs Chan walks away down the corridor, with her back to the camera, she suddenly freezes in mid-action while the camera pulls back in the opposite direction – a motif repeated later in the film with Mr Chow. This paradox – being both stationary and moving – is of a piece with Wong's other spatial paradoxes and the geographic and historic dislocations, displacements and transit zones which they express.

Mr Chow's journeys to and from Singapore and Cambodia also emphasise Hong Kong as a nodal point in an Asian and global network (the film itself was partly shot in Thailand). The spaces of Chow's Hong Kong and Singapore hotel rooms bleed into each other – the latter, filmed in shallow focus, appears blurry and indeterminate and in certain shots seemingly containing details, such as the red curtain and curving stairway banister, from the Hong Kong hotel.

In the coda, de Gaulle's visit to Cambodia heralds the end of another colonial era, a curtain call for France's relations with Indochina – an ominous reference to the ambiguous geo-political status of post-handover Hong Kong, no longer a British colony but now in a quasi-colonial relationship to China. Back then, even after France pulled out, Cambodia was still subject to colonial influences from China (which supported Cambodian communists, the Khmer Rouge) and America (whose war against communism in Vietnam spilled over into Cambodia). When Mr Chow breathes his secret into one of Angkor Wat's nooks, the overtly geo-political spaces of these concluding episodes retrospectively feed back, underlining how the 'politics of elsewhere' shapes even the most apparently closed spaces.[46]

Crouching Tiger, Hidden Dragon (Ang Lee, 2000)

A multinational blockbuster which ranks among the most successful foreign-language films ever released in the USA and winner of four Academy Awards, *Crouching Tiger, Hidden Dragon* belongs to the *wuxia pian* tradition and centres on two pairs of lovers. Yu Shu-Lien (Michelle Yeoh) loves *wu dang* swordsman Li Mu-Bai (Chow Yun-Fat), who is seeking to avenge his master, murdered by outlaw swordswoman Jade Fox (Cheng Pei Pei); but the couple remain celibate because of the codes of *jianghu*, the 'underworld of chivalrous, wandering outlaws', the background against which swordplay stories are typically set. These codes are steeped in Confucian values of 'filiality, fidelity, chastity, and respect for teachers and elders'.[47] Shu-Lien's betrothed, also killed by Jade Fox, was Mu-Bai's sworn 'brother', and the lovers must respect his memory. Governor's daughter Jen (Zhang Ziyi) and bandit Lo (Chang Chen), by contrast, are individualistic and impulsive in love as in their general conduct, transgressing barriers of class and ethnicity as well as Confucian

ethics. Jen steals Mu-Bai's powerful Green Destiny sword, casting suspicion on Jade Fox, Jen's fugitive governess and mentor.

The film is shot in Chinese Mainland studios and locations, with post-
production in Hong Kong. It is directed by Taiwanese émigré Ang Lee,
who established his reputation with films about the experiences of Chinese
overseas such as *The Wedding Banquet* (1993), then with US/UK films
such as the Jane Austen adaptation *Sense and Sensibility* (1995). *Crouching
Tiger*'s cast includes two Hong Kong actors (Chow Yun-Fat and Michelle
Yeoh), a Hong Kong choreographer (Yuen Woo-Ping), one mainland star
(Zhang Ziyi) and two Taiwanese actors (Chang Chen and former swordplay queen Cheng Pei Pei). Its unprecedented mainstream success worldwide puzzled East Asian audiences, as it did long-standing genre fans.
Before *Crouching Tiger*, kung fu had been more successful at breaking
through to non-Asian audiences – *A Touch of Zen* was the only previous
wuxia pian to do so. As usual, there were allegations that *Crouching Tiger*
pandered to the Orientalist tastes of 'Western' viewers, who were easily
seduced by 'the exotic beauty of martial choreography, but . . . incapable
of apprehending the "genuine spirit" of Chinese martial chivalry'.[48] For
some, the film's Oscars success was a sure sign of its surrender to the commercial values of 'American film culture' and the global superpower's 'cultural imperialism'. However, what such reactions miss is that the earlier
success of Hong Kong films paved its way in the West.

Like other *wuxia pian*, it inhabits a distant semi-fantastical past, where
temporal factors are blurred and anything is possible. Lee, moreover, establishes a cross-cultural mode of access, asserting: 'Family dramas and *Sense
and Sensibility* are about conflict, about family obligations versus free will
. . . In a family drama there is a verbal fight. Here, you kick butt.'[49] Unlike
regional audiences, who contested the film's cultural 'authenticity', international audiences focused on the physical grace of bodies in movement
and on the film's gender politics. Certainly, Lee's film is only following
generic precedent when it depicts such gravity-defying acts as scaling
walls, flurrying across rooftops and bounding across waves. Since the films
of Bruce Lee, global audiences have admired the 'speed and physical grace'
of Hong Kong action sequences.[50] But, as Tony Rayns points out,
Crouching Tiger utilises 'post-*Matrix* action choreography, which takes
weightless aerial combat literally to new heights' with a new generation of
digital effects deployed by Hong Kong's Asia Cine Digital for erasing wires
and pasting figures into landscapes.[51] Previously, in Hong Kong cinema,
wirework was 'lit out'.[52] In *Crouching Tiger*, and subsequently in *Hero*,
wirework, CGI and bodily performance are skilfully blended together.

What astonished international audiences further was that this physical power and movement was accessible to both men and women; indeed, it is the women who steal the show. Leon Hunt suggests that the centrality of fighting women was crucial to the response of Western audiences whose familiarity, if any, with Chinese martial arts genres was limited to Bruce Lee or Jackie Chan.[53] International audiences and critics have been fascinated by the film's gender politics, saluting the film's 'overtly feminist stance' as going beyond genre norms and identifying this as one of the film's key points of cross-cultural interest.[54] Ang Lee himself emphasises that women are the primary focus and men are secondary players, contrasting *Crouching Tiger*'s climactic fight scenes involving women with the 'real macho combat' for which Yuen Woo-Ping is renowned.[55]

Crouching Tiger in fact resurrects the swordplay heroine tradition, containing generic motifs such as a stolen sword, poisoned needles, disappearing tricks and 'a heroine who dresses as a boy'.[56] There are allusions to previous heroine films in the bamboo grove scene (*A Touch of Zen*) and the tavern scene (*Come Drink With Me*). But although swordplay heroines have featured in *wuxia pian* since the early twentieth century, they generally appear in secondary roles and rarely question patriarchal Confucian values.[57] In *Crouching Tiger*, by contrast, Jen and Jade Fox both express dissatisfaction with the patriarchal status quo. Jen wants to free herself from arranged marriage, believing that the world of *jianghu* lacks such constraints. She exclaims that Shu-lien cannot be married, because she would otherwise not be able to roam around so freely. However, Shu-Lien views *jianghu* differently, referring to herself as a woman bound by tradition. Indeed, she and Mu-Bai are depicted as being trapped by the Confucian ideals which they follow.

The film's title throws light on the film's gender politics. It alludes to the meanings of Jen's name ('Winsome Dragon') and Lo's name ('Little Tiger'); but 'Crouching tiger, hidden dragon' is also a well-known Chinese idiom, referring to 'hidden or unsuspected forces'.[58] One critic asserts, 'what is crouching is the traps of patriarchy. What is hidden is the law and order of the family.'[59] Female characters try to 'snatch, steal or protect' the Green Destiny Sword, thought to symbolise phallic power. Mu-Bai offers Jen *wu dang* training with the intention of subduing the 'poisoned dragon' which she could become without it, yet we know the *wu dang* has so far never accepted women. This is made clear in Jade Fox's story. Jade tells Mu-Bai, 'Your master had no respect for women. I was good enough to sleep with, but not to teach.' Because *wu dang* skills were barred to her, she stole the master's manual, but was unable to decipher it all due to her illiteracy. Jen, on the other hand, clandestinely reads the manual and hoards its secrets for herself, profiting from them since childhood, while Jade's own martial skills languish. Although portrayed as a villain, Jade Fox is in fact the film's 'most tragic figure', murdering to exact revenge for sex and class injustices, and finally betrayed by her own protégé.[60]

Crouching Tiger ends with Jen leaping from the cloud–capped *Wu dang* mountain, ostensibly following Lo's legend about the boy whose wishes came true when he did the same, floating 'far away, never to return'. This ending has been variously interpreted as a sacrifice to atone for Mu-Bai's death, as Jen's bid for independence, or as expressing the 'limited options' facing her, as a woman, despite being such a capable fighter.[61]

Notes

1. Li, 'Popular Cinema in Hong Kong', p. 708; Anon., 'Global Cinema Exhibition Markets', p. 303.
2. Abbas, *Hong Kong*, p. 25.
3. Bordwell, *Planet Hong Kong*, p. 32.
4. Rose, 'Hong Kong Phooey', p. 3.
5. Fore, 'Golden Harvest Films', p. 45.
6. Hunt, *Kung Fu Cult Masters*, p. 10.
7. Chan, *I Am Jackie Chan*, p. 174.
8. Li, 'Popular Cinema in Hong Kong', p. 710.
9. Ibid., p. 710.
10. Hall, *John Woo*, p. 4.
11. Ibid., pp. 34, 37.
12. Ibid., p. 55.
13. Ibid., pp. 6, 23.
14. Stringer, 'Tsui Hark', p. 348.
15. Chu, '*Swordsman II* and *The East Is Red*', p. 34.
16. Reynaud, '*Centre Stage*', p. 36.
17. Reynaud, 'I Can't Sell My Acting Like That', p. 24.
18. Louie, '*Floating Life*', p. 98.
19. See Bordwell, *Planet Hong Kong*, p. 282.
20. Abbas, 'The Erotics of Disappointment', p. 53.
21. Siegel, 'The Intimate Spaces of Wong Kar-Wai', p. 291.
22. See Yeh, 'Musical Discourses in Wong Kar-Wai's Films', p. 121.
23. Desser, 'Pan-Asian Youth', pp. 7, 14–15.
24. See Stringer, 'Scrambling Hollywood', pp. 229–42.
25. Hunt, *Kung Fu Cult Masters*, pp. 158, 181–2.
26. Ibid., p. 158.
27. Ibid., p. 180.
28. Stokes and Hoover, 'Hong Kong to Hollywood', p. 36.
29. Chu, *Hong Kong Cinema*, p. 126.
30. Ibid., p. 126.

31. Ibid., p. 124.
32. Rayns, 'Deep Cover', p. 26.
33. Bordwell, *Planet Hong Kong*, p. 100.
34. Desser, 'Pan-Asian Youth', pp. 7–8.
35. Ibid., p. 7.
36. Bordwell, *Planet Hong Kong*, p. 228.
37. Hall, *John Woo*, p. 28.
38. Ibid., p. 28.
39. Ibid., p. 44.
40. Ibid., p. 69.
41. Williams, 'Space, Place, and Spectacle', p. 79.
42. Teo, '*In the Mood for Love*'.
43. See *In the Mood for Love*, Tartan Special Edition DVD, 2001.
44. Teo, '*In the Mood for Love*'.
45. This 'forking path' narrative structure is associated with Argentinian writer Jorge Luis Borges, used in films by French New Wave director Alain Resnais, and recently popularised in hypertext internet fiction.
46. Orr, 'Wong Kar-Wai', p. 54.
47. Chen, '*Crouching Tiger*', p. 71.
48. Wu, '*CTHD* is Not a Chinese Film', p. 69.
49. Lee et al., *Crouching Tiger, Hidden Dragon*, p. 83.
50. Christopher, 'Fight Fantastic', p. 14.
51. Rayns, 'Crouching Tiger', p. 46.
52. Hunt, *Kung Fu Cult Masters*, p. 180.
53. Ibid., p. 117.
54. Rayns, 'Crouching Tiger', p. 46.
55. Lee et al., *Crouching Tiger, Hidden Dragon*, p. 42.
56. Hunt, *Kung Fu Cult Masters*, p. 118.
57. Leung, 'Crouching Sensibility', p. 51.
58. Chen, '*Crouching Tiger*', p. 71.
59. Cited in Wu, '*CTHD* is Not a Chinese Film', p. 73.
60. Hunt, *Kung Fu Cult Masters*, p. 138.
61. Ibid., pp. 138–9.

CHAPTER 7

South Asian Cinema

Among South Asia's film industries, India's is by far the most prolific, generating over 900 films annually. About a quarter of these are produced by the industry known as Bollywood or 'Hindi cinema', which is based in Mumbai (the city formerly named Bombay). Its films dominate the national market; and, of all the world's film industries, it faces the tiniest competition from Hollywood. It has been exporting its films successfully around the world (especially to parts of Africa, the Middle East, and Asiatic regions of the former Soviet Union) for more than half a century. Its current foreign sales moreover extend beyond these traditional export markets to emigrant communities in the UK, the USA, Canada and Australia. Bollywood is tipped to become the West's next Asian crossover phenomenon after Hong Kong cinema, although it has yet to convert mainstream Western audiences, who are allegedly put off by the melodramatic acting, song-and-dance sequences and non-linear plots. Within India and abroad, the traditional division between India's popular cinema and its 'art' or 'parallel' cinema, modelled after India's most prestigious film-director Satyajit Ray, often produced the uncritical assumption that Indian films are either 'Ray or rubbish'. Recent Indian film criticism has started to pay serious attention to India's popular cinema, assessing it on its own discursive terms. The spotlight on Bollywood, however, has often been at the expense of other South Asian cinemas, including India's many other film industries, making films in over fourteen regional languages, and the cinemas of Pakistan, Bangladesh and Sri Lanka, which this chapter briefly covers alongside a consideration of Bollywood's popular idiom.

Despite their linguistic and religious diversity, South Asian territories have often been linked by a shared history and culture, including an ancient Hindu and Buddhist cultural heritage. After the arrival of Islam (starting in the seventh century), Muslim rulers held sway over most of the region until it passed into the hands of the British, who maintained their grip over their subjects with the connivance of native (Hindu, Muslim and Sikh) rulers. The 200-year British Raj ended in 1947 with the partition of India into two independent states – India, where Hindus constituted the majority, and Pakistan, which was formed from the Muslim-dominant

North-west provinces (West Pakistan) and the eastern part of the province of Bengal (East Pakistan), liberated in 1971 as Bangladesh. Sri Lanka (then called Ceylon), where Buddhist Sinhalese are the majority and Tamils (mostly Hindus) are the minority, became independent in 1948.

In terms of aesthetics, South Asia displays an extraordinary cultural mixing which presents a 'striking discontinuity' with events in the political realm, including the sectarian religious riots that accompanied partition.[1] Yet this 'syncretism' derives from its history – including the intertwining of Hindu and Muslim influences in the cultural milieu during the centuries of Muslim rule as well as European influences mostly during the British Raj and globalising forces since then. Orthodox Muslims disapproved of music and dance as a form of entertainment, yet Muslim rulers patronised musicians, singers and poets, whose *ghazals* (a form of Urdu or Persian poetry) were set to music. Moreover, the Sufis, who helped to convert the subcontinent's poor and low-caste Hindus to Islam, spread their message through the medium of song and dance and other forms of folk culture.[2]

This cultural syncretism can be seen in the region's parallel cinema, which has a tradition of embracing intercommunal tolerance.[3] It is equally evident in Indian popular cinema's oft-recurring (though not always acknowledged) romance with Islam: as Shohat and Stam remark, films such as *Anarkaii* (1953) and *Mughal-e-Azam* (1960), which glorify Indo-Islamic culture, were produced in the aftermath of partition and 'adored by the same Hindu audience that was attacking Muslims in the streets'.[4] Many Muslim stars have remained 'wildly popular even at the height of Hindu–Muslim tensions' – including Dilip Kumar, Meena Kumari and Nargis during the 1950s and 1960s, and Shahrukh Khan and Aamir Khan in the 1990s. Moreover, despite its name, 'Hindi' cinema actually utilises Hindustani, a composite of Hindi and Urdu languages widely understood in the region by Hindu and Muslim audiences alike.

The underlying forms of Indian popular cinema – melodrama, spectacle, song and dance, and omnibus plots – have evolved from pre-cinematic roots in the Indian epics *Mahabharata* and *Ramayana* (which embody Hindu religious beliefs and the 'sacredness' of family institutions), classical and folk theatre (where drama takes the form of dance), and nineteenth- and early twentieth-century Parsi theatre (a European-influenced theatre which based its mass commercial appeal on a mix of 'realism and fantasy, narrative and spectacle, music and dance, lively dialogues and ingenious stagecraft' within a melodramatic framework).[5] Indian popular cinema has combined these 'local' sources with inspiration from 'international' forms including Hollywood (especially the glamour of its star system and the musical) and, since the late 1980s, from MTV. Indian popular films are sometimes called *masala* films (*masala* means 'mix of spices') because of the assorted elements – song and dance, action, comedy and melodrama – that can be found together in a single film. This *masala* feature is not exclusive to Indian popular cinema. As already seen, it is present in varying degrees in several other world cinemas, including Hong Kong cinema, and the 'something for everybody' formula – a sure blockbuster principle – is increasingly used in Hollywood, including the three-hour action/melo-drama/historical romance/disaster epic that is James Cameron's *Titanic*.

India's regional-language cinemas often use this popular idiom, adding their particular flavours to it. There are many exchanges between the region's film industries in terms of stars, directors and other personnel, although – with the exception of South Indian cinema – the distribution of regional-language films is largely restricted to their own region. The Indian idiom, which evolved when Pakistan and Bangladesh were part of India, has moreover defined the model of popular cinema in Pakistan, Bangladesh and Sri Lanka (where there were early links with the film industry based in the southern Indian state of Tamil Nadu). However, the market dominance of Indian popular cinema has been a formidable chal-lenge to South Asia's other cinemas; and, in order to win audiences for local films, the non-Indian territories have tried to distinguish their cinemas from the Indian model as well as imitating it. Tensions have also been polit-ically fuelled. From 1965 to 2003, Pakistan and India banned each other's films, but audiences in Pakistan watched Indian films on pirated prints and, later, on satellite TV.

There are remarkable convergences, too, between South Asia's parallel cinemas. These films consciously display an aesthetic restraint absent from Indian popular cinema, using codes of realism derived from European cinema, particularly Italian neorealism (for example, location shooting in natural light) and the minimalist aesthetic of Robert Bresson.

The rest of this chapter will analyse the norms and practices of the region's popular and parallel cinemas further, emphasising regional simi-larities and differences, including the common themes to which their over-lapping histories give rise – partition, communalism, the fragility of nationhood and independence, military confrontation, terrorism and relig-ious fundamentalism, with films sometimes using the family or the role of womanhood as metaphors for problems afflicting the nation.

Popular Indian Cinema

Indian filmmaking has its beginnings in the pre-Independence era, start-ing as early as 1896. Major film studios were established in the 1920s; the 'big three' of these were New Theatres in Calcutta, Prabhat in Pune and Bombay Talkies, which created a solid infrastructure, including distribution networks and star manufacture, before the Second World War, by which time Indian films already dominated the national market.[6] During the war, the film industry boomed – largely due to the entry of independent financiers wanting to launder money earned on the war's black market. After the war, the studio system collapsed, giving rise to a system of highly-paid freelance artists (actors, music directors and playback singers). Black money has continued to pour into the industry. Other finances come from presale to distributors and additionally, in the present era, from media conglomerates such as Polygram and the Amitabh Bachchan Corporation.[7]

Hindi film gained its nationwide audiences in the immediate post-independence era. At the same time, the 'All-India' aesthetic – the name given to Hindi film by eminent film critic Chidananda Dasgupta – came to be extended to regional film industries, including the Tamil, Telegu, Bengali and Marathi film industries.[8] In 1952, the new Indian government established the National Board of Censors, carrying over the tradition of censorship from the colonial government, which instituted it in 1918. India's strict censorship bears the colonial era's legacy, including its Victorian morality – nudity and 'profanity' are prohibited, and politically sensitive issues are off-limits.

Apart from this (and exhibition tax), the Indian government has not played an official role in the popular film industry, refusing to grant it 'industry status' until 2002, when it finally allowed producers access to bank loans and insurance.[9] Indian films have captured the national market without government help, taking as much as 97 per cent of the domestic box office even before state protectionist policies in the 1960s and early 1970s led America's Motion Picture Association to boycott the Indian market.[10] While the lifting of trade barriers in the 1990s has allowed Hollywood to earn more from India than it ever did in the past, it has not yet dented Indian audiences' overwhelming preference for local films. Filmmaking in India nevertheless remains a risky business with, on average, 90 per cent of Indian films flopping at the box office – of the remaining 10 per cent, 5 per cent do moderately well and another 5 per cent are blockbusters, keeping the industry afloat.[11]

There have been many attempts to explain Indian popular cinema's vast appeal not only across barriers of language, religion and caste in India but also to audiences in the Middle East and East Africa, where Indian popular cinema has crossed over from diasporic Indian audiences to mainstream audiences, who enjoy and identify with the films without knowing the language and without the benefit of dubbing or subtitles. The following account concentrates on aesthetics and narrative style, as these are the core elements of the cinema's national, regional and global appeal, leaving aside discussion of themes specific to contemporary Bollywood for Chapter 8.

Indian popular cinema's pan-Indian appeal has been analysed in terms of its roots in the *Mahabharata* and *Ramayana*, which have 'profoundly influenced the thought, imagination, outlook of the vast mass of Indian people'.[12] Their influence can be seen in the films' characters, narrative structure, ideologies and modes of address. Characters are frequently based on archetypes drawn from the epics; for example, the dutiful self-sacrificing mother or wife (like Sita in *Ramayana*) and the banished son (like the princes in both epics). Because they are recognisable archetypes, characters' psychological motives are generally not fleshed out; in any case, the collective (family or community) is always more important than an individual. Narratives are based on moral principles found in the epics: family obligation, duty and honour (notions of family honour being closely tied to a daughter's honour, i.e. chastity) and the omnipotence of 'fate'. Chance and coincidence play an emphatic role, sometimes with divine intervention producing the dénouement of the plot.

As this implies, codes of believability are quite different from the standards of 'realism' in Hollywood or European films. Yet there remains, as Rosie Thomas states, 'a firm sense of "acceptable realism and logic"' derived from moral principles:

> One is more likely to hear accusations of 'unbelievability' if the codes of, for example, ideal kinship behaviour are ineptly transgressed (i.e. a son kills his mother; or a father knowingly and callously causes his son to suffer), than if the hero is a superman who single-handedly knocks out a dozen burly henchmen and then bursts into song.[13]

K. Moti Gokulsing and Wimal Dissanayake remark that 'the central ideology underpinning the two epics is of preserving the existing social order and its privileged values' and that Indian popular cinema often 'legitimises its own existence through a reinscription of its values onto those of the two epics'.[14] Some have argued that films like Raj Kapoor's *Awaara* (1951) and the 1970s Angry Young Men films associated with superstar Amitabh Bachchan (*Zanjeer* [1973], *Deewar* [1975], *Sholay* [1975]), which critique social, political and economic injustices (the latter coinciding with Prime Minister Indira Gandhi's State of Emergency [1975–7], when she assumed dictatorial powers), question the status quo only ultimately to affirm it. Yet, as with any conservative-traditionalist films, there are many ways in which global audiences can, and do, read them.

In contrast to classical Hollywood narratives, which follow a linear, causal logic, the narratives of Indian popular cinema are episodic and digressive, often containing plots within plots and a flashback structure transporting viewers back and forth in time. This flashback structure is deployed in films as disparate as *Mother India* (1957), from Bollywood's 1950s 'golden era', and the contemporary Bollywood 'brat pack' film *Kabhi Khushi Kabhie Gham* (2001). The length of these is suitably epic – three hours or more, with a built-in halfway intermission. This affects how scripts are planned and structured; any given film will have two climactic 'turning points': one in the middle and one at the end.

Most of the films' narrative features stem from the epics, which were transmitted orally in endless repeated performances. However, Sheila J. Nayar has argued that these features, often seen as indigenously 'Indian', are common to oral storytelling practice more generally, and that this is what constitutes the appeal of Bollywood cinema across national borders.[15] In this respect, it is noteworthy that Indian films are popular in nations where there are 'significant numbers of non- or low-literate viewers' and that films that attempt to depart from oral storytelling characteristics do not succeed with non-elite, that is uneducated and rural, audiences. The appeal to oral cultures is not unique to Indian popular cinema – we have encountered it in Egyptian and other cinemas. It is even apparent in Hollywood films like *Titanic*, whose global success may be partly attributable to its use of oral storytelling flashback.

Indian popular films have a tendency to quote each other: 'an endless borrowing-cum-stealing of previous movies' tunes, lyrics, dialogue, iconic props, whole characters, and sometimes even entire plots'.[16] Nayar explains this 'intertextuality' with the fact that Indian popular films, like oral stories, are collectively owned by the group, which does not recognise the concept of plagiarism or copyright, both of which arise with print cultures. The narrative predictability of many popular Indian films can be seen in this context: their priority is to maximise emotion and spectacle, emphasising '*how* things will happen' rather than *what* will happen and 'familiarity and repeat viewings rather than "originality"'.[17] Their audiences are known to 'clap, sing, recite familiar dialogue with the actors' and – appreciatively – 'throw coins at the screen'.[18] Repeat value is built into films through the stars and songs, which keep audiences coming to see films again and again.

Sound is an essential element of oral cultures, as already noted (in Chapter 3). In India, the arrival of sound enabled Indian cinema to create features that protected it from Hollywood and sealed its distinctive appeal for audiences in India and abroad – the song sequences, music (a hybrid of light classical Indian music including *ghazals* and Western orchestral and popular music) and declamatory dialogue. In India, the popular music and film industries are intertwined. For core audiences, a film stands or falls on the basis of its songs. Actors rarely sing their own songs, so films deploy playback singers, with the actors lip-synching to lyrics – a practice dating back to the 1940s. Playback singers are stars in their own right – among the most famous are the sisters Lata Mangeshkar and Asha Bhosle, who have provided singing voices on Bollywood films from the 1950s to the present. Songs are released before the film; in the past on the radio, now on cassette and CD. Films can recover over half their budget by the presale of their music. In this respect, Indian popular cinema can be regarded as a model anticipating Western cinematic practice.[19] For, in European and Holly-wood cinema, popular music soundtracks are not only increasingly being used to market films, but have also come to define the appeal of many films to their audiences.

According to Nayar, sound is not the only element which is amplified in Bollywood cinema. Star performance, camerawork (which is flamboyant, unlike classical Hollywood's 'invisible style') and *mise en scène* (where 'the real' is abandoned in favour of 'the grand') resemble 'the mnemonic phrases of an oral epic' – commanded into a form that will 'render them permanently memorable'.[20] Bollywood stars are typically big and brash – not just icons of beauty and desire (although they are these too, for example, 1994's Miss World, Aishwarya Rai). Not for nothing is Amitabh Bachchan, whose superstar status remains unrivalled, also known as the 'Big B'. Bollywood stars, who present themselves on screen as stars rather than characters in roles, must 'stand out from the background; they cannot belong to it'.[21] There are, of course, other historical reasons why Indian film stardom is such a big phenomenon. Star power has been a key element in financing films since the arrival of independent financiers who lured stars with huge salaries; and, because of the high box-office failure rate, many contemporary Bollywood films are 'multi-starrers', featuring as many as five or six top stars in order to try to hedge bets on success.

In the 1980s and early 1990s, colour television, TV soap operas (including the massively popular serialisation of the *Ramayana* and *Mahabharata* on the state-run network Doordarshan), video piracy and multi-channel TV (including MTV) lured audiences away from cinema. Exposure to MTV and foreign influences created new expectations in Indian audiences. In order to sustain their mass appeal, filmmakers began to use MTV techniques, incorporating them into their popular idiom. Since the advent of MTV, 'song picturisations' (the industry term for song-and-dance sequences) or clips from films edited to the music have been shown on satellite channels as a marketing strategy.[22] The fact that the song-and-dance sequences circulate as self-contained items on music television makes visible aesthetic affinities between the films and music video, which has stimulated new ways of filming dance sequences, including the use of MTV-like cutting and camera angles. For pop video also involves performers lip-synching to pre-recorded music. In the films, song-and-dance sequences are often set against exotic backdrops completely unrelated to the narrative, regularly flouting spatial and temporal continuities so that 'heroines may change saris between shots and the scenery . . . skip continents between verses'.[23] This is not dissimilar in practice to pop video, where the relation between visual images and musical lyrics is often shifting and arbitrary. Also, if MTV embodies 'the look of sound', that, too, makes it an ideal import for a cinema based on oral storytelling tradition.

The song-and-dance sequences are a key site for the outpouring of emotions, including emotions which otherwise cannot be publicly professed, such as fantasy, eroticism and other forms of 'subversive' behaviour (including gender subversion). Lovers' fantasies in the form of dream sequences and stage shows are among the many means devised by filmmakers to express eroticism within restrictions imposed by censorship and public (or family) viewing contexts.[24] Also popular is the 'wet sari' routine, where the heroine rhapsodises about an absent lover while dancing in a downpour of rain or wading into a lake, her soaked clothes clinging to her body and revealing its sensuous contours. Elsewhere in the narrative, we often witness the 'withdrawal-of-the-camera technique', which Lalita Gopalan terms 'coitus interruptus' – that is, when 'steamy' love scenes are replaced by 'extra-diegetic shots of waterfalls, flowers, thunder, lightning and tropical storms'.[25]

India's Parallel Cinema

Parallel cinema, also called 'New Indian Cinema', defined itself against the norms of Indian popular cinema – initially, at least, it was songless, starless and low-budget.[26] The name 'parallel cinema' arose because it diverged so radically from the mainstream and seemed 'unlikely to intersect with it at any point'.[27] However, the two streams do have links and common roots which can be traced back to the Indian People's Theatre Movement (IPTA), a left-wing avant-garde collective of writers, dramatists, musicians and filmmakers founded in 1943 and based in Bombay. The IPTA influenced the political and aesthetic principles of some classic Bollywood actors, writers and directors including Bimal Roy and Raj Kapoor, as well as parallel cinema's ethos as a whole. In 1952, the First International Film Festival took place in India, exposing filmmakers to European film aesthetics, especially Italian neorealism, which impacted on 1950s Bollywood and parallel cinema alike.

Bengali director Satyajit Ray is variously regarded as either the forerunner or the founder of parallel cinema. His 'Apu Trilogy' – *Pather Panchali* (1955), *Aparajito* (1956) and *Apur Sansar* (1959) – has greatly inspired subsequent directors. Ray himself was influenced by Italian neorealism and French poetic realism, especially that of Jean Renoir, as well as by Bengali literature, particularly Rabindranath Tagore (literary influences are a characteristic feature of Bengali cinema, where there are fewer films derived from the epics than in other Indian cinemas). The Apu Trilogy charts the growth of Apu, a poor Brahmin boy, who experiences the hardships of rural poverty, urban migration and the deaths of all his family members through illness. The most famous is *Pather Panchali*, which won the Best Human Document award at Cannes in 1956. Ray's subsequent films have covered a wide range of genres and issues, including *The Chess Players* (1977) (a satire of British colonialism, the Mughal aristocracy and upper classes), musical comedies, children's detective stories, documentaries, and films that probe gender relations in Indian society, with films focusing on lonely married women (*Charulata* [1964]) and young middle-class men (*Days and Nights in the Forest* [1970]). Although Ray's cinema transcends regional cinema defined in the narrowest sense – his undisputed international reputation is testimony to this – most of his films *are* regional in accomplishing a trenchant dissection of Bengali middle-class sensibilities. *Kanchenjunga* (1962) and his final film *The Stranger* (1991) exemplify this vein.

The financing of parallel cinema is shared between regional and central state governments and various co-operatives. The Indian government established the Film Finance Corporation in 1960 (which became the National Film Development Corporation [NFDC] in 1980) and a National Film Institute in 1961 expressly to support parallel rather than popular cinema. Another Bengali filmmaker and precursor of parallel cinema, Ritwik Ghatak, whose *Cloud-Capped Star* (1960) depicted the aftermath of partition, was appointed director of the National Film Institute. Many parallel-cinema directors emerged under his guidance at the Institute, which also nurtured technical, acting and directorial talent flowing into mainstream cinema. In 1973, the government also set up the Directorate of Film Festivals (DFF) to organise international and national film festivals in the country, and to hold the annual National Awards ceremony.

The NFDC spread its funds thinly, resulting in low production values. It was also notoriously bad at distributing films, which often end up staying on shelves for months or years before going to festivals.[28] Bollywood's control over distribution networks poses a further disadvantage for parallel filmmakers. The privately produced soap operas which began to appear on state-owned network TV in the mid-1980s and the arrival of multi-channel TV in the 1990s were, initially, another setback, luring away parallel cinema's largely urban middle-class audiences. However, some parallel films are now funded by multinational companies involved in satellite and cable TV, creating new distribution outlets.[29] International co-productions form another new source of funding.

The parallel cinema of the 1970s and 1980s belongs to the Third Cinema model of radical collective filmmaking and includes the work of Bengali director Mrinal Sen, whose *Bhuvan Shome* (1969) is a landmark of the movement. Parallel cinema has since fractured into what is known as 'Middle Cinema' – which combines parallel cinema themes and popular cinema devices in order to appeal to a broader audience – and a cinema of *auteurs*.[30] The objective of presenting an 'authentic' version of Indian reality often takes parallel filmmakers to rural locations, telling regional stories using regional dialects. Some films employ regional songs and dances in place of popular cinema's fantasy song-and-dance routines; for example, Shaji Karun's *Vanaprastham* (1999) makes striking use of Kerala's classical dance-drama Kathakali, while Buddhadeb Dasgupta's *Uttara* (2000) features Bengali *natuas*, who sing and dance wearing masks.

Inspired by Marxist sympathies for India's exploited populations (including its Fourth World tribes) and the 1970s Women's Movement, parallel filmmakers have tended to focus on feudal, caste and gender oppressions, including Hindu customs which encourage widows to sacrifice their life and which forbid them to remarry. These themes can be traced from Ray's films to today's parallel filmmakers such as Gautum Ghosh, whose *In the Forest . . . Again* (2003), a sequel to Ray's *Days and Nights in the Forest*, shows the forest baring its 'teeth' – the anger of tribals whose forest habitat the rich use as a tourist destination. An interest in women and minority populations has been reawakened by the fiftieth anniversary of India's independence, which prompted some filmmakers to explore the attempts of marginals to enter the mainstream or to contest India's independence settlement on behalf of its minorities. Films in this category include Shyam Benegal's Muslim women trilogy (discussed below) and Rituparno Ghosh's *Chokher Bali* (2003).

The popularly acclaimed films of Shyam Benegal, who hails from Andhra Pradesh but works from Mumbai, have been seen as examples of Middle Cinema. Benegal made his debut feature *Ankur* in 1974. His films typically critique the stereotypes of the 'honourable' wife, mother and daughter in Indian cinema and are concerned with gender, caste and class issues, exploring periods of national or social transition from the perspective of minority or underprivileged classes. He has launched many actors who have either crossed into the mainstream (Smita Patil and Amrish Puri) or gone on to successful international careers (Shabana Azmi, Naseeruddin Shah and Om Puri). Benegal has also been a huge influence on several female directors who began making films addressing women's sexuality and desires during the 1980s, including his niece Kalpana Lajmi (whose *Rudaali* [1993] uses the format of popular cinema – glamour, song and dance, melo-drama – to examine the stereotype of the suffering Indian woman) and Bengali director Aparna Sen (discussed below).

For the trilogy focusing on India's Muslim minority – *Mammo/ Grandmother* (1994), *Sardari Begum* (1996) and *Zubeidaa* (2000) – Benegal collaborated with scriptwriter Khalid Mohammed, editor of the popular Indian film magazine *Filmfare*. The trilogy's last film *Zubeidaa* features Bollywood actress Karisma Kapoor, a popular soundtrack by A. R. Rahman, and dance sequences (most of them 'justified' within the diege-sis according to dictates of narrative realism). It has been Benegal's most commercially successful film yet – a sign of his recognition of the impor-tance of product packaging and branding in the new global market.[31] Its tag line, 'Zubeidaa – the story of a princess', highlights the film's fairy-tale romance and glamour qualities. The film exemplifies Benegal's ability to narrate appealing stories about real-life social causes, for the story of aspir-ing Muslim actress Zubeidaa who marries a Hindu prince is based on Khalid Mohammed's mother and set against the backdrop of a nation in transition (Indian Muslims fleeing across the border to Pakistan and former princes being forced to yield their feudal lands to the state). It shows a woman doubly marginalised by her community and class, and whose existence 'official' history has effectively erased.

The cinema of *auteurs* has flourished in Bengal and Kerala, partly sup-ported by these regions' Marxist governments and high literacy levels. Kerala's internationally acclaimed *auteurs* include Adoor Gopalakrishnan and Shaji Karun, while Bengal has the films of Aparna Sen, Buddhadeb Dasgupta, Gautam Ghosh and Rituparno Ghosh to testify to this regional film industry's resurgence. Bengal's film industry is based in Tollygunge, South Calcutta (hence known as 'Tollywood'), where a thriving 'commer-cial' sector exists alongside the *auteur* cinema, both sectors benefiting in recent years from increased private investment. There are crossovers between the two in the form of stars and crew, and also with the Bangladeshi film industry; for example, Tollywood actress Rituparna Sengupta has made films in Calcutta and Bangladesh (as well as in South India and Bollywood).

A former actress and daughter of renowned film critic Chidananda Das

Gupta, Aparna Sen made her directorial debut with *36 Chowringhee Lane* (1981). Her films typically focus on women and outsiders – here, an Anglo-Indian schoolteacher, and in *Paroma* (1984) a married woman who is abandoned by her lover. Sen won the Best Director prize at the 2003 National Films Awards for *Mr and Mrs Iyer* (2002), an English-language production like her debut. This film focuses on an encounter between a young Tamil Brahmin mother, Meenakshi Iyer (played by Sen's daughter Konkona Sensharma), and a Muslim photographer, Raja Chowdhury (Rahul Bose), on a bus hijacked by rioting Hindus. Although, prior to this, Meenakshi had abhorred him as 'unclean', she declares that Raja is her husband in order to save his life from threatened assault by the rioters. Vision and visuality are the film's key metaphors: Meenakshi learns to broaden her Hindu caste-bound perspective through the act of focusing through Raja's camera lens.[32]

Sen laid the framework for Rituparno Ghosh's films, including *Unishe April* (1994) (in which she stars), *Dahan* (1997), *Utsab* (2000) and *Chokher Bali* (also influenced in their style and subject matter by Ray). She has equally influenced a new generation of English-language (and non-Bengali) filmmakers including Dev Benegal, whose Mumbai-set *Split Wide Open* (1999) revolves around a confessional TV chat show and dissects a society reeling from the impact of globalisation and changing attitudes to sex, marriage and divorce. Rahul Bose, another actor, combines the influence of Dev Benegal and Sen in his directorial debut *Everybody Says I'm Fine!* (2001), whose telepathic hairdresser Xen analyses the rifts beneath the surface of Mumbai's high society.

Buddhadeb Dasgupta made his debut feature *Dooratwa* in 1978. He has won several prizes at the National Awards, including Best Director for *Uttara* (2000). Stylistically, his films break with the realist model of other Bengali films discussed here, transposing contemporary social concerns into dreamlike imagery. Set in rural Bengal, *Uttara* has magic realist and gothic elements reminiscent of British Victorian fairy-painter Richard Dadd, including a community of dwarves – representative of all marginals – who hope that the 'tall regime' will soon be over. The film explores the homoerotic relationship between Uttara's husband Balaram and his friend Nemai, who wrestle with each other on the hills, massaging each other's glistening bodies and rolling together in the sand, oblivious to a mob of Hindu militants who burn a Christian priest to death, execute one of the dwarves, and (it is implied) rape and kill Uttara.

Cinema of South India and Sri Lanka

Although Bollywood films claim the largest share of the national market, popular films from India's southern states – Andhra Pradesh, Tamil Nadu, Kerala and Karnataka – are gaining influence and reaching large nationwide audiences through dubbing. The regional languages of these states are Telugu (Andhra Pradesh), Tamil (Tamil Nadu), Malayalam (Kerala) and Kannada (Karnataka). Since the 1970s, the output of the southern industries has far exceeded Bollywood. The majority of southern Indian films, especially from Andhra Pradesh and Tamil Nadu, follow the popular song-and-dance idiom. Tamil cinema achieved its first all-India hit with *Chandralekha* (1948), and since then it has frequently remade its films in Hindi for all-India audiences. It has also obtained overseas success among Tamil populations in Singapore, Malaysia and Sri Lanka. The hub of film production in the south is Tamil Nadu's capital Chennai (Madras), which is where the industries of South India and Sri Lanka originated. In the past, a hierarchy between the northern and southern industries existed. For example, minor or fading northern stars would travel south in the hope of resuscitating their careers, while moving in the other direction was the sole prerogative of those female stars whose dance training and fairer skin made them more eligible for exchange.[33] Now the south is believed to excel the north in many respects and has gained a reputation for the quality of its technical infrastructure, including its colour labs, state-of-the-art digital technologies and sound-processing facilities (which have improved the dubbing of Tamil and other southern-language films into Hindi since the 1970s). The higher production values of Bollywood films since the 1990s are mostly due to using southern post-production labs. The careers of current stars also shows a different pattern from the past; for example, the Karnataka-born Aishwarya Rai made her breakthrough into the film industry with Mani Ratnam's Tamil film *Iruvar* (1997) and, since becoming one of Bollywood's top actresses, has returned to the south for *Kandukondain Kandukondain* (2000), a Tamil adaptation of Jane Austen's *Sense and Sensibility*. South India is renowned for its film stars going into state politics and political parties using cinema for political ends. *Iruvar* is based on the biggest of these star politicians, M. G. Ramachandran (known as MGR), and re-enacts excerpts from his films in its song-and-dance sequences.

Southern filmmakers like Mani Ratnam (whose work is discussed in Chapter 8), Ram Gopal Varma and Priyadarshan have altered the profile of India's 'national' cinema. So too have the south's technical specialists: cinematographers P. C. Sriram and Santosh Sivan, and music composer A. R. Rahman (who formed a highly successful team with Ratnam), have all attained star status in their own right. The Keralan Santosh Sivan, who is responsible for the distinctive visuals of *Rudaali* and some of Ratnam's 1990s films, has directed his own movies, notably *The Terrorist* (1999) and *Asoka* (2001). Inspired by Prime Minister Rajiv Gandhi's assassination, *The Terrorist* is shot in a realist style comparable to contemporary European films (see Chapter 1), using hyperactive camerawork and unbalanced perspective to access the subjectivity of Sri Lankan suicide bomber Malli. It famously gained the admiration of American actor John Malkovich, who personally negotiated its US distribution.

Sri Lankan cinema has strong historical links with South Indian cinema: many of the first Sri Lankan films were made in South Indian studios with South Indian crews, and shared common roots in myth, melodrama and song and dance. There were, however, early attempts to 'indigenise' Sri Lankan cinema, led by Sirisena Wimalaweera in the 1950s as part of the post-independence Sinhalese nationalist movement.[34] Due to subsequent divisions between the island's two main ethnic groups and the dominance of the Sinhalese majority, post-1950s Sri Lankan cinema has largely been Sinhala cinema in its language and outlook. Alongside the popular cinema, which continued to produce melodramatic films with song and dance, there emerged an art cinema favouring 'realistic' themes and dialogue conventions similar to Sinhala stage drama. Its pioneer was Lester James Peries – Sri Lanka's answer to Satyajit Ray – who received international acclaim for *Rekava* (1956) and has continued making films into his eighties. His wife Sumitra Peries became Sri Lanka's first female director in the late 1970s.

In 1972, when the new constitution renamed the island Sri Lanka, the state nationalised the film industry and put it under the monopoly of the State Film Corporation – now called the National Film Corporation (NFC). Despite liberalisation of Sri Lanka's economy and the release of Indian and other foreign films into the market in 1977, the NFC monopoly did not cease until 2000, and during the 1980s it typically held back the distribution of films unless they were classified as 'art' films.[35] This, together with competition from television, increased production costs and the burning down of theatres during the 1980s communal riots, has contributed to the declining output of the Sri Lankan film industry since the 1990s. Yet the 1990s also witnessed the emergence of new filmmakers such as Prasanna Vithange, Asoke Handagama and Somaratne Dissanayake, whose films explore Sri Lanka's sweeping economic, political and cultural changes since the 1980s, including violent conflict between Tamil separatists and the Sri Lankan government, through the theme of the family.

In Somaratne Dissanayake's *Saroja* (1999), a Sinhala family shelters a

Tamil girl, Saroja, and her Tamil Tiger father, eventually adopting her after his comrades kill her father. The arrival of the Tamil family into the Sinhala family's midst provokes a moral crisis and the outrage of other Sinhalese villagers, but the child's innocence enables her adoptive family to 'transcend ethnic barriers and to imagine a multicultural nation'.[36] Dharmasena Pathiraja has argued that the film portrays the conflict from a Sinhalese perspective, vindicating the Sinhala family as morally superior to its Tamil counterpart and accepting Tamils only in their most 'angelic' form. In Prasanna Vithange's *Walls Within* (1997), on the other hand, the protagonist is a divorced mother, who rekindles a relationship with an old boyfriend, earning her family's and her neighbours' opprobrium. After a botched home abortion plunges her into madness, her family sends her away for psychiatric treatment. However, the final shots of her being escorted away by her ex-boyfriend ambiguously suggest that her madness may be a ruse. By juxtaposing cultural expectations of the self-sacrificing mother with the image of a 'self-fulfilling mother', *Walls Within* exposes the family itself as an oppressive institution.[37]

Cinema of Pakistan and Bangladesh

Pakistan and Bangladesh each produce about eighty films a year, although their output is rarely shown outside their borders. Pakistan's main film industry is based in Lahore (therefore known as 'Lollywood') and makes films in Urdu and Punjabi. Lahore's film industry suffered irreparably from partition, as many of its talented personnel were Hindu and migrated to Bombay. Yet, with partition, an inflow of talent also arrived from Bombay. Among the newcomers was Noor Jehan (1926–2000), known as 'Melody Queen' – Pakistan's most famous singer and actress. The films in which she acted had a success ratio of 'well above 90%'.[38] She moreover became Pakistan's first female director with her film *Chanway* (1951), in which she also starred. She was still working as a playback singer in the 1990s.

Pakistan's post-independence history has featured a succession of military dictatorships. However, there have been interim democratic periods, including five years under Zulfikar Ali Bhutto, who promoted the development of arts and culture in Pakistan and established the National Film Development Corporation (NAFDEC) after the Indian model. However, following his ousting, NAFDEC's role has largely been 'ceremonial rather than real'.[39] In addition to lack of proper government support, strict censorship during periods of military rule has curbed freedom of cinematic expression. This has not only stifled the growth of an alternative, politicised cinema but has also given Pakistan's filmmakers a competitive disadvantage against Indian films.[40] The loss of East Pakistan, an important market for Urdu films, was also crippling. In the 1990s, however, some relief on Entertainment Tax and revenues from import duties enabled the production of several local successes including *Choorian* (1998) and *Yeh Dil Aap Ka Huwa* (2002). The latter has been classified as Pakistan's most expensive film and the first the country has released abroad.[41]

Bangladesh's capital Dhaka emerged as a film-producing centre after partition. At first supported by Pakistan's central development board, Bangladeshi films have been called a 'poor man's copy of the Bollywood *masala* films', although they tried to indigenise the popular idiom, for example with Bengali folk formats (*Jatras*) during the 1960s.[42] Like Pakistan since the mid-1970s, Bangladesh has veered towards Islamic fundamentalism and suffered military dictatorships for a period. After independence, film production continued under the tight control of the Dhaka-based Film Development Corporation.

As in Pakistan, there has been a lack of resources and facilities for alternative filmmakers. Unlike India's state-sponsored parallel filmmakers, Bangladesh's alternative filmmakers belong to an underground movement known as 'short films' because many – although not all – of their films are shorts or documentaries.[43] In order to have greater freedom of expression and avoid the commercial film industry's producer–distributor nexus, they use low-cost 16mm film and show their films around the country on mobile projection units. However, low production values were never means in themselves – filmmakers were always ready to move to more high-tech formats when these became available.[44]

Tanvir Mokammel is a leading 'short' filmmaker. Like many other films from Pakistan and Bangladesh, his feature-length *Quiet Flows the River Chitra* (1999) deals with the theme of partition, focusing on the Hindu minority who remained in Bangladesh (then East Pakistan) in the immediate aftermath. It evokes the idyll handed down through generations in Bengali families: 'a vision of a bounteous *Golden Bengal*, watered by eternally flowing blue rivers', with Hindus and Muslims living contentedly together on its banks.[45] Through typically understated means, the film explores the cracks appearing in this idyll. The opening images of water-reflected sunsets, the colourful costumes and children's games gradually yield to a menacing ambience. The river itself is highlighted as a place of danger, culminating in a gang rape of a Hindu girl on its banks, obliquely visualised as a sari unfurling across the screen.

A founding member of the Short Film Forum (established in 1986), Tareque Masud made a number of shorts and documentaries with his wife Catherine before their first feature *The Clay Bird* (2003), which their own

Dhaka-based production company Audiovision co-produced with the French company MK2. *The Clay Bird* became the first Bangladeshi film to compete at Cannes, where it won the International Critics' Prize in 2002. Like many films by other younger filmmakers from the short-film movement, it deals with events leading up to the 1971 liberation war, a trauma comparable to partition. The Pakistani army's repression led to genocide, and millions were forced to flee as refugees to India. An added motivation for this theme is that the values of the liberation war are exactly what the current political establishment – who use Islam for violent power politics – are set against.

In *The Clay Bird*, a boy nicknamed Anu is sent to a *madrasa* (Islamic seminary school) after his father, Kazi, an orthodox Muslim, discovers he has secretly been attending Hindu festivals with his uncle Milon, an activist for free elections (of which Kazi also disapproves). Through its child actors, the film combines the influences of Abbas Kiarostami (another MK2-sponsored filmmaker) and Ray, who – as a Bengali filmmaker, although from Hindu-dominant West Bengal – exerts a considerable force on Bangladesh's alternative cinema. The fate of Anu's sister Asma recalls that of Apu's sister, Durga, in Ray's *Pather Panchali* – she dies of a fever because Kazi, a homoeopathist by trade, refuses her allopathic medicine, tenaciously clinging to his beliefs just as he later refuses to leave his house despite warnings of the Pakistani army's crackdown. The echo of Ray in characters' names and plots is significant, as Anu (like Milon) is a Hindu name – he reluctantly switches to his official Muslim name at school. Milon makes a virtue of syncretism, saying at one point, 'the truth is that nothing is purely indigenous. Everything is mixed up.' The film itself vividly juxtaposes Hindu and Muslim iconography: the *madrasa*'s architecture and uniforms contrast with colourful, noisy Hindu festivals, including the kite-flying competition, where rivals try to cut down each other's kites – a 'millennium-old product of Hindu mythology' which has remained in Bangladesh and Pakistan.[46]

The Film Censor Board of Bangladesh banned the film due to its 'religiously sensitive material'.[47] However, others have praised the film for its nuanced view of Islam, expressed in song interludes of Bengali folk music at open-air concerts attended by Anu and his mother – including 'a debate song in the Baul (itinerant minstrel) tradition' which 'contrasts more traditional forms of Islam with Sufi ideology'.[48] At the *madrasa*, a moderate teacher takes issue with the head teacher's dogmatic approach, recalling that it was not by the sword that the people of the subcontinent embraced Islam but through the Sufis and dervishes, who used peaceful means.

Notes

1. Shohat and Stam, *Unthinking Eurocentrism*, p. 315.
2. Gazdar, *Pakistan Cinema*, p. 14. The Hindu caste system created a highly unjust social hierarchy whereby priests (Brahmins) hereditarily enjoyed the highest status in society and Dalits (once called 'Untouchables') the lowest. Dalits were thus deprived of their basic dignity of life. Caste discrimination has been outlawed in India since Independence, yet still prevails.
3. Shohat and Stam, *Unthinking Eurocentrism*, p. 315.
4. Ibid., p. 315.
5. Dissanayake, 'Rethinking Indian Popular Cinema', p. 208.
6. Rajadhyaksha, 'Indian Cinema', p. 153.
7. Subramanyam, 'India', p. 51.
8. Rajadhyaksha, 'Indian Cinema', p. 153.
9. Dwyer and Patel, *Cinema India*, p. 28.
10. Chapman, *Cinemas of the World*, p. 327.
11. Anon., 'Global Film Production and Distribution', p. 205.
12. Gokulsing and Dissanayake, *Indian Popular Cinema*, p. 17.
13. Thomas, 'Indian Cinema', p. 128.
14. Gokulsing and Dissanayake, *Indian Popular Cinema*, p. 18.
15. Nayar, 'Invisible Representation', p. 16.
16. Ibid., p. 19.
17. Thomas, 'Indian Cinema', p. 130.
18. Ibid., p. 129.
19. Creekmur, 'Picturizing American Cinema', p. 376.
20. Nayar, 'Invisible Representation', p. 20.
21. Ibid., p. 21.
22. Dwyer and Patel, *Cinema India*, p. 25.
23. Thomas, 'Indian Cinema', p. 127.
24. Dwyer and Patel, *Cinema India*, p. 37.
25. Gopalan, *Cinema of Interruptions*, p. 21.
26. Gokulsing and Dissanayake, *Indian Popular Cinema*, p. 91.
27. Guneratne, 'Introduction', p. 21.
28. Ibid., p. 21.
29. Subramanyam, 'India', p. 38.
30. Guneratne, 'Introduction', p. 21.
31. Datta, *Shyam Benegal*, pp. 15–16.
32. Ramnarayan, 'Mr and Mrs Iyer', p. 25.
33. Stephen Hughes, 'Made in Madras: The Place of Tamil Film within Indian Cinema', paper presented at the Institute of Contemporary Arts, London, 7 October 2000.
34. Dissanayake and Ratnavibhushnana, *Profiling Sri Lankan Cinema*, p. 7.
35. Abeyesekera, 'Fifty Years of Cinema in Sri Lanka', p. 8.
36. Pathiraja, 'The Filial Bond', p. 8.
37. Ratnavibhushnana, 'The Family as Paradox', p. 13.

38. Gazdar, *Pakistan Cinema*, p. 40.
39. Iqbal, 'Pakistani Cinema'.
40. Gazdar, *Pakistan Cinema*, p. 4.
41. Iqbal, 'Pakistani Cinema'.
42. Mokammel, 'Alternative Cinema', p. 29; Mokammel, 'Last Two and a Half Decades of Bangladesh Cinema', p. 30.
43. Mokammel, 'Alternative Cinema', p. 28.
44. Ibid., p. 30.
45. Amin, 'The Road to Homelessness', p. 18.
46. Ali, *Fundamentalisms*, p. 7.
47. Mohaiemen, 'Petition'.
48. Ramachandran, 'Clay Bird', p. 44.

CHAPTER 8

Indian Cinema

Bollywood films now have simultaneous international releases. Higher ticket prices in the UK, the USA, Canada and Australia ensure lucrative returns, generating up to 65 per cent of a film's total income.[1] In the UK, Bollywood releases routinely enter the weekly box-office top ten and score high screen averages. For example, in a UK box-office chart for a week in August 2003, the Bollywood hit *Koi Mil Gaya*, playing on just thirty-six screens, was listed as having the second best screen average after *Terminator 3*, which was in its second running week and showing in 477 theatres.[2] Reception contexts are also rapidly changing within India, where middle classes who attend air-conditioned city multiplexes are prepared to pay ticket prices several times higher than poor rural audiences. Today's Bollywood films are therefore constructed to appeal not only to the poor who traditionally formed their core audiences but also increasingly to the South Asian diaspora and India's middle classes. However, this is only one of the ways in which Indian cinema has reinvented itself for global audiences since the 1990s. In addition to dominant Bollywood genres, this chapter looks at the work of popular Tamil director Mani Ratnam and arthouse films by Indian expatriates.

In India's formerly closed, Soviet-style economy (introduced by India's first post-independence Prime Minister Jawaharlal Nehru), foreign products came on the market years after they became available in the West. Government reforms introduced in 1991 dismantled strict quotas, deregulated local industries and permitted multinationals to enter India. The nation underwent accelerated globalisation, flooded by foreign brands and satellite-TV channels, bringing the West, with its glittering promises of glamorous, modern lifestyles, straight into middle-class homes.[3] (In India, satellite-TV owners are mainly middle-class.) These rapid changes caused confusion and anxiety that traditional Indian values of belonging and support would be swept away – especially the institution of the joint (or extended) family whose interests had, for generations, been privileged over those of individuals. They gave rise to debates about who or what is 'Indian' and what is a foreign import.

Bollywood films have responded by reconciling global consumer lifestyles with traditional 'Indian' values – their mantra is similar to the song from Bollywood classic *Shri 420* (1955), where Raj Kapoor sings, 'My shoes are Japanese / These pants are British / The cap on my head is Russian / But my heart is Indian'. Indeed, one recent Bollywood film is actually called *Phir Bhi Dil Hai Hindustani/ The Heart Is Still Indian* (2000). Such films provide reassurance in a rapidly globalising world that 'Indian values are portable and malleable'.[4] In a pivotal move, films shift the diasporic Indian – known as 'non-resident Indian' (NRI) – to the centre of their narratives. NRI audiences living in the West can now see their pursuit of wealth and consumerism given a blessing in Bollywood narratives, and their nostalgic yearning for India acknowledged in the scripts. This is in stark contrast to earlier films, where NRIs never figured and the 'West was as dangerous as any Orientalist's East – seductive but spiritually fatal'.[5]

The Hindu nationalist (Hindutva) groups, such as the Bharatiya Janata Party (BJP) and Shiv Sena who rose to power in the 1990s, promote narrow conceptions of Indianness comparable to other tribal nationalisms discussed elsewhere in this book (for example, Sinhala and Tamil nationalism in Sri Lanka in Chapter 7 and rivalry between Croats, Serbs and Muslims in Yugoslavia in Chapter 1). The BJP believe that the Hindu nation is the one true Indian nation. They see the caste system as the 'natural' order, and they deny that Islam has made a significant impact on Indian culture. The Hindutva has many supporters in the South Asian diaspora as well as among India's middle classes. When in power, their neoliberal economic policies were popular with wealthy NRIs in the UK and North America, for whom they introduced generous tax-breaks to invest in 'the Motherland'.[6]

Women and women's desires are a particular focus of Hindutva debates on what constitutes Indianness. This is because, as we have seen elsewhere, women are traditional symbols of the nation – hence, the figure of 'Mother India'. In the Indian epic *Ramayana*, the virtuous wife Sita undergoes trial by fire in order to prove her sexual purity, stepping through a bonfire unscathed. The Hindu woman's purity has symbolised 'Indian' identity and resistance to the West.[7] Not surprisingly, this is a site of ideological anxiety in Bollywood films as well as in the hysteria surrounding the lesbian love story *Fire* (1996), directed by Indo-Canadian filmmaker Deepa Mehta. As will be seen, contemporary Bollywood endorses a sanitised version of the diaspora, counting the figure of the NRI within definitions of 'Indianness', while the values associated with the diasporic film *Fire* were perceived as a foreign import.

One theme established at the outset of this book is that the nation is a precarious and imaginary ideal, which works to conceal and contain differences. In India, there has been a spate of nationalist films, such as *Gadar*

(2001), *L.O.C. Kargil* (2003) and *Lakshya* (2004), appealing to a country racked by internal secessionist movements, with older tensions being re-ignited in Kashmir and the north-east together with a new flashpoint in the Punjab since the 1980s. In films like *Lagaan* (2001), another patriotic film, the contemporary era has witnessed a resurgence of All-India heroes, able to heal the nation's rifts. Bollywood has traditionally played a culturally unifying role, constructing a pan-Indian ethos and appeal seemingly able to unite every element of life in a land otherwise divided by differences of language, religion, class and caste. However, while targeting global audi-ences, Bollywood's dominant genres since the 1990s have retreated into narrow regional and/or ethnic preoccupations. In tandem with this, films from South India, especially Mani Ratnam's 'Terrorism Trilogy' – *Roja* (1992), *Bombay* (1995) and *Dil Se* (1998) – have risen to the challenge of tackling national themes, gaining nationwide distribution and, in the case of *Roja* and *Bombay*, wild popularity. Like *The Terrorist* (1999) (discussed in Chapter 7), which was directed by his cinematographer Santosh Sivan, Ratnam's films use the figure of terrorism to insert India into the global imaginary as well as drawing on regionalist and nationalist discourses. The rest of this chapter explores these topics more fully, engaging *Lagaan*, *Dil Se* and *Fire* in close analysis.

Bollywood Romance

The dominant Bollywood genre of the 1990s was romance mixed with comic subplots – a big departure from the action and revenge dramas which dominated in the 1970s and 1980s.[8] Its common features are: the love triangle, with two men falling in love with the same woman, or two women falling in love with the same man; the notion that love is based on friendship (also found in earlier films); the 'arranged love marriage', that is, love choices which gain parental approval; NRI characters; foreign loca-tions; and a style reminiscent of MTV and advertising, emphasising con-spicuous consumption and product placement.[9]

The arranged love marriage/'love is friendship' formula was minted by a young generation of directors known as the Bollywood Brat Pack. They include Sooraj Barjatya, Aditya Chopra, Karan Johar, Dharmesh Dhar-shan and Farhan Akhtar. The Bollywood film industry is full of acting and producing dynasties. Many Brat Pack directors are the sons of influential industry professionals. Sooraj Barjatya belongs to the family who own Rajshri Films, India's largest distribution network, which also produces films. Karan Johar is the son of producer Yash Johar and childhood friend of Aditya Chopra, the son of veteran director Yash Chopra. In fact, it is

Yash Chopra who is credited with originating 'the chiffon and roses' brand of romance and the focus on super-rich lifestyles in his early films, including *Waqt* (1965).[10] However, these featured older characters whereas contemporary romance focuses on youthful protagonists (usually young professionals or college-goers). In *Dil to Pagal Hai* (1997), Yash Chopra himself adopted the new formula, as has another veteran director Subhash Ghai, who made *Pardes* (1997).

Sooraj Barjatya's *Hum Aapke Hain Koun* (1994) broke Indian box-office records, returning audiences to the theatres in droves after the slump in attendance during the 1980s, when the arrival of colour TV and VCRs kept middle-class families at home, while cinemas catered for a lower-class male clientele with films containing 'higher doses of sex and violence' (another deterrent to family audiences).[11] *HAHK* was promoted and received as 'clean', 'wholesome' family entertainment. It enshrined the Hindu joint family myth in its narrative formula, where personal desires are subordinated for the good of the family, which unites around religious rituals and wedding celebrations. The tag line of a later blockbuster, Karan Johar's *Kabhi Khushi Kabhie Gham* (a.k.a. *K3G*) (2001), sums up the ethos of these Brat Pack films: 'it's all about loving your parents'. In contrast to love marriages, which are about rebellion against elders, the lovers in these narratives 'court family elders [for their blessings] with more ardour than the beloved'.[12] With each big hit outdoing the box-office performance of previous films, this has proved to be a commercially astute formula, affirming the tradition of the joint family and North Indian (particularly Punjabi) weddings and rituals as 'a bastion of stability and security in a rapidly changing world'.[13]

These are post-feminist films which have absorbed the discourses of feminism for their own purposes. In them, women inevitably set aside their desires for self-fulfilment in favour of the family, often following a *Taming of the Shrew*-type narrative model. For example, in the mega-hit *Kuch Kuch Hota Hai* (1998), the star Kajol is basketball-playing tomboy Anjali, who is unconcerned with acting or looking 'feminine' (a role which embodies Kajol's off-screen persona; she is often criticised for her lack of interest in maintaining her appearance by means of slimming, grooming, jewellery or fashion). However, in the course of the film we witness her spectacular metamorphosis, as her friend Rahul's recollection of her during their college days is cross-cut with shots of Anjali bejewelled and meticulously groomed for her engagement party. In Anne Ciecko's reading of the film, Anjali has tamed her rebellious youth and recognised her 'duty' to 'Indian' family values, thus proving her worthiness as Rahul's prospective wife. In the ending, her fiancé Aman hands her over to Rahul, sealing her transformation into a commodity exchanged between men and 'a self-sacrificing Sita-esque ideal of domestic goddess'.[14]

This custom of patriarchal exchange is embodied in the title of Aditya Chopra's *Dilwale Dulhania Le Jayenge/The Brave-hearted Will Take the Bride (DDLJ)* (1995), the longest-running movie in Indian film history.[15] *DDLJ*'s protagonists are second-generation British Asians Simran (Kajol) and Raj (Shahrukh Khan). When he discovers that the pair fell in love while on holiday in Europe, Simran's traditionalist father sends her back to the Punjab for an arranged wedding. In a moving scene, Simran's mother Lajjo, who sympathises with the lovers, speaks out against gender injustices. She relates how she was told that there are no differences between men and women, yet her own education was stopped so that her brothers' could continue; since then, she has never ceased making sacrifices as daughter, sister and wife. The film articulates feminist dissent, yet ultimately contains it through its resolution in which Simran is handed over from father to husband. Even when Lajjo encourages Raj to elope with Simran, Raj decides instead to win the respect of her parents, only accepting the father's authority to give away the bride. This is how Raj shows his Indian moral values, striking an iconic pose in his Harley Davidson jacket against a field of yellow flowers in the Punjab; despite outward signs, we find he is still 'Indian' at heart.

Male stars carry the box office in India, much as elsewhere. Top-ranking Bollywood stars include Shahrukh Khan, Aamir Khan, Hrithik Roshan and Amitabh Bachchan (who has made many comebacks since his Angry Young Man days). Like the Bollywood Brat Pack directors, many of today's young stars come from acting or producing dynasties. An exception to this is Shahrukh Khan, whose background is comparably humble. Previously a player of villains, Shahrukh retains a *badmaash* (wicked) or cocky element in his romantic roles. It was his first romantic role in *DDLJ* which made him a youth icon, both in India and abroad.

Through their use of stars, traditions and rituals, Bollywood films feed NRIs' nostalgia for their 'motherland'. They construct an imaginary or mythical India; for example, *DDLJ* presents an idyllic, virtually pre-industrial rural Punjab, airbrushed and shorn of violent conflict. At the same time, Bollywood makes prolific use of foreign locales, including Scotland, for song sequences in *KKHH* and the Lake District in *Mujhse Dosti Karoge* (2002). The craze for foreign locations is not new – Raj Kapoor's *Sangam* (1964) was the first Bollywood film to use European locations – but whereas foreign locations served largely as backdrops for songs in earlier films, contemporary films integrate them into their NRI-targeted narratives. Many have a dual-nation setting, set partly in India and partly abroad, including locations in London (*DDLJ*), New York (*Pardes*) and Sydney (*Dil Chahta Hai* [2001]). Some take place entirely abroad, like the New York-based *Kal Ho Naa Ho* (2003). These films solicit a global tourist's gaze from an economically aspiring Indian middle class as well as giving NRIs the pleasure of seeing their favourite stars touring their own cities or holiday destinations. However, while showcasing tourist sights, settings in contemporary Bollywood films are otherwise disconnected from social reality. Characters live in opulent mansions and loft-style apartments bearing little relationship to the living conditions of most Indians in India or even abroad.

Whereas before, wealth and the West signified corruption, today's films endorse global consumerism. Temples are among their recurrent settings, but so are shopping malls – temples of consumerism – providing reassurance to monied NRI audiences that their pursuit of wealth and material comforts is in keeping with 'Indian' traditions. After all, Hindus worship a god of business success – Ganesh – and a goddess of wealth – Lakshmi.

The Films of Mani Ratnam

Ratnam is South India's foremost director, who has also gained huge popularity in the all-India market. His films are renowned for their production values, stunning photography and well-choreographed song sequences. He is the director most closely associated with bringing MTV into Indian cinema (that is, by giving MTV a local inflection in song-and-dance sequences). He comes from a film-producing family – his father 'Venus' Gopalratnam was a producer, and his brother G. Venkatesan is a distributor and producer – although Ratnam himself worked as a management consultant before entering the film industry. Ratnam has made films in several Indian languages: his debut *Pallavi Anupallavi* (1983) in Kannada, *Unaroo* (1984) in Malayalam, *Geetanjali* (1989) in Telugu, *Dil Se* in Hindi, and the rest of his films in Tamil. The film that first brought him to national recognition was *Nayakan* (1987), financed by his brother's production company Sujatha Films. A gangster film inspired by Francis Ford Coppola's *The Godfather* (1972), *Nayakan* won National Awards for Cinematography and Art Direction for P. C. Sriram and Thotta Tharani respectively. Ratnam's national profile soared again when *Roja* and *Bombay* were dubbed into Hindi and released with great success all over India.

Ratnam is often accused of expressing simplistic, nationalist and Hindu-biased sentiments. He is by no means a 'radical' filmmaker, yet his films are astonishing for what they achieve within Indian popular-cinema conventions and censorship restrictions. Importantly, Ratnam has chosen to influence the mainstream not by operating *alongside* it – as India's parallel cinema (discussed in Chapter 7) traditionally has – but *inside* it, although his films would not be possible without parallel cinema's precedent.

The trilogy films all use real political conflicts as backgrounds to stories of passion and desire.[16] This is something of a breakthrough for Indian popular cinema, especially when compared to the dominant contemporary trend of Bollywood romance which, despite its globe-trotting, sometimes depicts India as a timeless present filled with feudal family weddings and rituals. *Roja* and *Bombay* mark a bold departure for South Indian cinema, as they place their Tamil characters in North Indian situations and take on the role of addressing national issues – namely the rise of separatist and independence movements within India's borders in *Roja* (also in *Dil Se*) and communalism in *Bombay*, where the terrorism in question is religious fanaticism. The Trilogy films explore the linkages between nations and their terrorists rather than depicting them in opposition.[17] Their stories of transgressive couples imagine empathy between the nation and its disaffected fragments. They also show a mirroring relationship between the state and terrorists, emphasising that state violence and oppression engenders terrorist violence.

Roja and *Bombay* have been massively influential, setting a trend for engaging with topical issues in some Bollywood films (for example, Khalid Mohammed's *Fiza* [2000]). In *Roja*, a code-breaker, Rishi Kumar, is kidnapped by Kashmiri terrorists in reprisal for their leader's capture by Indian security forces, and his distraught newlywed wife, Roja (another Sita-esque heroine), pleads with the state to secure his release. Rishi believes terrorists are mistaken in their aims of fighting for an independent Kashmir, as Kashmir is – according to him – part of India. Besides Rishi's stirring patriotic actions, the film emphasises the bond that develops between him and his captor Liaqat. The film is beautifully photographed by Santosh Sivan, and also marks the debut of music composer A. R. Rahman, whose soundtrack was a major ingredient in the film's success.

Marxist critic Madhava Prasad has argued that Ratnam's films are a sign of 'ideological reform' in Indian cinema – not, however, for their content, but for their form.[18] *Roja* opens with the capture of the terrorist leader and then cuts to Roja's first meeting and marriage with Rishi in a Tamil village. Although Ratnam generally prefers linear narrative, here he deploys something like a flashback, although it is not subjectively motivated as flashbacks in Indian popular cinema usually are, and its significance remains an enigma until later in the narrative. Prasad argues that the opening fragment therefore actually menaces the subsequent pastoral idyll – a compressed feudal family romance – forcing this dominant cinema convention to break out of its 'timeless frame' and stage the present.[19] Ratnam's method lays 'siege' to the dominant form and harnesses its pleasures to 'another narrative project', thereby 'staging . . . an ideological rehabilitation of its narrative elements'.[20]

Bombay, which was produced by the Amitabh Bachchan Corporation, is the first Indian popular film to centre on a Hindu–Muslim marriage. The couple face problems not only before but also after they marry, having eloped to Bombay, where they are caught in communal riots which broke out in December 1992 and January 1993 after the destruction of the Babri Masjid (mosque) at Ayodhya by armed Hindus mobilised by the BJP. The film underwent a wrangle with the Censor Board, which demanded cuts from an inflammatory speech by Bal Thackeray, leader of the Shiv Sena, then in power in the regional government of Maharashtra, whose capital is Bombay (since 1996 called Mumbai). In the speech, Thackeray allegedly talks about ethnically cleansing Bombay in order to preserve it for only Hindus of Maharashtrian origin.[21] Although Ratnam apparently took his dialogue directly from Thackeray's speeches, the Censor Board felt that the film's representation of Thackeray was too 'strong' and feared violent reprisals from the Shiv Sena if the film was shown in that form.[22]

Despite this, the film provoked protest from Hindus and Muslims, and Ratnam encountered death threats and an assassination attempt for making it. It was criticised for misrepresenting events, as it implies that Muslims started the riots, although this was not the case. The hero, Shekhar, tries to knock sense into the rioters, threatening to set himself alight unless they stop their bloodshed. He emphatically calls himself 'Indian' rather than Hindu or Muslim, highlighting a secular national identity that is being endangered by both state and terrorists. Despite its visible biases and 'simplistic' messages, one of the film's strengths is that it does recognise the responsibility of political parties for inciting violence and enmity in communities who 'have coexisted for decades' – carrying echoes of former Yugoslavia (see Chapter 1).[23]

After Indian audiences' unfavourable response to *Dil Se* (see below), Ratnam shifted away from national-political concerns for *Alaipayuthey* (2000). While Bollywood romances typically end with marriage, many of Mani Ratnam's films explore relationships and their complications *after* marriage. This is true of *Roja* and *Bombay* but especially of *Alaipayuthey* (which, however, was successfully remade as the Bollywood film *Saathiya* [2002]). In *Alaipayuthey*, Ratnam adopts a flashback structure (which, as noted above, he usually avoids). He uses non-linear storytelling here 'to explore the fragility of a marriage whose murky hopes for the future rests on a romantic past'.[24] Ratnam returned to explicit political topics in *Kannathil Muthamittal* (2002), which won Shweta Prasad Keertana recognition for her portrayal of nine-year-old Amudha at the 2002 National Awards. This is Ratnam's first film without dance sequences, where present-day conflict in Sri Lanka disrupts a South Indian family idyll. Having discovered she is adopted, Amudha ventures into the island's war zone in search of her biological mother, a trainer of Tamil Tiger suicide bombers. In a striking scene, Amudha finds herself in the midst of these 'daughters of death', girls of her own age, silently pointing rifles at her through the undergrowth – doubles of what she might have been.

Indian Expatriate Filmmakers

Indian expatriates such as Deepa Mehta and Mira Nair have gained a high profile making films with Indian casts and settings which appeal to international audiences outside the usual diasporic markets. A key feature of their work is the attempt to tackle aspects of Indian social reality left out of the hugely censored domestic cinema. This includes a bolder handling of sexuality, inevitably attracting controversy and leading Indian critics to dismiss their works as 'carefully crafted attempts to steal the limelight'.[25] In a competitive global market, 'the ability to manipulate content, aesthetics and perhaps, controversy' may be exactly what defines their approach – which, they themselves admit, is to provoke rather than merely entertain.[26] Yet the fact that they are expatriates no doubt bears on their hostile reception in India, especially at a time when 'suspicions about the influences of globalization can be stirred up against any and all foreigners'.[27]

A former Bollywood director, Shekhar Kapur ventured into this category of transnational filmmaking with his film *Bandit Queen* (1995), which was co-produced by Britain's Channel 4. He has since gone on to direct the UK production *Elizabeth* and other films abroad. *Bandit Queen*'s financiers are likely to have been attracted to the project by its conformity to Western ideas of 'realism' and its focus on the oppression of women.[28] It is a biopic of a real bandit, a Dalit ('Untouchable') who survived numerous humiliations meted out to her gender and caste. She came to be championed for looting on behalf of the poor, who called her 'Devi', meaning 'goddess'. After being jailed for eleven years, she entered politics and was assassinated in 2001. The film purports to be her 'true story', based on what she narrated to writer Mala Sen while she was in jail. As well as in the performance and shooting style, the film's 'realism' stands out in the graphic depiction of sexual abuse and violence. But although its degree of explicitness is new, *Bandit Queen*'s rape-revenge narrative is similar to an Indian popular-cinema formula from the 1980s. The real Phoolan Devi initially opposed the film, claiming that it was not the story she had given Sen. Because of this dispute, the Delhi High Court temporarily banned the film in India and withdrew it from the Oscars (it had been nominated as India's Oscar entry). Further to these complications, the Censor Board would not release the film without cuts, which Shekhar Kapur refused to make. The film was finally released after Phoolan Devi made an out-of-court settlement with Channel 4 and the producers agreed to some cuts.[29] Despite its favourable response in the West, which its financiers had carefully calculated, *Bandit Queen* came under attack from novelist Arundhati Roy, and others, who condemned its use of a feminist pretext for depicting explicit rape scenes.[30]

Mira Nair, who hails from Orissa, is the best-known Indian director outside India. She trained abroad, including with US documentary film-maker D. A. Pennebaker, and has lived in the USA and Africa. Nair believes that she had to leave India to make movies about India and that her US training allowed her to develop an independent style, which may have been restricted had she learnt filmmaking in India as an assistant to a male director.[31] Funding is another reason why she works from abroad – her films are mostly funded by the USA and Europe (especially the UK's Channel 4). Beginning with documentaries, then turning increasingly to fiction, her films express a feminist outlook and an interest in the disenfranchised (or 'the subaltern'). Her *Salaam Bombay!* (1988), a co-production between Channel 4 and India's NFDC, focuses on Bombay's destitute street kids, drug-addicts and prostitutes. It is shot in *cinéma-vérité* style on location with non-professional actors, combining documentary with narrative. It was Oscar-nominated and won the Caméra d'Or at Cannes 1988. Nair's later film, *Kama Sutra* (1996), named after the Indian erotic manual, is set in the sixteenth century and follows a female servant who rebels against feudal constraints. An erotic film with a feminist twist, it has sex scenes depicting erotic pleasure from a female point of view – a reaction against what Nair calls 'perverse sexual portrayals of women' in both US and Indian cinema, where 'rape is an accepted sexual expression, but sensual or spiritual pleasure [in sex] is not'.[32]

Kama Sutra's release was limited, and it was not particularly well received. *Monsoon Wedding* (2001), by contrast, turned out to be Nair's most popular film so far. It contains many ingredients common to contemporary Bollywood films: a Punjabi family wedding, 'filmi' music and dancing, super-rich lifestyles and an NRI character (Melbourne-returned Rahul). However, it also utilises a digital home-video aesthetic and narrative structure reminiscent of the Dogme 95 film *Festen* (1998) (see Chapter 2), enabling it to cross over to international audiences attuned to this kind of cinematic realism. Unlike contemporary Bollywood films, *Monsoon Wedding* reveals secrets behind the family façade – child abuse, pre-marital sex, financial problems, and technical hitches in the wedding preparations. Nair interweaves her interest in marginal characters into the story of a middle-class marriage by cross-cutting from them to wedding-manager Dubey and household servant Alice, whose marriage takes place on the sidelines of the big family event.

Deepa Mehta grew up in Amritsar, near India's border with Pakistan, and studied philosophy at the University of New Delhi. Her father was a film-distributor and exhibitor, which gave her the chance to watch many Hindi films from early on. She herself learned filmmaking by working for a company producing documentaries for the Indian government. She emigrated to Canada in 1973, directing for television before making her debut feature film, *Sam & Me* (1991), which won the Caméra d'Or at Cannes. *Fire* (1996), the start of a trilogy, is her third feature and the first film she made in India. The second trilogy film *Earth* (1998) is adapted from Bapsi Sidwa's novel *Cracking India*, which narrates the trauma of partition through the eyes of a polio-ridden Parsi child, Lenny, living in what is now Pakistan. The film, however, focuses more on the love triangle between Lenny's Hindu Ayah, Shanta (Nandita Das), and two Muslim men, Masseur and Ice Candy Man (Aamir Khan), using partition as a dramatic backdrop for a tale of passion. Insofar as it uses stars and this kind of narrative structure, it resembles mainstream Indian cinema (although not in other respects). *Water*, the third trilogy film, has a story about widows taking refuge in a house in the holy city of Benares during the 1930s, in which one widow is forced into prostitution. Widowhood has traditionally been bound by Hindu customs, as mentioned in Chapter 7. Already provoked by the controversial *Fire* (see below), Hindu fundamentalists destroyed *Water*'s set even before shooting began, believing that the story sullied the image of widowhood, and spread rumours about the film's 'lurid and anti-Hindu content'.[33] Mehta faced death threats, and her effigy was burned by protesters. The BJP, then in government, did nothing to stop the demonstrations – so Mehta halted the production, hoping to return to it upon a change of political climate.

Close Analysis

Lagaan (Ashutosh Gowariker, 2001)

The Bollywood film *Lagaan* takes place in a drought-stricken central Indian province in 1893, where Captain Russell (Paul Blackthorne), the commanding officer of the local British cantonment, challenges a group of Indian villagers to a game of cricket, promising to waive the entire province's land tax (*lagaan*) for the next three years if they win; the forfeit if they lose, however, is triple *lagaan*. A village lad, Bhuvan (Aamir Khan), accepts the challenge, although the Indians have never played cricket before. The film contains a subplot involving a love triangle between Bhuvan, the village belle Gauri (Gracy Singh) and Russell's sister Elizabeth (Rachel Shelley), who believes Russell has been unfair and teaches the Indians how to play. The film was an international break-through – the first Bollywood film to be Oscar-nominated since *Mother India* (1957) – signalling a shift towards mainstream Western acceptance. It was also popular in India, where cricket is a well-known national passion.

For *Lagaan*, Gowariker studied films by Guru Dutt, Bimal Roy and Mehboob Khan from Bollywood's 1950s era, from which he draws his iconography of a poor rural community. Although *Lagaan* assembles a star-filled production team – including music director A. R. Rahman – Aamir Khan is the only star in the cast and the only one to have previously performed song-and-dance numbers. Aamir initially rejected the script as a risky departure from formula, but eventually agreed not only to act in the film but to produce it himself, setting up a production house for the purpose. This was his first venture as a producer, although he comes from a famous film-producing family.

Aamir's roles in art-house films such as *Earth* have given him the reputation of being a 'thinking actor'.[34] He brings production practices from *Earth* into *Lagaan*, which was shot on a single schedule on location using direct sound, while Bollywood films are usually shot discontinuously depending on schedules of stars who are booked into several films simultaneously, with sound dubbed in studios after production. Direct sound considerably added to the cost and length of the shoot – every shot had to be good for both camera and dialogue delivery, therefore increasing the number of retakes. This, together with its large multinational cast, made *Lagaan* a very high-budget film by Bollywood standards. Much more time was spent on it than is the norm for Bollywood – the film was in post-production for a whole year, mainly for editing which, also unusually for Bollywood, closely follows continuity rules.

Just as unusually, *Lagaan* strives for period authenticity, although it does not recreate a historical India but rather a 'mythical' one, as suggested in its subtitle: *Once Upon a Time in India*. Despite its influences from Western realist codes – including linear narrative – it contains many traditional motifs and conventions. Although the outcome is inevitable – we know the Indians are going to win – the film aims to deliver a spectacular presentation

of a 'larger-than-life' situation, where it is not *what* happens but *how* it
happens that is important.

Our first sight of Bhuvan is as he is protecting animals in the forest from
the British hunters. An eye-line match with Russell aiming his gun makes
it appear as if it is Bhuvan who is being hunted; he is simultaneously discovered by Russell's men and indeed finds a gun pointing at him. This early
scene underlines that the British have the power of the gun – odds are
stacked against the Indians. Furthermore, the Indian team are presented as
a motley bunch – consisting of a deaf mute, a crazy fortune-teller and a polio-
stricken cripple and contrasting with the well-turned-out British team, who
are experienced cricketers. The theme of underdogs who overcome a might-
ier foe is recognisably universal and common to other leading film export
industries (Hong Kong as well as Hollywood).[35] In *Lagaan*, however, it is significant that this is done not through conventional means of combat but
through a cricket match, which becomes a metaphor for the anti-colonial
struggle against the British, who invented cricket and spread it throughout
their empire. Although the Indians initially think that cricket is just child's
play – like their own *golli danda* – they start to see its 'complex rules and
power' and learn to beat the imperialists at their own game.[36] In this way, the
film also constructs an origin myth about the Indian passion for cricket, and
references to historic Indian cricketers are scattered throughout.

Bhuvan overcomes the villagers' initial reluctance to take on the British
challenge and assembles his cricket team by harnessing their native or
vocational talents. The film details each recruit's specific qualities: for
example, Bhura the chicken-keeper dives to catch the ball as he does his
runaway hens, and Kachra, the 'Untouchable' with a withered arm, is a
fantastic spin-bowler. The team is multicultural – including a Muslim
(Ismail), a Sikh (Deva) and an 'Untouchable' (Kachra). Under Bhuvan's
paternalistic leadership, people set aside their religious and caste differences for their common goal of defeating the British. The film upholds
India's secular traditions by emphasising that they 'go back in history', at
the same time using its All-India hero to perform the ideological work of
smoothing out present divisions.[37]

Due to an investment in period authenticity, *Lagaan*'s song-and-dance
sequences are not in the usual MTV style and are filmed mostly in long
takes. Each song fulfils a specific function. For example, in 'Ghanan
Ghanan', the villagers' joy at seeing rain-clouds, which promise to end
their two-year drought, heightens their subsequent despair when no rain
falls. 'O Paalanhaare' occurs with the villagers praying to the gods after the
match's second day concludes badly. Although *Lagaan* avoids the use of
coincidences and acts of fate characteristic of Indian epics and popular

cinema, it shows the 'workings of destiny' operating on the cricket pitch the next day.[38] However, the film also cleverly allows Western audiences to ascribe the Indian team's successes to 'good fortune', while Indian audiences may 'thank divine intervention for the same fortuitous events'.[39]

To configure the cross-racial love triangle, *Lagaan* uses the Hindu myth of Radha and Krishna. Radha and Krishna are the model of spiritual love: they were not married to each other yet they loved each other passionately, although legends also gave out that Krishna was a philanderer. In Song Three, 'Radha kaise na jale' ('Why is Radha Jealous?'), Bhuvan is shown in overhead shot as Krishna, playing his flute and encircled by maids, flirts with each one equally. The song positions Gauri as the Radha figure, jealous of Elizabeth. Yet, after Elizabeth's tearful farewell at the end of the film, we are told in voiceover that Elizabeth returned to England and never married, remaining Bhuvan's Radha all her life. Radha thus becomes a mutable, shifting identification, figuring the impossibilities of their love – both serving and destabilising the film's 'desire to form an Indian couple'.[40]

In 'O Rey Chhori' ('Oh my Love'), Bhuvan tries to dispel Gauri's jealousy, yet the film reminds us of the triangular nature of their desire by cutting to Elizabeth in the cantonment. Earlier, Elizabeth confesses to Bhuvan that she loves him – in true Bollywood fashion, she does it in English (Bollywood characters often say 'I love you' in English, the language difference heightening the utterance's forbidden status). Her words fall on deaf ears, as Bhuvan does not understand English. What cannot be expressed in language has outlet in song. The sequence becomes a three-way fantasy, increasingly blurring the characters and their settings. Elizabeth appears in superimposition in the dusty plains with Bhuvan and Gauri, then rematerialises in Gauri's clothes; later, Gauri appears with her hair looking deceptively like Elizabeth's.

Fire (Deepa Mehta, 1996)

In *Fire*, sisters-in-law Radha (Shabana Azmi) and Sita (Nandita Das) fall in love in a joint middle-class family household. Adapted from 'The Quilt' (1942), a short story by Urdu writer Ismat Chughtai, the film was shot in English and executive-produced by Mehta's Canadian husband David Hamilton. It was viewed at international film festivals and Western arthouse venues, principally by lesbian and gay and South Asian diasporic audiences, before its 1998 release in India, where it opened to packed houses in forty-two theatres.[41]

Fire is the first Indian film to present explicitly a relationship between women as lesbian. It provoked violent reactions from the Shiv Sena, who considered it 'alien to Indian culture' and vandalised theatres showing the film.[42] The Indian Censor Board had passed it without cuts, but the Shiv Sena removed it from screens and returned it to the Censor Board, which passed it a second time. In the wake of *Fire*, explicitly gay characters also emerged on the Bollywood screen (for example in *Girlfriend* [2004], which, too, aroused Hindu fundamentalist ire), although prior to this Bollywood provided space for homoeroticism under conditions of cross-dressing and masquerade, as well as in male-buddy films and indeed under the banner of 'love is friendship'.

As Gayatri Gopinath observes, the issues of *Fire*'s diasporic origin and its lesbian content were conflated in its reception.[43] On both counts, *Fire* was considered 'un-Indian' (ironically for Mehta, her Trilogy films are not considered 'Canadian' either, since they are shot in India, which disqualifies them for funding by the Canadian government). Resurging through anxieties about globalisation and the forces of Hindu fundamentalism, the myth of homosexuality as a foreign import brought to India by either Muslim invaders or European colonisers has been in currency since at least the late nineteenth century.[44] In reaction to the Shiv Sena protests, Indian lesbian groups demonstrated on the streets proclaiming that 'lesbianism is our Indian heritage', evoking homoerotic traditions in Indian literature, paintings and erotic sculptures, partly suppressed during the colonial era.[45] According to this argument, it is homophobia, not homosexuality, which is the 'foreign import'. Ruth Vanita writes: 'The rhetoric of modern Indian homophobia (with concepts . . . like unnatural and sinful) draws directly on a Victorian version of Judeo-Christian discourse'.[46] This can be seen in *Fire*, when Ashok reacts using biblical language to seeing his wife, Radha, and Sita together in bed: 'What I saw is a sin in the eyes of God and man.'

Ashok, who has vowed celibacy, lies in bed next to Radha only to test his own strength; he believes that, by helping him attain his spiritual goals, Radha is doing her duty as his wife. His brother Jatin, succumbing to family pressures, has agreed to an arranged marriage with Sita, whom he expects to play the dutiful wife, while he continues to see his Chinese girlfriend Julie. Rendered immobile and speechless by a stroke, Radha's and Sita's mother-in-law Biji personifies the paralysing effects of traditions in the joint family household, making her demands known by ringing her bell. Mehta believes that Hindu fundamentalists reacted to *Fire* because it questions tradition.[47] She sees her film as being about choices which women have traditionally been denied, not about lesbianism per se. In promoting this view, she risks presenting a one-dimensional view of Hindu tradition, and the reading that her characters make their choice solely because of their bad deal in their marriages. The film itself suggests another reading.

Whereas the men pursue their desires outside – Jatin with Julie, and Ashok with his *swami* (spiritual mentor) – the women make the interior space of the house their own, bonding over the preparation of food in the kitchen, meeting at first on the rooftop, then in the bedroom. As Gopinath argues, Radha's and Sita's relationship emerges from 'those spaces of female homosociality that are sanctioned by normative sexual and gender arrangements'.[48] Together they undertake *karva chauth*, a North Indian Hindu ritual where married women observe a day-long fast so that their husbands may enjoy a long life. We see them drying out orange-coloured saris on the roof, the colour orange signifying their growing passion. Everyday female homosocial activities, such as oiling hair and foot-massage, become suffused with eroticism. This gains meaning in connection with Radha's dream of herself as a child sitting with her parents in a field of yellow flowers. This opens the film with a parable in which her mother tells her: 'What you can't see, you just have to see without looking.' Towards the end of the film, we cut back to this scene in which the young Radha finally says she can 'see' the ocean; that is, Sapphic desire hidden within the interstices of the known and the visible.

Gopinath suggests that the real reason why *Fire* incurred the Shiv Sena's wrath was because it depicts lesbian desire in the joint family home. Radha and Sita implicitly reject the Hindu nationalist project which aims to harness women's sexuality, particularly their sexual conduct and repro-ductive capacity, to the propagation of the nation.[49] Their names evoke sanctified notions of Hindu womanhood, as the film underlines in its re-enactments of Sita's trial by fire from *The Ramayana*, which Biji watches on video. Radha is another Hindu mythological archetype (also seen in *Lagaan*), representing a steadfast ideal, for Radha remains devoted to Krishna despite his womanising. Not only do both women defy their namesakes, they leave the Hindu joint family home and reunite in an Islamic shrine. Radha's sari catches fire as she attempts to escape her husband, but she steps through the fire and joins Sita unscathed.

Dil Se (Mani Ratnam, 1998)

In *Dil Se*, the final instalment in Ratnam's 'Terrorism Trilogy', a reporter for All-India Radio, Amar Verma (Shahrukh Khan), becomes obsessed with an Assamese militant, Meghna (Manisha Koirala), who is plotting to blow up India's president at Delhi's Republic Day parade. The film is inspired by real events: Rajiv Gandhi's assassination by a female suicide bomber, the activities of the militant group ULFA (United Liberation Front of Assam) who have been fighting for an independent state since 1979, and the fiftieth anniversary of India's independence.

Indian audiences had great expectations for *Dil Se*, Ratnam's first Hindi film, after the success of *Roja* and *Bombay*. *Dil Se*, however, flopped at the Indian box office. Yet, in the UK, it broke box-office records, becoming the first Indian film to enter the Top Ten, and proving the 'box-office muscle' of UK South Asians.[50] Audiences drawn to it mainly for the songs and their favourite star Shahrukh Khan packed out the twenty cinemas showing *Dil Se* several times a day. *Dil Se* also became a favourite with international critics. For example, Jacob Levich writes in *Film Comment* that *Dil Se* is Ratnam's 'darkest, finest, and least conventionally satisfying work'.[51]

All the Trilogy films, Sumita Chakravarty notes, 'stage fantasmatic encounters with the other'.[52] Desire leads the hero to 'the outside', reversing the more common scenario in Bollywood films where desire remains inside the community. As Chakravarty argues, 'it is the seductiveness of the stranger (not love of the national mainstream) that propels these films' narrative energies and photographic powers'.[53] This goes some way to explain the troubled reception of *Dil Se*, visually and musically ravishing like the other Trilogy films, but where the love of the stranger is the most obsessive and ends in a bomb-embraced death.

In *Dil Se*, Ratnam dramatises the attraction between a character from the heart of India and another from a peripheral state. Just after meeting Meghna (but as yet unaware of her affiliation), Amar embarks on an assignment to interview people in the north-east about what freedom means to them after fifty years of Indian independence, receiving answers such as 'What freedom? We have no freedom'. They believe they are oppressed by India's central government. Amar decides to pose the same questions to an Assamese terrorist, who tells him, 'Delhi thinks it is India,' intimating that India's central government does not care about 'small far-flung states'. In interview, Ratnam emphasises that this scene is crucial to understanding the film: 'if you claim that this [the north-east] is as much India as say, UP [Uttar Pradesh], it needs as much attention.'[54]

As Chakravarty states, the Trilogy films use terrorism as 'a means of interrogating national ideals gone awry, and of evoking the faces and voices of the estranged who must be brought back to the mainstream'.[55] However, while *Dil Se* certainly shares this aim, it shows an awareness which the other films lack – namely that the All-India hero's claim to represent the nation is tenuous at best. Its apocalyptic ending spectacularly refuses to offer the ideological reassurance of *Roja* and *Bombay*, where the rift between the nation and its fragments is healed through love and affection. In *Dil Se*, romance is interrupted and fails; but, rather than making this a bleak film, the emphasis on failed resolution highlights a problem that must be faced.

Interruption becomes the defining strategy throughout the film. Not only is the romance between Meghna and Amar interrupted, but also the marriage between Amar and Preeti (Preity Zinta), whom Amar agrees to marry after Meghna has repelled his advances several times. The wedding invitations, all printed and ready to go, pile up uselessly. However, it is through the song-and-dance sequences themselves that the interruptions are most powerfully registered – making use of the song-and-dance sequence form *as* an interruption. The first song, 'Chaiya Chaiya', occurs just after Amar and Meghna have met, with Meghna boarding a train before Amar has a chance to buy her a cup of tea. 'This has got to be the shortest love story,' he murmurs, and the rain-soaked railway station segues into a dance atop a moving train in Ooty (a hill-station in Tamil Nadu). This exhilarating sequence showcases Ratnam's MTV style, with the female dancer's sensual hip and belly thrusts accentuated by camera angles.

Although he used the Seychelles in *Alaipayuthey*, Ratnam generally avoids foreign locations, setting his films 'within the geographical space endorsed by the nation-state'.[56] *Dil Se* uses locations all over India – from the backwaters of Kerala, South India, where Amar and Preeti dance on rice-boats, to the snow-capped landscapes of Ladakh in India's far north-west. The song-and-dance sequences configure the nation-state as a space of fantasy and dreaming, evoking the utmost borders of its 'imagined cartography', yet also – through their hybrid styles – open to the pleasures of global cultural exchange and fluidity.[57]

Notes

1. Willis, 'Locating Bollywood', p. 255.
2. Anon., 'Charts', p. 19.
3. Chopra, *DDLJ*, p. 55.
4. Ibid., p. 72.
5. Ibid., p. 11.
6. Ali, 'Enemies of the Hindutva', p. 6.
7. Virdi, *The Cinematic Imagination*, p. 207.
8. Willis, 'Locating Bollywood', pp. 263, 265.
9. 'Arranged love marriage' is a phrase coined by Patricia Uberoi, 'The Diaspora Comes Home', pp. 305–36.
10. Rao, 'Globalisation and Bollywood'; Dwyer and Patel, *Cinema India*, p. 71.
11. Chopra, *DDLJ*, p. 13.
12. Rao, 'Globalisation and Bollywood'.
13. Virdi, *The Cinematic Imagination*, p. 193.

14. Ciecko, 'Superhit Hunk Heroes', p. 123.
15. Chopra, *DDLJ*, p. 8.
16. Chakravarty, 'Fragmenting the Nation', p. 232.
17. Ibid., p. 232.
18. Prasad, *The Ideology of Hindi Film*, p. 218.
19. Ibid., p. 230.
20. Ibid., p. 224.
21. Pendakur, 'India's National Film Policy', p. 159.
22. Ibid., p. 159.
23. Ibid., p. 158.
24. Gopalan, *Cinema of Interruptions*, p. 183.
25. Joshi, 'India's Art House Cinema'.
26. Levitin, 'An Introduction to Deepa Mehta', p. 274; Foster, 'Mira Nair', p. 264.
27. Levitin, 'An Introduction to Deepa Mehta', p. 281.
28. Wayne, *Political Film*, p. 93.
29. Pendakur, 'India's National Film Policy', p. 162.
30. Gopalan, 'Indian Cinema', p. 380.
31. Redding and Brownworth, *Film Fatales*, p. 160.
32. Ibid., p. 162.
33. Levitin, 'An Introduction to Deepa Mehta', p. 280.
34. Ciecko, 'Superhit Hunk Heroes', p. 130. See also Bhatkal, *Spirit of Lagaan*, p. 28.
35. Miller et al., *Global Hollywood*, p. 96.
36. Mishra, *Bollywood Cinema*, p. xix.
37. Raghavendra, 'Indian Cinema as Global Entertainment', p. 4.
38. Ibid., p. 3.
39. Ibid., p. 4.
40. Gopalan, 'Indian Cinema', p. 386.
41. Patel, 'On *Fire*', p. 223.
42. Gopinath, 'Local Sites/Global Contexts', p. 150.
43. Ibid., p. 150.
44. Vanita, *Queering India*, p. 127.
45. Ibid., p. 3.
46. Ibid., p. 3.
47. McGowan, 'Excerpts from a Master Class', p. 288.
48. Gopinath, 'Local Sites/Global Contexts', p. 155.
49. Ibid., p. 158.
50. Goldberg and Dodd, 'The Indians Are Coming', p. 7.
51. Levich, 'Fearless Bollywood Picks', p. 52.
52. Chakravarty, 'Fragmenting the Nation', p. 231.
53. Ibid., p. 232.
54. Ratnam, 'Straight from the Heart', p. 23.
55. Chakravarty, 'Fragmenting the Nation', p. 232.
56. Gopalan, *Cinema of Interruptions*, p. 129.
57. Ibid., p. 129.

Bibliography

Abbas, Ackbar (1997a), *Hong Kong: Culture and the Politics of Disappearance*, Minneapolis, MN: University of Minnesota Press.

Abbas, Ackbar (1997b), 'The Erotics of Disappointment', in Jean-Marc Lalanne, David Martinez, Ackbar Abbas and Jimmy Ngai, *Wong Kar-Wai*, Paris: Dis Voir, pp. 39–81.

Abeyesekera, Sunil (1996), 'Fifty Years of Cinema in Sri Lanka', *Cinemaya* 35: 4–10.

Acland, Charles (2003), *Screen Traffic: Movies, Multiplexes, and Global Culture*, Durham, NC: Duke University Press.

Ali, Tariq (2003), *The Clash of Fundamentalisms: Crusades, Jihads and Modernity*, London: Verso.

Ali, Tariq (2004), 'Enemies of the Hindutva', *London Review of Books* 26.13: 6–8.

Amin, Sonia (1999), 'The Road to Homelessness: Thoughts on *Chitra Nadir Pare*', *Celluloid* 21.3: 18–21.

Anderson, Benedict (1991), *Imagined Communities: Reflections on the Origins and Spread of Nationalism*, London: Verso.

Ang, Ien (1996), *Living Room Wars: Rethinking Media Audiences for a Postmodern World*, London: Routledge.

Anon. (2003a), 'Global Film Production and Distribution', *Screen Digest* (July): 201–8.

Anon. (2003b), 'Charts', *The Guardian*, Section 2, 15 August.

Anon. (2003c), 'Global Cinema Exhibition Markets', *Screen Digest* (October): 297–304.

Armes, Roy (2001), 'Cinema in the Maghreb', in Oliver Leaman (ed.), *Companion Encyclopedia of Middle Eastern and North African Cinema*, London: Routledge, pp. 420–517.

Arroyo, José (2000), 'Pedro Almodóvar', in John Hill and Pamela Church Gibson (eds), *World Cinema: Critical Approaches*, Oxford: Oxford University Press, pp. 107–10.

Asfour, Nana (2000), 'The Politics of Arab Cinema: Middle Eastern Filmmakers Face Up to Their Reality', *Cineaste* 26.1: 46–8.

Austin, Guy (1996), *Contemporary French Cinema: An Introduction*, Manchester: Manchester University Press.

Berry, Chris (2003a), 'Hero', *Cinemaya* 58: 22–4.

Berry, Chris (2003b), 'Dazzling', *Cinemaya* 58: 24–5.

Berry, Chris (ed.) (2003c), *Chinese Films in Focus: 25 New Takes*, London: BFI.

Bhatkal, Satyajit (2002), *The Spirit of Lagaan*, Mumbai: Popular Prakashan.

Björkman, Stig (1996), 'Naked Miracles', *Sight and Sound* 6.10: 10–14.

Bordwell, David (1997), 'Art-Cinema Narration', in David Bordwell, *Narration in the Fiction Film*, London: Routledge, pp. 205–33.

Bordwell, David (2000), *Planet Hong Kong: Popular Cinema and the Art of Entertainment*, Cambridge, MA: Harvard University Press.

Bransford, Stephen (2003), 'Days in the Country: Representations of Space and Place in Abbas Kiarostami's *Life and Nothing More, Through the Olive Trees* and *The Wind Will Carry Us*' <http://www.sensesofcinema.com/contents/03/29/kiarostami_rural_space_and_place.html> (14 June 2004).

Bresheeth, Haim (2001), 'Telling the Stories of *Heim* and *Heimat*, Home and Exile: Recent Palestinian Films and the Iconic Parable of the Invisible Palestine', *New Cinemas: Journal of Contemporary Film* 1.1: 24–39.

CDMI [Coalition for Cultural Diversity in Moving Images] (December 2000), 'Overview of the Screen Quota System in Korea', <http://www.screen-quota.org/menupage/newsPage_disp.asp?num=42&gotopage=1> (19 July 2004).

Chakravarty, Sumita (2000), 'Fragmenting the Nation: Images of Terrorism in Indian Popular Cinema', in Mette Hjort and Scott MacKenzie (eds), *Cinema and Nation*, London: Routledge, pp. 222–37.

Chan, Jackie (1999), *I Am Jackie Chan*, London: Pan.

Chapman, James (2003), *Cinemas of the World*, London: Reaktion.

Chaudhuri, Shohini and Howard Finn (2003), 'The Open Image: Poetic Realism and the New Iranian Cinema', *Screen* 44.1: 38–57.

Chen, Pauline (2001), '*Crouching Tiger, Hidden Dragon*', *Cineaste* 26.4: 71–2.

Chopra, Anupama (2002), *Dilwale Dulhania Le Jayenge*, London: BFI.

Chow, Rey (1995), *Primitive Passions: Visuality, Sexuality, Ethnography, and Contemporary Chinese Cinema*, New York: Columbia University Press.

Christopher, James (2003), 'Fight Fantastic', *The Times*, 21 July.

Chu, Rolanda (1994), '*Swordsman II* and *The East Is Red*', *Bright Lights* 13: 30–5, 46.

Chu, Yingchi (2003), *Hong Kong Cinema: Coloniser, Motherland, and Self*, London: Routledge.

Ciecko, Anne (2001), 'Superhit Hunk Heroes for Sale: Globalization and Bollywood's Gender Politics', *Asian Journal of Communication* 11.2: 121–43.

Collins, Noreen (1997), 'Against the Tide', *Film West* 27: 47.

Cowie, Peter (1992), *Scandinavian Cinema*, London: Tantivy Press.

Creed, Barbara (1993), *Monstrous-Feminine: Film, Feminism, Psychoanalysis*, London: Routledge.

Creekmur, Corey K. (2001), 'Picturizing American Cinema: Hindi Film Songs and the Last Days of Genre', in Pamela Robertson Wojcik and Arthur Knight (eds), *Soundtrack Available: Essays on Film and Popular Music*, Durham, NC: Duke University Press, pp. 375–406.

Crofts, Stephen (2000), 'Concepts of National Cinema', in John Hill and Pamela

Church Gibson (eds), *World Cinema: Critical Approaches*, Oxford: Oxford University Press, pp. 1–10.

Dabashi, Hamid (1999), 'Mohsen Makhmalbaf's *A Moment of Innocence*', in Rose Issa and Sheila Whittaker (eds), *Life and Art: The New Iranian Cinema*, London: BFI, pp. 114–28.

Dabashi, Hamid (2001), *Close Up: Iranian Cinema: Past, Present, and Future*, London: Verso.

Danish Film Institute (19 December 2003), 'Success for Danish Cinema', <http://www.dfi.dk/sitemod/moduler/generelle_moduler/presse_modul/index.asp?pid=280&id=1151> (17 July 2004).

Danks, Adrian (2002), 'The House that Mohsen Built: The Films of Samira Makhmalbaf and Marzieh Meshkini', <http://www.sensesofcinema.com/contents/0/22/makhmalbaf. html> (14 June 2004).

Datta, Sangeeta (2002), *Shyam Benegal*, London: BFI.

De Castella, Tom (2004), 'Way out West', *Sight and Sound* 14.1: 8–9.

Desser, David (2001), 'New Kids on the Street: The Pan-Asian Youth Film', text of the 2001 Sir Stanley Tomlinson Memorial Lecture delivered at the University of Nottingham, 21 February, <http://216.239.59.104/search?q=cache:nTrplR7H5uoJ:www.nottingham.ac.uk / iaps / NewKids.pdf+desser+pan+asian+youth&hl=en&ie=UTF-8> (19 July 2004).

Dissanayake, Wimal (ed.) (1993), *Melodrama and Asian Cinema*, Cambridge: Cambridge University Press.

Dissanayake, Wimal (2003), 'Rethinking Indian Popular Cinema', in Anthony R. Guneratne and Wimal Dissanayake, *Rethinking Third Cinema*, London: Routledge, pp. 202–25.

Dissanayake, Wimal and Ashley Ratnavibhushnana (2000), *Profiling Sri Lankan Cinema*, Sri Lanka: Asian Film Centre.

Donald, Stephanie Hemelryk (2002), '*Beijing Bicycle*: The Awkwardness of Being Seventeen', *Metro* 133: 190–2.

Dwyer, Rachel and Divia Patel (2002), *Cinema India: The Visual Culture of Hindi Film*, London: Reaktion.

Ehrlich, Linda and David Desser (eds) (1994), *Cinematic Landscapes: Observations on the Visual Arts and Cinema of China and Japan*, Austin, TX: University of Texas Press.

Ehteshami, Anoushiravan (1995), *After Khomeini: The Second Iranian Republic*, London: Routledge.

Ezra, Elizabeth (ed.) (2004), *European Cinema*, Oxford: Oxford University Press.

Farahmand, Azadeh (2002), 'Perspectives on Recent (International Acclaim for) Iranian Cinema', in Richard Tapper (ed.), *The New Iranian Cinema: Politics, Representation, and Identity*, London and New York: I.B. Tauris, pp. 86–108.

Fawal, Ibrahim (2001), *Youssef Chahine*, London: BFI.

Finnish Film Foundation (n.d.), 'Cinema Statistics / Finland 1990–1999', <www.ses.fi/data/tilastot/gener98.htm> (24 October 2000).

Forbes, Jill and Sarah Street (2000), *European Cinema: An Introduction*, Basingstoke: Palgrave.

Forde, Leon (2002), 'The Winning Team', *Screen International*, 26 July.

Fore, Steve (1994), 'Golden Harvest Films and the Hong Kong Movie Industry in the Realm of Globalization', *Velvet Light Trap* 34: 40–58.

Foster, Gwendolyn Audrey (2002), 'Mira Nair', in Yvonne Tasker (ed.), *Fifty Contemporary Filmmakers*, London: Routledge, pp. 263–72.

Freidberg, Freda (1996), '*Akira* and the Postnuclear Sublime', in Mick Broderick (ed.), *Hibakusha Cinema: Hiroshima, Nagasaki and the Nuclear Image in Japanese Film*, London: Kegan Paul, pp. 91–104.

Fu, Poshek and David Desser (eds) (2000), *The Cinema of Hong Kong: History, Arts, Identity*, Cambridge: Cambridge University Press.

Gaonkar, Dilip (ed.) (2001), *Alternative Modernities*, Durham, NC: Duke University Press.

Gazdar, Mushtaq (1997), *Pakistan Cinema 1947–1997*, Karachi: Oxford University Press.

Gokulsing, K. Moti and Wimal Dissanayake (1998), *Indian Popular Cinema: A Narrative of Cultural Change*, Stoke-on-Trent: Trentham Books.

Goldberg, Suzanne and Vikram Dodd (1998), 'The Indians Are Coming', *The Guardian 2*, 3 September.

Gopalan, Lalita (2003a), *Cinema of Interruptions: Action Genres in Contemporary Indian Cinema*, London: BFI.

Gopalan, Lalita (2003b), 'Indian Cinema', in Jill Nelmes (ed.), *Introduction to Film Studies*, London: Routledge, pp. 359–88.

Gopinath, Gayatri (2003), 'Local Sites/Global Contexts: The Transnational Trajectories of Deepa Mehta's *Fire*', in Arnaldo Cruz-Malavé and Martin F. Manalansan IV (eds), *Queer Globalizations: Citizenship and the Afterlife of Colonialism*, New York: New York University Press, pp. 149–61.

Guneratne, Anthony R. (2003), 'Introduction: Rethinking Third Cinema', in Anthony R. Guneratne and Wimal Dissanayake, *Rethinking Third Cinema*, London: Routledge, pp. 1–28.

Hall, Kenneth E. (1999), *John Woo: The Films*, Jefferson, NC: McFarland.

Hames, Peter (ed.) (1995), *Dark Alchemy: The Films of Jan Svankmajer*, London: Flicks Books.

Hamid, Nassia (1997), 'Near and Far', *Sight and Sound* 7.2: 22–5.

Hammond, Andrew (21 August 1997), 'The Incoherence of Destiny', <http://www.cairotimes.com/content/issues/Islists/incoh13.html> (10 June 2004).

Harris, Sue (2004), 'The *Cinéma du Look*', in Elizabeth Ezra (ed.), *European Cinema*, Oxford: Oxford University Press, pp. 219–32.

Hayward, Susan (2001), *Cinema Studies: The Key Concepts*, London: Routledge.

Heath, Stephen (1998), 'God, Faith and Film: *Breaking the Waves*', *Literature and Theology* 12.1: 93–107.

Hebron, Sandra (2003), 'At Five in the Afternoon', *The London Film Festival Catalogue*, 22 October to 6 November 2003, p. 19.

Higson, Andrew (1995), 'British Film Culture and the Idea of National Cinema', in Andrew Higson, *Waving the Flag: Constructing a National Cinema in Britain*, Oxford: Clarendon, pp. 4–25.

Hill, John (2000), 'Film and Postmodernism', in John Hill and Pamela Church Gibson (eds), *Film Studies: Critical Approaches*, Oxford: Oxford University Press, pp. 94–103.

Hjort, Mette (2000), 'Themes of Nation', in Mette Hjort and Scott MacKenzie (eds), *Cinema and Nation*, London: Routledge, pp. 103–17.

Hjort, Mette and Ib Bondebjerg (2001), *Danish Directors: Dialogues on a Contemporary National Cinema*, Bristol: Intellect.

Hjort, Mette and Scott MacKenzie (eds) (2003), *Purity and Provocation: Dogme 95*, London: BFI.

Horton, Andrew (2002), 'No Man's Land', *Cineaste* 27.2: 38–9.

Hoskins, Colin, Stuart McFadyen and Adam Finn (1997), *Global Television and Film*, Oxford: Clarendon.

Hu, Sheldon Hsiao-peng (ed.) (1997), *Transnational Chinese Cinemas: Identity, Nationhood, Gender*, Honolulu: University of Hawai'i Press.

Hunt, Leon (2003), *Kung Fu Cult Masters: From Bruce Lee to Crouching Tiger*, London: Wallflower Press.

Iordanova, Dina (2001), *Cinema of Flames: Balkan Film, Culture and Media*, London: BFI.

Iordanova, Dina (2003a), *Cinema of the Other Europe: The Industry and Artistry of East Central European Film*, London: Wallflower Press.

Iordanova, Dina (2003b), 'East of Eden', *Sight and Sound* 13.8: 26–8.

Iqbal, Sajid (n.d.), 'Pakistani Cinema', <http://imagineasia.bfi.org.uk/guide/surveys/pakistani/> (21 June 2004).

Jäckel, Anne (2003), *European Film Industries*, London: BFI.

Jameson, Fredric (1992), *The Geopolitical Aesthetic: Cinema and Space in the World System*, Bloomington and Indianapolis, IN: Indiana University Press.

Joshi, Lalit Mohan (n.d.), 'India's Art House Cinema', <http://imagineasia.bfi.org/guide/surveys/india-arthouse/index.html> (21 June 2004).

Kelly, Richard (2000a), *Name of this Film is Dogme 95*, Channel 4, 12 August.

Kelly, Richard (2000b), *Name of this Book is Dogme 95*, London: Faber.

Kennedy-Day, Kiki (2001), 'Cinema in Lebanon, Syria, Iraq and Kuwait', in Oliver Leaman (ed.), *Companion Encyclopedia of Middle Eastern and North African Cinema*, London: Routledge, pp. 364–406.

Kim, Kyung Hyun (2004), *The Remasculinization of Korean Cinema*, Durham, NC: Duke University Press.

Kong, Rithdee (2002), 'Cinematic Revival in Thailand', *Film Comment* 38.5: 12–13.

Kristeva, Julia (1982), *Powers of Horror: An Essay on Abjection*, New York: Columbia University Press.

Kronish, Amy (1996), *World Cinema: Israel*, Trowbridge: Flicks Books.

Krstić, Igor (1996), '"Showtime Brothers!" A Vision of the Bosnian War: Srdjan

Dragojević's *Lepa sela lepo gore*', in Andrew James Horton (ed.), *The Celluloid Tinderbox: Yugoslav Screen Reflections of a Turbulent Decade*, Central Europe Review: Telford, pp. 43–61.

Lacan, Jacques (1993), *Écrits*, trans. Alan Sheridan, London: Routledge.

Lang, Robert (2001), 'Choosing to Be "Not a Man": Masculine Anxiety in Nouri Bouzid's *Man of Ashes*', in Peter Lehman (ed.), *Masculinity, Bodies, Movies, Culture*, New York: Routledge, pp. 81–94.

Lang, Robert (2003), 'Le colonisé et le colonisateur dans *Les silences du palais*', *IBLA: Revue de l'Institut des belles lettres arabes* 192: 189–204.

Lau, Jenny Kwok Wah (2003), 'Globalization and Youthful Subculture', in Jenny Kwok Wah Lau (ed.), *Multiple Modernities: Cinemas and Popular Media in Transcultural Asia*, Philadelphia, PA: Temple University Press, pp. 13–27.

Lee, Ang, James Schamus, Richard Corliss and David Bordwell (2001), *Crouching Tiger, Hidden Dragon: Portrait of the Ang Lee Film*, London: Faber.

Leung, William (2001), 'Crouching Sensibility, Hidden Sense', *Film Criticism* 26.1: 42–55.

Lev, Antonia (1996), *Samurai from Outer Space: Understanding Japanese Animation*, Chicago, IL: Open Court.

Levich, Jacob (2002), 'Fearless Bollywood Picks from Our Contributors', *Film Comment* 38.3: 52.

Levitin, Jacqueline (2003), 'An Introduction to Deepa Mehta: Making Films in Canada and India', in Jacqueline Levitin, Judith Plessis and Valerie Raoul (eds), *Women Filmmakers: Refocusing*, London: Routledge, pp. 273–83.

Li, Cheuk-To (1996), 'Popular Cinema in Hong Kong', in Geoffrey Nowell-Smith (ed.), *Oxford History of World Cinema*, Oxford: Oxford University Press, pp. 704–11.

Li, David Leiwei (2003), '*Yi Yi*: Reflections on Reflexive Modernity in Taiwan', in Chris Berry (ed.), *Chinese Films in Focus: 25 New Takes*, London: BFI, pp. 198–205.

Loshitzky, Yosefa (2001), *Identity Politics on the Israeli Screen*, Austin, TX: University of Texas Press.

Louie, Kam (2003), '*Floating Life*: Nostalgia for the Confucian Way in Suburban Sydney', in Chris Berry (ed.), *Chinese Films in Focus: 25 New Takes*, London: BFI, pp. 97–103.

Louvish, Simon (1996a), 'The White Balloon', *Sight and Sound* 6.1: 57.

Louvish, Simon (1996b), 'Letters', *Sight and Sound* 6.4: 64.

Lu, Alvin (2002), 'Horror Japanese-style', *Film Comment* 38.1: 38.

Macnab, Geoffrey (2001), 'House Rules', *Sight and Sound* 11.6: 32–4.

Macnab, Geoffrey (2003), 'A Woman's Place', *The Guardian 2*, 19 May.

McGowan, Sharon (2003), 'Excerpts from a Master Class with Deepa Mehta', in Jacqueline Levitin, Judith Plessis and Valerie Raoul (eds), *Women Filmmakers: Refocusing*, London: Routledge, pp. 284–91.

Malik, Sarita (1996), 'Beyond "The Cinema of Duty"? The Pleasures of Hybridity: Black British Film of the 1980s and 1990s', in Andrew Higson (ed.), *Dissolving Views: Key Writings on British Cinema*, London: Cassell, pp. 202–15.

Martin, Fran (2003), '*Vive l'amour*: Eloquent Emptiness', in Chris Berry (ed.), *Chinese Films in Focus: 25 New Takes*, London: BFI, pp. 175–82.

Miller, Toby, Nitin Govil, John McMurria and Richard Maxwell (2001), *Global Hollywood*, London: BFI.

Mishra, Vijay (2002), *Bollywood Cinema: Temples of Desire*, London: Routledge.

Mohaiemen, Naseem (n.d.), 'Petition: Remove the Ban on *Matir Moina*', <http://www.petitiononline.com/moina/petition.htm> (2 July 2004).

Mokammel, Tanvir (1998), 'Last Two and a Half Decades of Bangladesh Cinema', *Celluloid* 20.3: 30–4.

Mokammel, Tanvir (1999), 'Alternative Cinema in Bangladesh: Points to Ponder', *Celluloid* 21.1: 28–32.

Möller, Olaf (2002), 'Shameless', *Film Comment* (January/February 2002): 45.

Mulvey, Laura (1998), 'Kiarostami's Uncertainty Principle', *Sight and Sound* 8.6: 24–7.

Murphy, Robert (ed.) (2000), *British Cinema of the 90s*, London: BFI.

Naficy, Hamid (1994), 'Veiled Vision/Powerful Presences: Women in Post-Revolutionary Iranian Cinema', in Mahnaz Afkhami and Erika Friedl (eds), *In the Eye of the Storm: Women in Post-Revolutionary Iran*, London: I. B. Tauris, pp. 131–50.

Naficy, Hamid (1998), 'Iranian Cinema under the Islamic Republic', in Sherifa Zuhur (ed.), *Images of Enchantment: Visual and Performing Arts of the Middle East*, Cairo: American University of Cairo Press, pp. 220–46.

Naficy, Hamid (2001), 'Iranian Cinema', in Oliver Leaman (ed.), *Companion Encyclopedia of Middle Eastern and North African Cinema*, London: Routledge, pp. 130–222.

Napier, Susan (2001), *Anime from Akira to Princess Mononoke: Experiencing Contemporary Japanese Animation*, New York: Palgrave.

Nayar, Sheila J. (2004), 'Invisible Representation: The Oral Contours of a National Popular Cinema', *Film Quarterly* 57.3: 13–23.

Neale, Steve (1981), 'Art Cinema as Institution', *Screen* 22.1: 11–39.

Orr, John (2000), 'Wong Kar-Wai: In the Mood for Reflection', *Film West* 42: 52–4.

Orr, John (2002), 'Out of Dreyer's Shadow? The Quandary of Dogme 95', *New Cinemas: Journal of Contemporary Film* 1.2: 69–77.

Orr, John (2004), 'New Directions in European Cinema', in Elizabeth Ezra (ed.), *European Cinema*, Oxford: Oxford University Press, pp. 299–317.

Osmond, Andrew (2003), 'Gods and Monsters', *Sight and Sound* 13.9: 34–5.

Patel, Geeta (2002), 'On *Fire*: Sexuality and its Incitements', in Ruth Vanita (ed.), *Queering India: Same-Sex Love and Eroticism in Indian Culture and Society*, London: Routledge, pp. 222–33.

Pathiraja, Dharmasena (2003), 'The Filial Bond: The Nation in Sri Lankan Film', *Cinemaya* 58: 6–10.

Payami, Babak (2004), 'Necessary Illusions', *Sight and Sound* 14.6: 28–30.

Pendakur, Manjanath (1996), 'India's National Film Policy: Shifting Currents in the 1990s', in Albert Moran (ed.), *Film Policy: International, National and Regional Perspectives*, London: Routledge, pp. 148–71.

Petrie, Duncan (2000), *Screening Scotland*, London: BFI.

Prasad, Madhava (1998), *The Ideology of Hindi Film*, Delhi: Oxford University Press.

Pusan International Film Festival (2000), *Salaam Cinema: The Films of the Makhmalbaf Family*, South Korea: Pusan.

Raghavendra, M. K. (2001), 'An Unmarried Woman: Abbas Kiarostami's *Through the Olive Trees*', *Deep Focus* 9.1: 77–81.

Raghavendra, M. K. (2002), 'Indian Cinema as Global Entertainment', *Bollywood and Beyond: A Guide to Teaching Indian Cinema*, BFI Education CD-ROM, Catalogue No. BR040.

Rajadhyaksha, Ashish (2000), 'Indian Cinema', in John Hill and Pamela Church Gibson (eds), *World Cinema: Critical Approaches*, Oxford: Oxford University Press, pp. 151–6.

Ramachandran, Naman (2003), 'Clay Bird', *Sight and Sound* 13.8: 43–4.

Ramnarayan, Gowri (2002), 'Mr and Mrs Iyer', *Cinemaya* 56–7: 24–5.

Rao, Maithili (n.d.), 'Globalisation and Bollywood', <http://imagineasia.bfi.org.uk/guide/surveys/globalisation/index.html> (21 June 2004).

Rapfogel, Jared (2001), 'Don't Look at the Camera: Becoming a Woman in Jafar Panahi's Iran', <http://www.sensesofcinema.com/contents/01/15/panahi_jared.html> (14 June 2004).

Ratnam, Mani (1998), 'Straight from the Heart', Interview with Gautam Padamanabhan, *Asian Eye*, 3 October.

Ratnavibhushnana, Ashley (2003), 'The Family as Paradox: Modern Sri Lankan Cinema', *Cinemaya* 58: 10–11.

Rayns, Tony (1993), 'Story of Qiu Ju', *Sight and Sound* 3.5: 55.

Rayns, Tony (2001), 'Crouching Tiger, Hidden Dragon', *Sight and Sound* 11.1: 45–6.

Rayns, Tony (2004), 'Deep Cover', *Sight and Sound* 14.1: 26–9.

Redding, Judith M., and Victoria A. Brownworth (eds) (1997), *Film Fatales: Independent Women Directors*, Seattle, WA: Seal Press.

Rentschler, Eric (2000), 'The Post-Wall Cinema', in Mette Hjort and Scott MacKenzie (eds), *Cinema and Nation*, London: Routledge, pp. 260–77.

Reynaud, Bérénice (1997), 'I Can't Sell My Acting Like That', *Sight and Sound* 7.3: 24–6.

Reynaud, Bérénice (2003), '*Centre Stage*: A Shadow in Reverse', in Chris Berry (ed.), *Chinese Films in Focus: 25 New Takes*, London: BFI, pp. 31–8.

Rich, B. Ruby (26 March 2003), 'Divine Comedy', <http://www.sfbg.com/37/26/art_film_divine.html> (10 June 2004).

Ridgeon, Lloyd (2000), *Makhmalbaf's Broken Mirror: The Socio-political Significance of Modern Iranian Cinema*, Durham: University of Durham.

Roberts, Les (2002), '"Welcome to Dreamland": From Place to Non-place and

Back Again in Pawel Pawlikowski's *Last Resort*', *New Cinemas: Journal of Contemporary Film* 1.2: 78–90.

Robins, Kevin and Asu Aksoy, 'Deep Nation: The National Question and Turkish Cinema Culture', in Mette Hjort and Scott MacKenzie (eds), *Cinema and Nation*, London: Routledge, pp. 203–21.

Romney, Jonathan (2004), 'A Silky Sadness', *Sight and Sound* 14.6: 20–3.

Rose, Steve (2003), 'Hong Kong Phooey', *The Guardian*, 11 July.

Rosen, Philip (1996), 'Nation and Anti-Nation: Concepts of National Cinema in the "New" Media Era', *Diaspora* 5.3: 375–402.

Rutherford, Anne (2000), 'Arrested Motion in the Korean Detective Film', <http://www.sensesofcinema.com/contents/00/7/arrested.html> (19 July 2004).

Rutsky, R. L. (1999), *High Techne: Art and Technology from the Machine Aesthetic to the Posthuman*, Minneapolis, MN: University of Minnesota Press.

Saeed-Vafa, Mehrnaz and Jonathan Rosenbaum (2003), *Abbas Kiarostami*, Urbana, IL: University of Illinois Press.

Said, Edward (1978), *Orientalism*, London: Penguin.

Schrader, Paul (1972), *Transcendental Style*, Berkeley, CA: California University Press.

Sciolini, Elaine (2000), *Persian Mirrors: The Elusive Face of Iran*, New York: Free Press.

Shafik, Viola (1998), *Arab Cinema: History and Cultural Identity*, Cairo: American University of Cairo Press.

Shohat, Ella (2003), 'Post-Third-Worldist Culture', in Anthony R. Guneratne and Wimal Dissanayake (eds), *Rethinking Third Cinema*, London: Routledge, pp. 51–78.

Shohat, Ella and Robert Stam (1994), *Unthinking Eurocentrism: Multiculturalism and the Media*, London: Routledge.

Shohat, Ella and Robert Stam (1996), 'From the Imperial Family to the Transnational Imaginary: Media Spectatorship in the Age of Globalization', in Rob Wilson and Wimal Dissanayake (eds), *Global/Local: Cultural Production and the Transnational Imaginary*, Durham, NC: Duke University Press, pp. 145–70.

Siegel, Joshua (1998), *Baby It's Cold Outside: Films from Finland 1917–1997*, New York: Museum of Modern Art.

Siegel, Marc (2001), 'The Intimate Spaces of Wong Kar-Wai', in Esther Yau (ed.), *At Full Speed: Hong Kong Cinema in a Borderless World*, Minneapolis, MN: University of Minnesota Press, pp. 277–94.

Sinka, Margit (n.d.), 'Tom Tykwer's *Lola Rennt*: A Blueprint of Millennial Berlin', <http://www.dickinson.edu/departments/germn/glossen/heft11/lola.html> (16 July 2004).

Soila, Tytti, Astrid Söderbergh Widding and Gunnar Iversen (1998), *Nordic National Cinemas*, London: Routledge.

Solanas, Fernando and Octavio Getino (1976), 'Towards a Third Cinema', in Bill

184 CONTEMPORARY WORLD CINEMA

Nichols (ed.), *Movies and Methods, Volume One*, Berkeley, CA: California University Press, pp. 44–64.

Stephens, Chuck (1996), 'Intersection: Tsai Ming-liang's Yearning Bike Boys and Heartsick Heroines', *Film Comment* 32.5: 20–3.

Stephens, Chuck (2001a), 'Kingdom Come', *Film Comment* 37.1: 33–40.

Stephens, Chuck (2001b), 'Tears of the Black Tiger', *Film Comment* 37.3: 16–17.

Stephens, Chuck (2001c), 'Another Green World', *Film Comment* 37.5: 64–72.

Stephens, Chuck (2002), 'High and Low: Japanese Cinema Now: A User's Guide', *Film Comment* 38.1: 35–46.

Stevenson, Jack (2002), *Lars von Trier*, London: BFI.

Stevenson, Jack (2003), *Dogme Uncut: Lars von Trier, Thomas Vinterberg, and the Gang that Took on Hollywood*, Santa Monica, CA: Santa Monica Press.

Stokes, Lisa Oldham and Michael Hoover (1999), 'Hong Kong to Hollywood', *Cinemaya* 46: 30–9.

Stone, Rob (2002), *Spanish Cinema*, Harlow: Pearson.

Stringer, Julian (1997), '"Your Tender Smiles Give Me Strength": Paradigms of Masculinity in John Woo's *A Better Tomorrow* and *The Killer*', *Screen* 38.1: 25–41.

Stringer, Julian (2002), 'Tsui Hark', in Yvonne Tasker (ed.), *Fifty Contemporary Filmmakers*, London: Routledge, pp. 346–53.

Stringer, Julian (ed.) (2003a), *Movie Blockbusters*, London: Routledge.

Stringer, Julian (2003b), 'Regarding Film Festivals', Ph.D. thesis, Indiana University.

Stringer, Julian (2003c), 'Scrambling Hollywood: Asian Stars/Asian American Star Cultures', in Thomas Austin and Martin Baker (eds), *Contemporary Hollywood Stardom*, London: Arnold, pp. 229–42.

Subramanyam, Radha (2000), 'India', in Gorham Kindem (ed.), *The International Movie Industry*, Carbondale, IL: Southern Illinois Press, pp. 36–59.

Suner, Asuman (1998), 'Speaking the Experience of Political Oppression with a Masculine Voice: Making Feminist Sense of Yilmaz Güney's *Yol*', *Social Identities* 4.2: 283–300.

Suner, Asuman (2005), 'Horror of a Different Kind: Dissonant Voices of the New Turkish Cinema', author's manuscript, forthcoming in *Screen* 46.1.

Teo, Stephen (2001), 'Wong Kar-wai's *In the Mood for Love*: Like a Ritual in Transfigured Time', <http://www.sensesofcinema.com/contents/01/13/mood.html> (26 June 2003).

Thomas, Rosie (1985), 'Indian Cinema: Pleasures and Popularity', *Screen* 26.3–4: 116–31.

Uberoi, Patricia (1998), 'The Diaspora Comes Home: Disciplining Desire in *DDLJ*', *Contributions to Indian Sociology* 32.2: 305–36.

Vanita, Ruth (ed.) (2002), *Queering India: Same-Sex Love and Eroticism in Indian Culture and Society*, London: Routledge.

Vincendeau, Ginette (2000), 'Designs on the *banlieue*', in Susan Hayward and

Ginette Vincendeau (eds), *French Film: Texts and Contexts*, London: Routledge, pp. 310–27.

Virdi, Jyoti (2003), *The Cinematic Imagination: Indian Popular Films as Social History*, New Brunswick, NJ: Rutgers University Press.

Von Bagh, Peter (2000), *Drifting Shadows: A Guide to the Finnish Cinema*, Helsinki: Otava.

Ward, Nada (2001), 'Audition', *Film Ireland* (June/July): 39–40.

Wayne, Mike (2001), *Political Film: The Dialectics of Third Cinema*, London: Pluto.

Williams, Kevin (2003), *Why I [Still] Want My MTV: Music Video and Aesthetic Communication*, Cresskill, NJ: Hampton Press.

Williams, Tony (1997), 'Space, Place, and Spectacle: The Crisis Cinema of John Woo', *Cinema Journal* 36.2: 67–84.

Willis, Andrew (2003), 'Locating Bollywood: Notes on the Hindi Blockbuster', in Julian Stringer (ed.), *Movie Blockbusters*, London: Routledge, pp. 255–68.

Wu, Chia-Chi (2002), '*Crouching Tiger, Hidden Dragon* is Not a Chinese Film', *Spectator* 22.1: 65–79.

Xiaoping, Lin (2002), 'New Chinese Cinema of the "Sixth Generation": A Distant Cry of Forsaken Children', *Third Text* 16.3: 261–84.

Yeh, Yueh-Yu (1999), 'A Life of Its Own: Musical Discourses in Wong Kar-Wai's Films', *Postscript* 19.1: 120–36.

Yeh, Yueh-Yu (2001), 'Politics and Poetics of Hou Hsiao-Hsien's Films', *Postscript* 20.2–3: 61–76.

Zhang, Yingjin (2002), *Screening China: Critical Interventions, Cinematic Reconfigurations, and the Transnational Imaginary in Contemporary Chinese Cinema*, Ann Arbor, MI: Centre for Chinese Studies.

Žižek, Slavoj (1997), *The Plague of Phantasies*, London: Verso.

Žižek, Slavoj (1999), 'Death and the Maiden', in Elizabeth Wright and Edmond Wright (eds), *The Žižek Reader*, Oxford: Blackwell, pp. 206–21.

Zuhur, Sherifa (ed.) (1998), *Images of Enchantment: Visual and Performing Arts of the Middle East*, Cairo: American University of Cairo Press.

Useful Journals

(For coverage of the most recent world cinema)
Cineaction
Cineaste
Cinemaya (dedicated to Asian cinema)
Film Comment
Film Quarterly
Screen Digest (source of business data on global audiovisual media)
Screen International (weekly film trade paper)
Sensesofcinema (online journal)
Sight and Sound

Useful Websites

Internet Movie Database <www.imdb.com>
The British Film Institute website <http://www.bfi.org.uk> contains study guides and has extensive film links.

Video/DVD purchase

Facets Multimedia, Chicago <http://www.facets.org>
Moviemail, UK <http://www.moviemail-online.co.uk> specialises in world cinema.

Index